THE MACEDONIA[N]
The arrows indicate the final advance in 1918

[R]UMANIA

•BUCHAREST

Danube

THE

BLACK

SEA

[BUL]GARIA

Adrianople

TURKEY
IN
EUROPE

Bosphorus

Scutari

CONSTANTINOPLE

SEA OF
MARMORA

Kavalla

Dedeagatch

[Ser]rai

Mt.
Athos

MUDROS

Gallipoli

Dardanelles

TURKEY

IN ASIA

EGEAN SEA

THE GARDENERS OF SALONIKA

Alan Palmer

THE GARDENERS
OF SALONIKA

To Libra

Alan Anderson

Dec - 1966 -

J Howard

A present. Not a Christmas one

ANDRE DEUTSCH

FIRST PUBLISHED 1965 BY
ANDRE DEUTSCH LIMITED
105 GREAT RUSSELL STREET
LONDON WC1
COPYRIGHT © 1965 BY ALAN PALMER
ALL RIGHTS RESERVED
PRINTED IN GREAT BRITAIN
BY EBENEZER BAYLIS AND SON LIMITED
THE TRINITY PRESS
WORCESTER AND LONDON

Acknowledgements

In writing this book I have profited greatly from the reminiscences of my father, who served in Salonika for nearly three
years. Since he first aroused my interest in the campaign in
Macedonia it seems right that this book should be dedicated
to him.

I am grateful, also, for the assistance and encouragement of
my wife, Veronica, who accompanied me on both my journeys to the old Salonika front. Mr G. E. Willis of the Salonika
Reunion Association kindly suggested a number of books for
me to consult and gave me permission to quote from the excellent quarterly magazine, *The Mosquito*, of which he is the
Honorary Editor. Professor J. B. Hoptner helped me with
information about the only United States battalion to serve in
the Balkan theatre of war. I thank the staff of the Imperial
War Museum (and particularly of the photographic reference
department) for their invaluable assistance. This book could
not have been written if I had not been able to borrow gene-
rously from the London Library. Among written authorities
I must express an especial obligation to the two volumes of the
Official History of the War, *Macedonia*, by Professor Cyril
Falls, from which I have quoted through the courtesy of Her
Majesty's Stationery Office. Permission to include copyright
material has also kindly been granted by the following:
Librairie Flammarion for *Franchet d'Espérey* by General Paul Azan;
The Beaverbrook Foundations for *War Memoirs* by D. Lloyd
George; Messrs Allen and Unwin Ltd for *The Supreme Command*
by Lord Hankey; and Le Service Historique de l'Armée, for
volume III of *Les Armées Françaises dans la Grande Guerre*. The
letters from *King George V* by Sir Harold Nicolson are quoted
here by gracious permission of Her Majesty The Queen. The
bibliographical notes show how great is my debt to the authors
of other books and articles.

I should like to thank my publishers for their wise counsel

and patience. Naturally, I alone am responsible for the interpretations of character and the assessment of events printed in this book. Perhaps I might add that my admiration for the men who served in Macedonia, which was high when I began my researches, was intensified as I read more and more about the campaign. At a time of revived interest in the Great War I fail to understand why so little attention has been given to their achievement or honour paid to their sacrifice.

A.W.P.

Contents

1   The Arrival   11

2   Plans and Policies   17

3   Winter War   38

4   'The Greatest Internment Camp'   51

5   The Battle for Monastir   71

6   Politics and Knavish Tricks   92

7   Spring Offensive   108

8   Conspiracy, Mutiny and Fire   131

9   The Fall of Sarrail   153

10   Guillaumat   165

11   'Desperate Frankie'   179

12   'The Enemy is in Retreat'   197

13   Orient Express   221

14   'Without the Laurel'   237

    Notes on Sources   245

    Bibliography   269

    Index   275

Illustrations

between pp 48 and 49

Serbian cavalry in the Albanian retreat
The Serbian retreat, 1915: Voivode Putnik in a
sedan chair
The Serbian retreat, 1915: climbing the Babuna
Pass
General Sarrail and General Sir Bryan Mahon,
April 1916
Transporting a motor boat across the mountains for
service on Lake Langaza
Serbian battle honours: troops dancing a traditional
Kolo round a cairn of stones carrying the names of
their victories
Winter War: a Serb mounts guard near the Albanian
frontier

between pp 112 and 113

Albania: part of Essad Bey's private army
Annamites in Salonika: French colonial infantry
from Indo-China
Russian troops disembarking, Salonika, 1916
Russian troops moving up to the front
The Voivode Mišić and General Sir George Milne
Serbian infantry, adequately re-equipped
The liberation of Monastir: Russian troops entering
the town

between pp 176 and 177

Salonika from the air, January 1917
Venizelos inspecting Greek Nationalist troops,
November 1916

British mule-sleigh in the Struma mud
Newsvendor, Salonika 1916
The Black Watch lead the 77th Brigade up into the hills
Doiran: Pip Ridge from the British lines

between pp 240 and 241

Grand Couronné, showing the 'Devil's Eye' (arrowed)
Salonika, 1917: the aftermath of the Great Fire
General Todorov and officers of the Bulgarian High Command
Serbian signaller in the Moglena mountains
The Serbian front line: deep trenches are impossible on the rocky hills of Macedonia
General Franchet d'Espérey inspects a British Guard of Honour at Constantinople, February 1919: General Sir Henry Maitland Wilson behind
Spahis of the Jouinot-Gambetta Brigade

All photographs are reproduced by permission of the Imperial War Museum

MAPS

1. The Macedonian Front   Front end papers
2. The Great War 1914–18
   Showing the main battle areas   Back end papers
3. The Allied Offensive, September 1918   p. 188
4. The Moglena Front, September 1918   p. 198
5. The Battle of Doiran, September 1918   p. 207

(The maps on pp. 188 and 198 may also be of assistance to the reader of Chapter 5. The map on p. 207 may be helpful to the reader of Chapter 7)

To
W. L. P.

1 / The Arrival

ON OCTOBER 5TH 1915 two small transports steamed past
Cape Paliouri, turned north-eastwards through the narrows
off the mouth of the river Vardar, and dropped anchor off
the breakwater protecting the Greek port of Salonika. Other
transports and the British battleship *Albion* followed in the
course of the morning, slipping in behind the hastily constructed
anti-submarine nets to berth in the crowded rectangle of a
harbour or send pinnaces to the east quay. The vessels were
packed with men in khaki and steel-grey blue – the troops of
Britain and France were about to experience for the first time the
frustration of warfare in the Balkans.

The British and French came to Salonika as neither allies nor
enemies of the Greeks. It was a curious situation, without precedent at that time. The major European powers had been at war
for over a year. Greece had declared herself neutral but the
Greeks were well disposed towards their neighbours and former
allies in Serbia, who were the first victims of Austrian aggression.
It was this geographical proximity to Serbia that made Greek
neutrality precarious. Serbia had no sea-coast; hence, if the
Entente Powers (Britain and France) wished to send effective aid
to the Serbs they could do so only through the largest port in
Greek Macedonia, Salonika. Moreover, the Entente Powers con-
sidered that international law entitled them to send a military
force to Greece since, when Greece won independence from
Turkey in the early nineteenth century, a formal treaty had given
Britain, France and Russia the right to land troops, by agreement
among themselves, in case of violent upheaval in the Balkans.
The British had, indeed, already set up a base in the Aegean at
Mudros, on the Greek island of Lemnos, for operations against
the Turks at Gallipoli. Now, in concert with the French, they
sought to establish themselves on the mainland as well. For by
October 1915 the position of the Serbs was becoming desperate.
They anticipated an attack in the near future, not only from the
Austro-Hungarian armies, but from the Germans and Bulgars as

well. Only an inter-allied force could check an offensive of this
magnitude; and the route to Serbia was by way of Salonika and
the single track railway up the river Vardar. Yet how would the
Greeks react to the landing of belligerent troops on their soil?
Their prime minister, Venizelos, favoured the Entente and had
promised the British and French every facility in Salonika; but it
seemed unlikely that the provincial garrison commanders and
local governors would continue to support him. 'I fear the Greeks
even though they offer gifts:' the sentiment with which Virgil
credited Laocoon was expressed with less elegance but equal
brevity by the senior officers arriving at Salonika. As the convoy
moved up the Gulf, the glinting steel of the Krupp guns at Fort
Karaburun looked ominous even if the troops manning the
battery were Greek and not German.

Although it was a Tuesday and a working day when the
transports sailed in, the waterfront of the Greek city filled with
onlookers in the afternoon, for the habit of a siesta persisted,
despite the cool wind that was blowing down the Vardar. Moreover, the arrival of the troops was not unexpected. On the previous
Friday the destroyer *Scourge* had brought senior British and
French staff officers to the port to make preparations for the
allied troops. The town was full of rumours, speculation on the
size of the force and its intentions. Some maintained that the
newcomers would take over the administration of the city from
the Greek authorities; others that they would move off within
a few days into the mountains of Serbia. Salonika, which until
three years before had been a Turkish garrison town, was accustomed to the presence of the military. Indeed, there were already
two Greek divisions encamped on the outskirts, pledged to uphold
Greek neutrality. Feelings about the imminent arrival of belligerent forces were divided, that first weekend in October. The
civil administration was openly hostile, but the merchants and
shopkeepers were uncertain. Occupying troops, with their high-
handed requisitioning of buildings and transport, were a burden
for some; but for others they were a source of profit. Everyone
knew that the purchasing power of the *poilu*, and even more of
the Tommy, was greater than that of the Greek militia. The
bazaar-men and the brothel owners awaited the Allies, if not
with open arms, then at least with interest. For, like everyone
else in Salonika, they considered themselves by now connois-
seurs of soldiery.

The observers along the waterfront (who included the German

and Austrian and Turkish consuls) were far from impressed by their first sight of Allied military power. The British troops, the headquarters staff of the 29th Brigade and two battalions of Irish infantry – some 1,400 men in all – were an advance guard of the 10th Division. They were veterans of the Gallipoli campaign and, only nine weeks before, had stormed ashore in pitch blackness below the heights of Suvla, two hundred miles away. The Division reached Salonika under strength and battle-weary. Some men were wearing regulation serge, others were in shorts. A few had greatcoats, others tropical drill uniform. They had come without waggons and lorries, and were to be seen, in the fitful sun of the late afternoon, lugging their tents off eastwards from the harbour, puzzled and perplexed. Brought post haste from the peninsula of Gallipoli to the island base of Mudros they had, at once, been put aboard the ships for Greece. So swift had been the move that little regard had been given to their immediate requirements. The units of the French 156th Division, which had also been serving at Gallipoli, were in better shape, but they too had left their transport in Mudros for later shipment. Gradually, as vessel after vessel disgorged its human cargo amid rumours of political crisis in distant Athens, the whole landing assumed the unmistakable air of an afterthought, and the attitude of the Greeks hardened. It was a dismal beginning.

If the Greeks watched the coming of the Allies with sullen passivity, the soldiers themselves were hardly more impressed by the town on which they had descended. After weeks on the beaches and cliffs of Gallipoli, Salonika had looked attractive from the sea. The vessels had turned northwards beneath the snow-capped sentinel of Olympus itself. Across the bay a long line of low buildings had come into view stretching the length of the water-front to the massive stump of the White Tower, an isolated pivot of the old ramparts. A fleet of caiques rode at their moorings and further back two dozen minarets pointed skywards, slim white pencils above the domes of Byzantine churches which the Turkish conquerors had converted into mosques. Low hills came down to the outskirts of the town, offshoots of the Rhodope range, which loomed, a distant grey smudge, far away to northwards. It had seemed, at any rate, a livelier base than Mudros.

Closer acquaintance dispelled many illusions. Salonika in 1915 was an ancient city almost mocking her own history. Sixteen hundred years ago the Emperor Galerius had erected a triumphal

arch commemorating his victories over the Persians and spanning
the Via Egnatia, Rome's highway to the East. Now the bas-
reliefs on the arch rose thirty feet above a busy road, with a
copper-smith's shop behind it and a tram passing less than five
yards from the carved legionaries. The old town was a maze of
winding streets. Behind it climbed the terraces of the Turkish
quarter, alleys clinging to the sides of a hill, low houses with
balconies enclosed with lattice-work and a teeming population
who would squat suspiciously on the uneven pavement. Near the
port, which had been modernized at the turn of the century, there
were cobbled streets, divided by tram-lines, garish cafés on the
pavement, and drab hotels with grandiloquent names ('Splendid',
24 rooms; 'Olympus Palace', 20). It was a dusty and a noisy
town; and it was also an overcrowded one, for Salonika had not
yet absorbed the refugees thrust down upon it by the upheavals
of the Balkan Wars. There were Greeks and Slavs and Albanians
and Turks in the streets. But above all there were Jews of Spanish
origin, sixty thousand of them, proudly independent even after
centuries of exile, and forming a third of the population. Salonika,
once the second centre of Byzantium, was by now a bustling,
clanging, strident city on the make. To the Frenchmen of the
156th Division, it had all the appearance of a Balkan Marseilles.
To the men of the British regiments, it was a second-rate Port
Said, with Alexandrine undertones, neither in Europe nor in
Asia, but of both.

More British troops disembarked on October 6th, mainly
Irishmen but including a battalion of the Hampshire Regiment.
They were even unluckier than the first arrivals. By now the
weather had broken, and the rain beat down with tropical force.
The troops were encamped three miles north-east of the town,
and the heavy rain churned up the ill drained soil. Brigadier-
Gerneral Hamilton, who had accompanied the staff officers in
the *Scourge*, had already found that the Greeks had requisitioned
most of the buildings which the Allies required and were not
prepared to assist them in any way. Horses and mules arrived
from Mudros on the Thursday, short of nosebags and guiding
ropes. It was still pouring and the mules, with characteristic
sensitivity, saw no reason for leaving the sheltering vessels for the
mud-bespattered streets. Three years later a Bulgarian general,
coming to negotiate the surrender of his army, was to admire and
envy the British mule-packs, a tribute duly noted by the military
commentators. But on that October morning, as men and beasts

struggled on the rain-swept quayside, such a sentiment would have seemed as ironical as it was improbable.

By five o'clock on the Saturday when a destroyer brought General Mahon, the commanding officer of the British Salonika Force, to his base, Brigadier Hamilton had his cup filled to over-flowing with vexatious frustration. It was a relief to pass some of his problems on to other shoulders. Sir Bryan Mahon was a familiar figure to the men of the 10th Division. He was a very senior lieutenant-general, a fifty-three year old Irish landowner, a cavalryman, set in his ways and by now naturally cautious, but an officer for whom his troops felt genuine affection. Mahon had been imposed on the division by Lord Kitchener late in 1914 when it might have been wiser to entrust the command to a younger man of greater energy. Yet Mahon had something more than the traditional 'distinguished record of service' behind him. There had been a time when he enjoyed a few weeks of popular adulation, for in the Boer War it was Mahon's flying column which finally relieved Mafeking. The hysteria of Mafeking Night lay now in another age, even if by the calendar it was only fifteen years ago. Mahon reached Salonika under a cloud, for at Suvla his hesitancy after the initial assault had provoked criticism, not only from his immediate superiors, but from Colonel Hankey who had been sent by the prime minister to make an assessment on the spot and had visited Mahon's headquarters within a few hours of the landing. Poor Mahon (who paid his Turkish opponents the compliment of assessing them as 'regular Boers') was puzzled by this strange warfare of combined operations in which famous regiments, deprived of their auxiliary services, clung to the very cliff face of Europe.

Yet, although Mahon himself may have lacked dynamic enter-prise, it is questionable whether even a young Bonaparte could have fired the 10th Division into action under the conditions in Salonika. There were no howitzers, only a few batteries of field artillery, and little transport. The men looked as if they were fitted out for an Egyptian expedition, but they were expected to advance into a region more impenetrable than Snowdonia and, at this time of year, just as wet. The local population was coldly uncooperative; Mahon's instructions from London contradictory and vacillating; and, when Mahon disembarked, his senior French colleague had only just sailed from Toulon. As Mahon inspected his makeshift camp on the Seres Road, it is hardly surprising if he began to wonder what these veteran troops were doing on the fringe of the

Balkans. It was a question others were asking at conference tables far distant from the mud of Macedonia – and it was a question that was to be posed many times in the following three years, before the men in Macedonia themselves supplied the triumphant answer.

2 / Plans and Policies

In august 1914 there seemed little likelihood of Salonika becoming a centre of military operations. War burst on Europe over a question of such little concern to the combatants in the west that it was thrown into the back of men's minds and virtually forgotten. For the manœuvrings of two rival armed camps among the Great Powers in the preceding decade had not merely accustomed people to the possibility of war, but had determined both the probable composition of the contending forces and the fields of battle. As the troop trains brought the millions of recruits to their war stations the last amendments were being made to plans long since drawn up for just such a contingency. There was an awful resignation in the Ministries of each of the capital cities – even British civil servants rubber-stamped documents 'War, Germany, act' with the imperturbability of postal officials franking the evening mail. This was the testing time which French generals and British admirals had anticipated with confidence ever since the German Emperor made his bellicose speech at Tangier in 1905. This was the conflict which Count von Schlieffen, that master strategist who never fought a battle, played out on paper each Christmas for the last seven years of his life. The army and navy staffs knew, in Paris and Berlin and London, that the fate of Europe would be determined probably within a month on the plains of Flanders and Poland or the seas around the British Isles. To their way of thinking the Balkan Peninsula lay on the periphery of the military arena, geographically remote and politically irrelevant. It was a habit of thought which persisted.

Yet the immediate occasion of hostilities in 1914 was not the tension of naval or colonial rivalry nor the ambition of the French to recover Alsace and Lorraine; it was the explosion of pent-up forces of nationalism in that most cosmopolitan of Balkan cities, Sarajevo. Soon the war would assume the guise of a crusade for the sanctity of treaties but it began over an issue which was essentially Slav and hence, to some extent, antipathetic to the British. There was little knowledge of Serbia in London and virtually no sympathy with her political aspirations. It was not appreciated that while the youth of Britain were shedding their blood for a courageous little Belgium ravaged by the despicable Hun, their Serbian co-belligerents were waging a lonely war on the Danube for a cause which, in their eyes, was no less noble – the liberation of their fellow Slavs from Teutonic and Magyar regimentation. In Paris, on the other hand, there was a strong tradition of Serbian friendship, reaching back to the travels of the romantic poet, Lamartine, early in the nineteenth century, emphasized by the services rendered by King Peter to France in the war of 1870, and fostered by commercial contacts in the preceding decade and a half. This difference in outlook between London and Paris was, in time, to prove significant.

Initially, however, the war in the Balkans was a separate conflict distinct from the great setpieces on the Western Front and in East Prussia. Thus, as Ludendorff was fighting his way into Liège on August 12th, Austrian troops were crossing the river Drina into Serbia, only to encounter strong resistance. And on August 20th, as the Belgians fell back on Antwerp, the Austrians were making a desperate effort to break through the defences of Sabac, and the Serbs were still holding firm. By August 25th, when the Germans on the Eastern Front were beginning the encirclement of Samsonov's army at Tannenberg, the Austrians had been forced to evacuate Serbian territory, and the Serbian commander-in-chief was poised for an impudent (and possibly imprudent) incursion into Austrian-held Bosnia.

By October the momentum of the first offensives in the West and East had run down, and the old assertion that 'It would all be over by Christmas' was sounding grimly hollow. The Russians had lost the decisive battle in East Prussia but had stabilized their front; the Germans had fallen back from the Marne; and, although heavy fighting persisted in Flanders, the armies were entrenching themselves for a winter of war. Then, in the first week of November, the conflict spread. The Turkish military leaders, who had never disguised their admiration for the German war machine, authorized two Turkish vessels to participate in a bombardment of Russian ports in the Black Sea. There was only one possible reaction from the Entente Powers: Britain, France and Russia declared war on Turkey on November 2nd. New battle zones were thus created in the Caucasus, in Mesopotamia, and in Egypt. But Turkey was no less isolated from her allies in the West than was Serbia. Bulgaria and Greece interposed a

barrier of neutrality between the combatants. It was inevitable
that the diplomats of both sides should seek to entice the Balkan
States into the fray.

The attitude of each of the Balkan neutrals to the greater European conflict was largely determined by the achievements and
the failures of the two brief wars of 1912–13. Two years previously,
in October 1912, the Russians had induced Greece, Bulgaria,
Serbia and the tiny mountain kingdom of Montenegro to make
common cause against Turkey. In a series of swift victories the
Turks had been thrown back to the hinterland of Constantinople.
Then the Balkan allies had fallen out among themselves. The
Bulgars claimed that they had suffered three-quarters of the
casualties but had been robbed of their due reward by the
machinations of the Serbs and Greeks. In a six week campaign
in the summer of 1913 the Bulgars failed to dislodge either of
their rivals from their new conquests and were, in turn, invaded
by the Roumanians from the north. The resultant treaty of
Bucharest (August 1913) doubled the size of Serbia, made Greece
the most important power on the Aegean, and left the Bulgars
bitterly resentful. Their troops had been only four hours behind
the Greeks in entering Salonika, but all they acquired for their
efforts was a line of mountain summits in eastern Macedonia and
a couple of second-rate harbours on the Aegean, Port Lagos and
Dedeagatch. Subsequent Bulgarian policy accordingly showed
rare singleness of purpose: Bulgaria would support whichever side
afforded her the better prospect of revising the treaty of Bucharest.
Although there was deep antagonism between Bulgar and Serb,
it was not beyond the bounds of possibility that Bulgaria might
support the cause of the Entente, for the Bulgars had influential
friends in London and traditions of sympathy with Russia and
hatred towards Germany's new ally, Turkey. For nearly a year
the British Foreign Office made representations to the Serbs in
the hope of inducing them to hand over to Bulgaria regions in
Macedonia which the Bulgars claimed they had been promised
before the Balkan Wars; but, until it was far too late, the Serbs
would not budge. From the start, however, the Entente Powers
could offer Bulgaria substantial gains at the expense of Turkey.
The Germans, on the other hand, while counselling friendship
with Turkey, could promise Bulgaria everything that she wanted
from Serbia. Not unnaturally, Bulgaria's ruler – King Ferdinand,
the fox of the Balkans – determined to stay out of the war until

he could see which of his neighbours, Serbia or Turkey, would end up on the losing side.

Greek policy was more equivocal. Since October 1910 the Greek Government had been headed by the Cretan revolutionary, Eleutherios Venizelos. As a student thirty years before, Venizelos had hung a map on the wall of his study showing the boundaries of the new Greek Empire which 'was his national 'vision – its limits ran from Lake Ochrid through Monastir to Constantinople itself and stretched along the coast of Asia Minor to Smyrna and the Dodekanese. Many of his ambitions had already been realized: the Greek frontier in 1914 lay less than thirty miles short of the Ochrid–Monastir line in Macedonia and had crept along the Aegean to within two hundred miles of the Turkish capital. Venizelos was prepared to forego the small segment of Macedonia which the Serbs had occupied if he could secure the greater prize of Constantinople. But Venizelos had many enemies in Greece. He had reformed the financial administration, purged the army, revised the constitution. Moreover, George I, the Danish-born king who had ruled Greece for fifty years and had entrusted Venizelos with the formation of a government, was assassinated in Salonika in March 1913. He had been succeeded by his son, Constantine. George's sympathies had been with Britain; he was, after all, the brother of Queen Alexandra. Constantine's family links were with Germany; he had married the Kaiser's sister. And, as a successful general in the Balkan Wars, Constantine shared the distrust of the High Command for Venizelos' reforming activities and their admiration for the militaristic traditions of Prussia. Yet Constantine too had ambitions, not dissimilar from those of Venizelos. George may have entered Salonika in triumph; but there was one city whose very name called for liberation by his son.

On August 8th 1914 Venizelos persuaded the King (with some difficulty) to decline his brother-in-law's invitation to participate in 'an united crusade against Slav domination in the Balkans'. A fortnight later Venizelos offered to put all Greece's military and naval resources at the disposal of Britain. This overture caused embarrassment to the British Foreign Secretary, Sir Edward Grey, and his French opposite number, Delcassé. They had no wish to drive Greece's old enemies Bulgaria and Turkey (who was not then at war) into the arms of Germany, for this would have made the Balkans a major area of conflict for which the Western Powers could not spare troops. But if Grey and

Delcassé were perplexed by Venizelos' importunity, their Russian colleague, Sazonov, was angry. For the Russians had no intention of allowing the Greeks to enter Constantinople. If the cross were restored to St Sophia, it must be placed there by the Russian branch of the Orthodox Church, not the Greek. Venizelos' offer was turned down, and Greece continued to maintain an uneasy neutrality, with tension mounting between king and minister. Venizelos left no doubt where he thought Greece's true interests lay. He reminded Constantine that, by a military convention of June 1913, Greece was bound to assist Serbia if she were attacked by Bulgaria, provided that the Serbs could concentrate an army of 150,000 men against the Bulgars. We shall find, in due course, that figure of 150,000 becoming almost a talisman of success; but, for the moment, apart from unauthorized raids by *komitadji* guerrillas, all remained quiet in Macedonia.

While the Foreign Office and the Quai d'Orsay were conducting their complicated manœuvres, other public figures, less closely associated with the niceties of diplomatic etiquette, were seeking to offset the military stalemate in France. To one senior French commander, General Franchet d'Espérey at Fifth Army Head-quarters north of Rheims, it seemed foolish to concentrate on breaking through the heavily fortified positions on the Western Front. The General was steeped in French military history. In private letters he recalled the grand strategy of the revolutionary wars: 'Remember 1796–97', he wrote, 'It was not the mighty armies of the Rhine and Sambre-Meuse that succeeded; it was the little army in Italy.' Was there, perhaps, a possibility of making a surprise thrust against Germany from a direction against which the Germans had no ready-made fortifications? He was mesmerized by the thought of a great cavalry advance across the open plains of Hungary. Strategically, there seemed to be a case for linking France with the Balkan Front. Did the route to Berlin lie through Budapest, Vienna, Olmütz, Prague and Dresden? It was a Bonapartist vision. Was its author a Napoleon?

Outwardly, Louis Felix Marie François Franchet d'Espérey was an orthodox French commander, a good Catholic from a family with royalist traditions but despising political intrigue. His career looked, on the face of it, the typical success story of a French general who now, at 58, was past his prime. A graduate of Saint Cyr, he had served in Algeria and Tunis and Indochina, spent a couple of years in the Operations Department in Paris, returned to Saint Cyr as an instructor, joined in the international force

which had suppressed the Boxer Rising in China, assisted Lyautey
to pacify Morocco, and distinguished himself in the first weeks
of the war. But Franchet d'Espérey, unlike most of his colleagues,
had never been obsessed by the frontier of the Rhine. He had
travelled profitably. He knew Austria-Hungary well. Not only
had he visited the twin capitals and made a dutiful pilgrimage to
the Napoleonic battlefields, but he also travelled down the
Dalmatian coast, meeting in Trieste the redoubtable Conrad von
Hötzendorf, the most gifted strategist in Francis Joseph's army.
And he had gone even further afield. Shortly after Venizelos
came to power, he went to Greece. Once again he was not content to remain in the capital. He took a trip to Larissa, inspected
the frontier posts in Thessaly, spent some days in the small port
of Volo and got to know many of the Greek officers. Now, when
a lull fell on the Western Front, his thoughts returned to the
journey he had undertaken four years before.

In the first week of October 1914 President Poincaré visited
d'Espérey's headquarters in Champagne. The President mentioned in conversation the possibility that Turkey might enter the
war and the General seized the opportunity to give his views on
Balkan strategy. The President was impressed and invited him to
put his ideas on paper. With the assistance of his chief of staff and
of a Major who had served with the French mission in the Balkan
Wars, Franchet d'Espérey drafted a lengthy memorandum. The
plan proposed the despatch to Salonika of five army corps (some
185,000 men) whence they would be transported along the
Vardar–Morava valleys to Belgrade so as to mount an offensive
aimed at Budapest in the spring of 1915. Franchet d'Espérey
admitted that there were two grave military obstacles to be overcome before the force could be mustered in Serbia: the inade-
quacy of the harbour resources at Salonika and the limited capacity of the railway, a single track through difficult country. He
suggested that Kavalla might be used as an additional base to
Salonika and that engineers should begin work improving the
resources of the railway. Even so, he calculated that it would take
two months for the army to be moved from Greece to the Danube.

The plan was entrusted to a parliamentary deputy serving
with the Fifth Army, Bénazet, and handed over to Poincaré on
December 1st. It was a bad moment to discuss a Balkan offensive
and for the time being the President took no action. The Austrians
had launched an attack which threatened Belgrade late in November and on December 2nd the city fell. But the Serbs were a fierce

warrior people steeled by an intensive national patriotism. Instead
of falling back under the impact of the Austrian assault, they
counter-attacked along the river Kolubara and broke the Austrian front. Within a fortnight Belgrade had been liberated and
the Serbian High Command was able to issue the proud communiqué, 'Not one enemy soldier remains at liberty on the soil of
the Serbian Kingdom'. Yet the Serbs had to pay a heavy price
for this triumph: some 170,000 men killed in battle and possibly
as many as 50,000 in hospital from typhus. A victorious army
stood on the threshold of the Austrian Empire but lacked the
strength to cross it.

London and Paris remained in ignorance of Serbia's true position. The 'miracle of the Kolubara' had awakened interest in the
Balkans on both sides of the Channel. On January 1st 1915
Poincaré discussed a possible offensive with the French prime
minister, Viviani, and his principal colleague, Briand, the Minister of Justice. Briand was enthusiastic and Viviani, though less
sanguine, at any rate not hostile to the idea. They agreed to put
proposals for an offensive on the lines of d'Espérey's plan to the
commander-in-chief of French armies in the north-east, the imperturbable 'Papa' Joffre, who was to lunch with them a week
later.

Meanwhile, entirely independently of the French (and, indeed,
of each other) two British observers spent the Christmas of 1914
drafting memoranda on the war situation. The first of these was
Colonel Hankey, secretary of the Committee of Imperial Defence
since 1912. Hankey was surprised at what he termed 'the remarkable deadlock which has occurred in the western theatre of
war'. He sought 'some other outlet' for the employment of the
newly raised armies. Among his proposals was an attempt to
unite the Balkan States by vigorous action against Turkey and
'the possibility of some co-operation with the Serbian Army
against Austria'. The plan was duly laid before the War Council,
a body of ten Cabinet ministers and military leaders which had
been established in August 1914 to assume responsibility for the
general strategy of the war and of which Hankey was secretary.

Hankey's note was a general survey of the whole strategic
scene; some commentators have suggested that it contained the
genesis of the Dardanelles expedition. The second memorandum,
a formidable document of nearly 4,000 words, was specifically
related to the Balkan situation. It was the work of a member of
the War Council, Lloyd George, the Chancellor of the Exchequer.

Lloyd George was not popular with the army and navy chiefs; they had mastered the mysteries of war, he (they felt) was a demagogue. What did this Merlin from Snowdonia know of logistics or of the obstacles imposed by geography to the movement of armies? In their opposition they were less than just to Lloyd George. With his Celtic imagination, he was the least insular member of the Liberal Government. He had travelled widely in Canada and South America and knew more of Europe than any of his colleagues did. He had even had the enterprise to undertake a motoring expedition through Germany, Switzerland, Austria-Hungary and France. And, as his letters to his brother show, ever since the outbreak of the Balkan Wars he had made a point of reading all the military information that was put before the cabinet. He had not, indeed, visited the Balkans but his romantic radicalism had been fired by the image of Venizelos, an interest stimulated by his friendship with Sir Arthur Crosfield who had married a wealthy Greek, a close acquaintance of the Venizelos family. All these influences combined to attract his mind to the Balkans; and he came forward with a proposal for a general offensive against Austria in combination with the Serbs, Greeks and Roumanians. The Western Powers were to participate either through landing a force at Salonika or by an amphibious operation on the Dalmatian coast. 'It might be advisable', he wrote, 'to send an advance force through Salonika, to assist Serbia.' For the first time a note of urgency was coming into these Balkan proposals. The memorandum was dated January 1st 1915, and circulated at the same time as that of Hankey.

In the first week of 1915, then, the leaders of France and Britain were considering a possible extension of the war in the Balkans, assuming that Greece could be tempted to abandon her neutrality. The military chiefs on both sides of the Channel instinctively disliked the whole project. One tenth of metropolitan France was in enemy occupation; and the Germans were entrenched less than sixty miles from Paris, as near to the Arc de Triomphe as Oxford to the City of London or Gettysburg to Capitol Hill. The French High Command needed sublime confidence in the defensive ring around the capital to contemplate a speculative venture in a distant corner of Europe. Joffre, a veteran of the 1870 disaster, was not the man to take such a risk. And he had other reasons, apart from caution bred of experience. His strategic plan for 1915 provided for the maximum number of divisions concentrated as battering-rams at three points along the German defensive line in Artois and Champagne. Joffre believed (and it remained the one article in his Credo) that the war would not be won until the main German army had been defeated in the field of battle which the Germans had themselves selected for their principal effort. He had, under his direct command, over one and a quarter million men and they were supported by more than two hundred thousand British and Belgian troops. Never before had such a huge army been gathered on a single front. But behind the nests of barbed-wire and the machine gun emplacements lay 85 German divisions, almost equal in numbers to the Allied force. Casualties would be heavy – the British, for example, had lost 50,000 men in little more than a month's fighting around Ypres – and Joffre would need every division he could raise. He made it clear to Poincaré that he could not accept the withdrawal of men from the decisive theatre of war for many months to come. Not everyone agreed with Joffre – General Galliéni, who had been nominated as successor to Joffre should the commander-in-chief be killed in battle, favoured a landing at Salonika – but it was still Joffre's hour; and the French Government accepted his decision. For the moment, nothing more was heard of Franchet d'Espérey's plan.

The British generals were almost as adamant. They had little difficulty in shooting down Lloyd George, though it can hardly be said they silenced him. The Chancellor of the Exchequer, they maintained, 'had discovered the Balkans in an atlas'. He did not understand that it would take six months to fit out a Balkan Expeditionary Force. He was thinking (and there was some truth in this criticism) of a paper triumph for political objectives, of a fillip to lagging morale at home. This, they intimated, was all that could be expected from a vote-catching politician; in war, it was the final victory that mattered, and final victory could only be achieved by wearing down the German army in France. Hankey's paper they treated with a little more respect, but they refused to accept his contention that it was impossible to break through the German lines by a direct attack. Given less rain and fog and more shells, the German front could still be broken; until the military commanders on the spot were convinced that the Allies could not make a breach in France, no offensive should be launched elsewhere. Sir John French, the commander of the British Expeditionary Force, grudgingly admitted that, 'An attack with Greece and Serbia was, perhaps, the least objectionable proposal, but the lines of communication would be long and difficult'. And so, too, he might have added, would be the conversion of the commanders in the field.

There were, nevertheless, good reasons why the 'Easterners' were not routed at this early stage. The War Office and the Admiralty were still dominated by Titans, Kitchener (the War Minister) and Admiral Fisher (the First Sea Lord) – and neither was completely convinced of the absolute priority of the Western Front. But action was forced on the Asquith Government from another quarter. On January 2nd 1915 a message was received from the Russian commander-in-chief urging 'a demonstration of some kind against the Turks' to ease the position of the Russian armies. Generals, admirals and ministers in London weighed the merits of rival theatres of war. A final decision was to be taken at the War Council of January 13th.

This day-long conference has rightly fascinated historians. The records of its participants retain, even today, the tension of high drama. We seem to catch the very gestures and inflexions of the principal actors: the nagging uncertainties of Lloyd George and Balfour about the Western Front; the long cross-examination of Sir John French on his proposed offensive in Flanders; the gruff interventions of Kitchener, finally convincing even the Chancellor of the Exchequer that at present not a single division could be spared from France; Grey's plea for a naval raid in the southern Adriatic (to which few councillors gave their attention); and, as the curtains block out the murky evening, the magnetic appeal of Churchill's masterly exposition of the Dardanelles problem, the sudden consciousness that in the long arm of the navy is salvation. Here, surely, is the true alternative for Britain to the soldiers' war of attrition, an assault from the sea rather than an overland trek to central Europe. Here lies the key to southern Russia; this must be the victory to swing Balkan opinion in favour of the Entente and hand to the British public a triumph that meant something for them. 'The Admiralty should prepare for a naval expedition in February to bombard and take the Gallipoli Peninsula with Constantinople as its objective', ran the final decision of the conference. It was a magnificent directive, resolute in its laconicism, filled with the confidence of centuries of sea power. Thus spoke Britannia. Another six weeks were to elapse before the First Sea Lord penned the damning minute, 'The Dardanelles futile without soldiers'.

Commitment to operations in the Dardanelles did not, however, necessarily exclude an expedition to Salonika. Lloyd

George's thesis had prevailed sufficiently for the Council to re-
solve that, should there still be stalemate in France and Flanders
in the spring, British troops would be sent 'to another theatre of
war'. Moreover, Grey hoped that Greece might now be tempted
to enter the war; if Greece moved, it was essential to safeguard
that slender lifeline to Serbia along the Vardar and Morava.
After characteristic prevarication, Venizelos offered support, provided that Greece was safeguarded from a Bulgarian attack by the
presence of an allied force at Salonika and by the mobilization
of the Roumanian army on Bulgaria's northern frontier.

This overture from Venizelos gave Lloyd George another opportunity. The General Staff continued to hedge: Salonika was,
indeed, the best place to send troops but it was useless to despatch
them until the snow had melted. Lloyd George persisted. There
was much coming and going between London and Paris. Churchill
and Lloyd George both made visits to France to win support for
an Aegean diversion. 'We ought not to dilly-dally any longer',
urged Lloyd George on his return. The French reluctantly agreed
to send a division to Salonika. Kitchener wanted Russian troops
as well, believing that the presence of their fellow Slavs would be
a greater deterrent to the Bulgars than a purely Western force;
but the Russians could offer only a thousand Cossacks and it
would have taken them several months to reach Salonika from
Archangel. The Roumanians were unresponsive. But finally, on
February 9th, Kitchener agreed to send the 29th Division to
Salonika. A strong telegram was sent to Venizelos:

'Every obligation of honour and interest renders it necessary
that Greece should go to the assistance of Serbia. In order to
help them to do so effectively, and to secure their communications, Britain, France and Russia propose to send a division to
Salonica. Even if there is delay in the despatch of the Russian
contingent, the British and French divisions will be despatched
immediately'.

'Might have beens' are a temptation for the historian, and this
one is particularly hard to resist. Had an inter-allied force landed
in the Balkans in February 1915 rather than in October, the
balance of the war would have been drastically altered. This
would have been an act of reinsurance, not of succour. Linked
with the naval assault on the Dardanelles, it could have rolled
back the German map of Europe from its south-eastern corner.

With Italy, too, joining the belligerents (as she did) and with Russia encouraged, the Central Powers would have been forced on the defensive on four fronts. This was the true policy of 'encirclement', the strategy the Germans had most feared since the days of Bismarck. It was the first, but hardly the last, of the lost opportunities.

Mistiming in Whitehall and mistrust in Athens effectively prevented Greece from 'going to the assistance of Serbia'. Grey had believed that the naval bombardment of the Dardanelles forts would begin on February 11th; the British and French diplomatic representatives were to press acceptance on Venizelos four days later. But bad weather and technical problems postponed the naval action for over a week. The diplomats therefore waited on Venizelos too soon. They were not able to say to him, 'If you seek confirmation of our determination to press on with the war, go to Mudros and listen to the roar of the guns'. Venizelos himself favoured intervention; but without some tangible evidence of allied power he could not carry Constantine and the General Staff with him. Hence the Greeks fell back on a technicality. They had asked that Roumania must threaten Bulgaria's northern flank before Greece marched; the Roumanians would never enter the war until they saw a sound prospect of Allied victory; and the Greeks accordingly declined to move. The Salonika project fell into the background.

The tragic tale of courage and confusion which is Gallipoli has been brilliantly told elsewhere, most recently by Mr Alan Moorehead, and it is, properly speaking, beyond the scope of this present book. Yet such an enterprise cannot be totally omitted from any narrative of events in 1915. For there are moments in the months which precede the creation of the Salonika Army when the historian feels that for Whitehall the war *was* Gallipoli. The War Council was superseded by the Dardanelles Committee; and it was the Dardanelles which led to the demise of the Liberal Government in May, 1915, and became the first problem of the Asquith Coalition which replaced it. Gallipoli, with its high hopes so nearly realized and its bitter disappointments, profoundly influenced British policy towards south-eastern Europe for many years ahead – and imposed blinkers on imaginative strategy for a generation.

By the end of February naval shells had silenced the outer forts of the Dardanelles. The political reaction to the news was electric.

Venizelos sought to turn about, and promptly offered three divisions for an advance on Constantinople. Kitchener began to scrape up divisions in case the Navy needed backing up. Even the French, jealously guarding their influence in the Levant, proposed to despatch troops, while the Russians unearthed from their archives a well-worn project for landing men on the Bosphorus. To the young volunteer officers bringing war back to the Hellespont and revelling in romantic classicism it seemed as if they were witnessing an historical climacteric.

It was, alas, one of the turning points when history failed to turn. In mid-March the optimism began to evaporate. There were political disappointments: Venizelos was forced out of office by the General Staff and replaced by a pro-German government. Far more serious was the calling off of the naval attack when it was within a hair's breadth of success. For the Allies thus drifted into a land campaign for which their military chiefs grudged every man and every shell. As the men sweltered in the heat of summer, the tip of the peninsula became a microcosm of established infantry practice, criss-crossed by trenches, four thousand of the attackers dying to gain four hundred yards on a mile front. The inconclusive futility of France and Flanders against which Franchet d'Espérey and Hankey and Lloyd George had railed was repeated in a very different terrain. Fresh divisions landed at Suvla in August suffered 38,000 casualties in three weeks of battle without being able to consolidate their position. By the autumn Gallipoli was a symbol of tragedy, not of triumph, for the Asquith Government. Nobody yet breathed the word 'Evacuation'; but it was at the back of everyone's mind. Unless, of course, another army, fresh men and new divisions, could sweep through those Turkish defences.

The war was going grimly for the Allies elsewhere that summer. The Germans and Austrians were rolling the Russians back through Poland. The Italians were immobile on the Adriatic; the Serbs static on the Danube. Joffre's offensive in Artois lost the French 100,000 men in ten days of fierce combat and penetrated little more than two miles into the German defences. Joffre might dolefully pat his head and repeat his pet-phrase, 'I keep nibbling at them', but it was tempting to ask, 'How strong are your teeth?'.

Nor was the political prospect any brighter. The Roumanians, who had contemplated intervention when all was going well in the Dardanelles, had second thoughts. The Bulgars seemed about

to commit themselves to the Central Powers: an ominous telegram from the Sofia Legation early in August informed the
Foreign Office that an influential colonel on the General Staff had
slipped off to Berlin in high secrecy. Only in Athens was there
some glimmer of hope; for on June 13th the Greek electorate,
despite intimidation, gave an overwhelming mandate to Venizelos' Liberal Party (184 seats in a chamber of 310). But another
ten weeks were to elapse before Venizelos was invited to form a
Ministry, for the King was seriously ill and constitutional propriety demanded (or was made to appear to demand) that until
he was well enough to send for the victorious Liberal leader, the
existing government should remain in office. Constantine's convalescence coincided with the low ebb of Allied military fortunes,
and by the time Venizelos was back in office the whole of Greece
was politically split between the Entente party (which backed
Venizelos) and the neutralists (who relied on King and army to
keep the tiger from their gates).

It was at this point that political considerations in France began
to exert an influence on the Balkans, for better or worse. For on
the Western Front there had been a development among the
military leaders of more than local interest. On July 22nd Joffre
dismissed General Sarrail from command of the Third Army.
There were good grounds for Joffre's action and plenty of prece-
dents. The Third Army had recently suffered a serious reverse,
losing five thousand men killed and another four thousand taken
prisoner in what were, strictly speaking, limited skirmishes. Yet it
was a bold stroke of Joffre's, for Sarrail was no mere field commander out of luck but the military idol of the dissident Left, a
political general down to his infantryman's boots.

Maurice Sarrail was born in south-western France, at Carcas-
sonne in 1856, the same year as Franchet d'Espérey (and, indeed
as two other French commanders, Nivelle and Pétain). He gradu-
ated from Saint Cyr in 1877, as did Franchet d'Espérey, but his
character and personality marked him out for a different career.
While many brother officers were devout Catholics, often affecting
a sentimental royalism, Sarrail was an uncompromising radical,
a Freemason and a freethinker. As a battalion commander in the
eighteen-nineties he did not hide his sympathies for the martyred
Dreyfus and the subsequent political victory of Dreyfus' champions
ensured Sarrail's promotion. His contacts with politicians became
closer after a period as commandant of the guard at the Palais

Bourbon, the home of the Chamber of Deputies, and in due course he was put in charge of infantry instruction at the rankers' training college of Saint-Maixent, the poor man's Saint Cyr. There his name became associated with the unpopular system by which confidential reports on the religious practices of officers and cadets were forwarded to the War Ministry, but this did not impede Sarrail's career for by now he had powerful patrons in one wing of the Radical Socialist Party. When, in the summer of 1911, his friend Joseph Caillaux became prime minister, Sarrail was promoted General and given a command of a division. Of his contemporaries, Franchet d'Espérey (whom it was generally agreed had a brilliant record) waited another year to attain a similar rank, while Pétain and Nivelle were still colonels when the war began.

It would, nevertheless, be unfair to suggest that Sarrail owed his advancement entirely to the happy coincidence of his views with those of M. Caillaux. Sarrail was a gallant soldier who had shown initiative on the Marne and at Verdun in the autumn of 1914; and it was for his abilities in the field that Joffre had appointed him to the Third Army in the first place. Indeed Caillaux, so far from assisting Sarrail on that occasion, was content to secure the general's backing for his own ambition of becoming Paymaster to the Forces (having resigned as a Minister when his wife emptied a revolver into the editor of *Figaro* who, in a bitter campaign against her husband, had unchivalrously cast aspersions on her pre-marital status). But if Sarrail had won his own way to the top, his friends could at least prevent his dismissal banishing him to the obscurity of a provincial garrison. Though Caillaux was out of office, his lieutenants were in Viviani's Government and Viviani could not afford a breach with the Radical Socialists if he were to continue as prime minister.

Fortunately for Viviani, there was a post for Sarrail. The general in command of the two French divisions at the Dardanelles had been seriously wounded by Turkish shell fragments. On the day after his dismissal, Sarrail was summoned before Viviani and the War Minister, Millerand, and offered the Gallipoli command. He was reluctant to accept a post which he considered to be inferior to his rank and dignity, but was allowed two days grace to make up his mind. With typical self-confidence, he then sought a further interview with Millerand and accepted the appointment, but on his own terms: the French force to be increased from two to six divisions; complete independence from the British command; and recognition that these 100,000 French-men should constitute 'the Army of the Orient'. Millerand con-ceded these points in principle, but he too insisted on one con-dition: 'Do not go canvassing Deputies', he said to Sarrail. And, for once, Sarrail did not.

Sarrail never went to Gallipoli. The situation in south-eastern Europe deteriorated rapidly in the early autumn. For during those months of wrangling between Easterners and Westerners in the allied capitals, the Germans had become aware that the Serbian Front, though silent, was potentially dangerous. Falkenhayn and Conrad, the chiefs of the German and Austrian General Staffs, decided in August on action in the Balkans: the Serbian obstacle must be swept from the middle Danube; and, if Turkey were to be an effective partner, men and munitions must move freely along the great trans-European railway through Belgrade and Niš to Constantinople. Hence on September 6th they signed a secret convention with Bulgaria for the total elimination of Serbia as a military force. A German army and an Austrian army were to attack across the Danube and the Sava and were to be supported, within a week, by two Bulgarian armies advancing on Serbia's flank to cut the Vardar–Morava link to the south. The Serbian army, sick of typhus and short of artillery, would thus be encircled by a force of over 400,000 men. A sledge-hammer was to be used to crack a small, but irritatingly tough, nut.

All this, although hardly unexpected, remained unknown to the Allies. Five days after the Bulgars had committed themselves to Falkenhayn's design, a conference was held at Calais to discuss the despatch of four French divisions under Sarrail to the Dar-danelles. Kitchener headed the British delegation, Joffre and Sarrail the French. There was still no sense of urgency. It was agreed that the French troops should only be sent eastwards after Joffre's autumn offensive at Loos, which was to be launched in the last week of September. Should the German line be broken, as Joffre hoped, the four divisions were to be retained on the Western Front. The tardiness of the Allies defies belief. As late as September 16th, Hankey was still working on a cabinet paper for sending a nominal force to Salonika to deter the Bulgars from entering the War. Nor did the French show any greater resolution. The Army of the Orient still existed only in Sarrail's ambitious imagination. Joffre had agreed on August 4th to send a French mission to Salonika to survey harbour installations and railway facilities; it did not reach its destination until September 22nd, a delay of seven weeks. By then it was far too late.

It was, in fact, on September 22nd that King Ferdinand signed the decree ordering general mobilization of the Bulgarian Army within three days. The Serbs promptly telegraphed an appeal for 150,000 French and British troops to be sent to Salonika and entrained for Serbian Macedonia. This, it will be remembered, equalled the number of men whom the Serbs were bound by the 1913 Convention with Greece to put into the field against Bulgaria to ensure Greek participation in a joint military enterprise. A similar request was received from Venizelos on the same day. In Paris, political sentiment and commercial interests dictated a swift acceptance of the demand for help even if the General Staff had no idea where they would find the troops. But in London there was dismal prevarication. Disillusionment with Gallipoli had strengthened the hands of the Westerners in Whitehall. Reluctantly the War Office looked around for men and material to form its quota (75,000) of the force. But the Foreign Secretary even refused to believe that Bulgaria had decided to intervene. Pathetically conjuring up the old Liberal image of enlightened Bulgaria, Grey took the disastrous step of advising Kitchener to veto a Serbian proposal to launch an attack on her neighbour before mobilization was complete and, a few days later, he enraged opinion in Serbia and Greece by holding out an olive branch to Sofia in the House of Commons.

London and Paris still behaved as if they had some time in which to muster an army. Sarrail was told by the historian Alphonse Aulard on September 25th that his destination was Salonika; another three days were to elapse before he received official notification. And it was not until a week after the Bulgarian mobilization that preparations were begun at the Dardanelles for the despatch of two British divisions to Salonika. Several weeks must pass before they could reach even the southernmost tip of Serbia. It was as if the whole notion of maintaining an army at Salonika had fallen on the Government out of the blue.

Yet had Falkenhayn been content to go through all the traditional motions of mounting an offensive, Allied counter-measures, although meagre, might at least have been in time. The Germans, however, had counted on swift action. In the previous spring Falkenhayn had organized the transference of troops for his Polish offensive with remarkable speed and secrecy but, even so,

the presence of fresh German regiments in the line had become
known to the Russians five days before the storm burst. Now he
would strike with even greater surprise. The infantry was not to
be massed along the Danubian Front until the very eve of the
offensive. In Falkenhayn's own words, the troops would have
'practically nothing to do but march up and proceed instantly
with the crossing'. Hence, although intelligence reports at the end
of September noted the movement of troop trains through southern Hungary, neither the Serbs nor the British and French had any
clear indication that an attack was actually imminent. When it
came, on the morning of October 6th, Allied aid still seemed
painfully far away. The first British and French divisions began to
disembark at Salonika just fifteen hours before the artillery
opened up on Belgrade. And between Salonika and Belgrade lay
nearly four hundred miles of hills and mountains.

The greatest obstacle to Allied policy in these crucial weeks
was, however, the political uncertainty in Athens. Even after
half a century it is not possible to discover exactly what happened
from day to day. Certain incidents stand out clearly enough. We
know, for example, that Venizelos attended King Constantine on
the afternoon of September 23rd, when the Bulgars were mobili-
zing. The two men met alone and their versions of the interview
are at variance with each other. Venizelos claims to have told the
King that the electorate had shown its support of his policy of not
permitting Bulgaria to destroy Serbia. 'Your Majesty,' he said, 'as
representative of the sovereign people, I must tell you that you
have no right on this occasion to differ from me'. To which the
King, with equal spirit, allegedly replied, 'As long as it is a question of internal affairs I must bow to the people's will; but in
foreign affairs I must decide what shall or shall not be done for
I feel responsible before God'. Venizelos maintains that he thereupon tendered his resignation which the King refused to accept,
agreeing to mobilize the army as a precautionary measure and to
seek the aid of the British and French. Constantine, on the other
hand, claims that he was only informed of the request for Allied
troops by letter one hour after Venizelos had seen the British and
French diplomatic representatives and denies that the audience
was so dramatic as Venizelos' account would suggest. Yet,
though neither Venizelos nor Constantine may have used these
actual words, they represent their differing points of view. Moreover, there remains one incontrovertible fact about the meeting:

the King decided to call the 180,000 men in his army to their war stations.

The confusion in Greek politics was reflected, at the time, in the messages reaching London: Venizelos would like troops to be sent as speedily as possible to Salonika; Venizelos thought troops should go to Mudros for later shipment to Salonika; Venizelos was afraid he must protest if belligerent forces landed at Salonika, etc., etc. The climax was reached on September 28th when two telegrams from Athens arrived within a short time of each other: the first thanked the British Government for its offer of troops but maintained that, since Serbia and Bulgaria had both given pacific assurances, these would not now be needed; the second insisted that no notice should be taken of the earlier message. Nor were matters made any easier by the arrival of Brigadier General Hamilton with the advance party on October 1st. For a message from the Salonika garrison commander to Athens stated that 'General Hamilton' had declared that he would occupy the city. Venizelos, assuming that the British officer was none other than the commander-in-chief at the Dardanelles, Sir Ian Hamilton, promptly complained to the Allies that they were violating Greek neutrality by transferring the whole of their Aegean army to Salonika in order to force concessions from the Greeks. Venizelos felt he had been deceived and, enjoying as he did the full Cretan temperament, did not hide his feelings from Sir Francis Elliott, the British Minister in Athens. So tense was the situation that Elliott urged Brigadier General Hamilton to prepare to leave Greece and insisted that the embarkation of the main force for Salonika should be halted until Venizelos had been re-assured about Allied intentions (and the movements of poor Sir Ian). By the evening of October 2nd, when this particular misunderstanding had been sorted out, it is small wonder if the British Government was regarding the whole enterprise with marked distaste.

A further scene in the Athenian tragi-comedy was played on the Sunday afternoon (October 3rd). Venizelos again summoned Elliott and his French colleague to his office and asked that troops should be landed at Salonika, promising that all the facilities of the port should be at the disposal of the Allies. But, at the same time, he solemnly read out a formal protest at the breach of Greek neutrality, handing a written copy of the note to the French Minister. The situation was still obscure. Influential newspapers were openly hostile to the proposed arrival of the Allies, but Venizelos was preparing to defend his policy in the Chamber and the Allied authorities, feeling that Venizelos was behind them, decided to go ahead with the landing. Had they hesitated for a few more hours, there would in all probability have been no army at Salonika, for between the Sunday and the Tuesday Venizelos suffered political defeat.

All went well in the Greek Parliament. Venizelos made a rousing speech, making it clear that for Greece Bulgaria remained the paramount enemy and that he intended to stand by the 1913 Convention. 'Greece has no immediate quarrel with Germany or Austria', he said, 'but if in the course of events in the Balkan Peninsula, she should find herself faced by other Powers, she will act as her honour demands'. He carried the Chamber with him; but it was too much for the King. On October 5th, at the very moment the Allied transports were sailing into the Gulf of Salonika, Venizelos had a further stormy audience with Constantine. The General Staff maintained that military intervention was tantamount to political suicide, and the King agreed with them. That evening Venizelos resigned, and Constantine entrusted the government to Zaimis, an able political manager who shared the King's convictions. It was too late to stop the French and British divisions. Disembarkation continued in a country in which resentment was changing to apprehension with each hour that passed.

Dramatic events were also taking place elsewhere on October 5th. In Sofia the British and French Ministers asked for their passports, thus formally recognizing the breach between Bulgaria and the Allies. Along the Danube and the Sava the new German and Austrian infantry regiments at last moved into position. In Calais an inter-allied conference between Joffre and Kitchener revealed the extreme reluctance of the British to press on into the interior of Macedonia. And all this while at Loos the casualty-list was rising grimly, as division after division was thrown against the German lines on the Western Front.

Not for many decades had a British Government embarked on a military undertaking with greater repugnance. Among Cabinet ministers only Lloyd George and Carson and Bonar Law believed in a supreme effort to rescue the Serbian Army. The General Staff disliked and distrusted the operation. On his return from Calais, Kitchener left no doubt about the feelings of the staff officers. It was an absurd risk to send 150,000 men to Serbia 'on the slender hope of being able to stop munitions from reaching the Turks'. A campaign of this nature might develop in such a way that it would become an 'unendurable strain by land and sea'. The only real alternative to using troops to gain a decision in France was to defend Britain's empire in the East and that could be done only at the Dardanelles. For the moment, the General Staff recognized that it was politically impossible to abandon Serbia because of France's pledges to render her assistance. But it was abundantly clear that the Government was far too timid to undertake a general action in the Balkans. The 10th Division might be in Salonika; but it was anyone's guess how long it would remain there.

3 / Winter War

GENERAL SARRAIL SAILED from Toulon in a fast destroyer on October 7th and arrived at Salonika five days later. He had been refused the completely independent command for which he had asked but was directly subordinate to the Minister of War rather than to Joffre at his headquarters in Chantilly. Nevertheless Joffre had already made his general views known in a directive dated October 3rd, which is printed in the official French collection of military documents. 'I consider,' he wrote, 'that it is in France, the main theatre of war, that we must seek a decision', although he admitted that, 'the Entente clearly has an obligation which it cannot shirk to prevent Serbia from being wiped off the map'. The immediate objective of the Allied troops must be the safeguarding of Serbian communications along the river Vardar as far as Skopje. He added, 'In my view Britain must subsequently galvanize the Balkan powers into military action; she has the necessary resources for the task and her troops, less committed than ours to the offensive (in France) are also less essential than ours in the decisive theatre of operations'. Joffre clearly grudged every man sent to the Balkans – except, perhaps, Sarrail himself whom he was glad to see removed from the vicinity of the Paris politicians. Unfortunately, the British were not prepared to play the rôle for which Joffre had cast them. Indeed, the first instructions sent to Sir Bryan Mahon, in command of the 10th Division at Salonika, were to remain near the port until it became clear whether or not the Greeks would participate with the British and French in rescuing the Serbs. The inference was that if the Greeks continued to be obdurate now that Venizelos had fallen, Mahon and his men would be evacuated from Salonika.

Until Sarrail reached Salonika the French 156th Division was under the command of General Bailloud. He, too, had received orders from Paris, drawn up before Joffre's directive. Bailloud was told to link up with the Serbs as quickly as possible, protecting the railway as far as Niš. This was a far more ambitious pro-

ject. Niš was the temporary seat of the Serbian government and
was a further hundred miles along the twisting railway from
Skopje. To reach Niš, Bailloud would have to move his men as
far as Plymouth from London along a single-track line which,
at several points, lay less than a dozen miles from the Bulgarian
border and which, on a good day, might manage a train every
four hours. This was a difficult enough task, but it was made no
easier by the fact that the line south of the Serbian frontier was
already being used by the Greeks to mobilize their own army.
Nevertheless, Bailloud got under way with commendable prompt-
itude. The division started on its long journey within thirty
hours of landing. A peremptory order from Paris recalled the
division before the end of the day. Bailloud was to remain at
Salonika until he had been reinforced by the 57th Division,
which was on its way from France and would not arrive for
another week. Niš, meanwhile, hopefully awaited the coming of
the French; it was still awaiting them on November 5th, when
the town fell to the Bulgars.

Sarrail, too, was determined to make a move as soon as he
could. Three battalions of infantry, with supporting artillery,
were transported some fifteen miles across the Greek-Serbian
frontier on October 14th, the day upon which the first units of
the 57th Division began to disembark. More troops and guns
followed in the course of the week, and the French went into
action against a Bulgarian column on October 21st. The brief
skirmish, in which the Bulgars were repulsed without much
difficulty, is militarily unimportant, but it well illustrates the
geographical confusion within the Balkans at this time, for the
French defended the railway station of Strumica, in Serbia,
against a Bulgarian force which had come from the town of
Strumica, a dozen miles away over the mountains in Bulgaria itself.

So far all was going well and Sarrail sent a brigade further up
the railway to Negotin, a village halfway between Strumica
Station and Veleš, the town upon which the main Serbian army
in Macedonia was based. But contact could not be made with
the Serbs. It was difficult country. The only bridges over the
Vardar were those carrying the railway and they had no foot-
way, the rails being bolted to slats which were precariously held
by a steel frame above the mountain stream. There were virtually
no roads, only bridle paths and tracks that had been worn down
by the bullock-carts over the years. North of Negotin the map
showed a road bridge across the Vardar. When the French

reached this position, they found that the bridge had been in ruins since the First Balkan War. To move their guns to the higher ground up river they were dependent upon a venerable ferry, operated by a Turkish Charon. This improbable obstacle, which no staff officer in distant Chantilly could have envisaged, prevented any effective aid from reaching the Serbs. For by the time engineers had thrown a bridge across the Vardar, Veleš had fallen and the Serbs were in retreat to the west.

Sarrail's men continued to take some of the pressure off the Serbs by engaging twenty-four battalions of the Bulgarian Second Army, but they had made too little progress into Serbia for their actions to effect the outcome of the campaign. The French eventually penetrated another nine miles and engaged the flank of the Bulgarian Army beyond the river Crna. Heavy fighting took place between November 11th and November 14th and the French had to give some ground, but they were still strongly placed when the Bulgars broke off the action to tighten the noose around the Serbian forces which had fallen back from the Babuna Pass. Skopje by now seemed as remote and unattainable as Belgrade.

If the French attempt to aid the Serbs was paltry, the British was almost derisory. Not until October 22nd, seventeen days after the disembarkation, was Mahon authorized to leave Salonika and even then he was instructed not to go beyond the Greek frontier. Two brigades of the 10th Division were moved up to the west of Lake Doiran, their progress being impeded by the uncooperative attitude of the Greek railway authorities. Four days later, Kitchener telegraphed an order to Mahon that he was to support Sarrail fully, even crossing the frontier if necessary. Mahon accordingly sent a detachment of engineers to assist the French along the Vardar but, apart from this handful of men, the British did not take over any section of the front in Serbia until November 10th. By then the whole of the old kingdom of Serbia had been overrun and the Serbs were preparing to retreat to the historic plateau of Kosovo, which they had liberated from the Turks only three years before. Even when the 10th Division moved over the frontier, it encountered few Bulgars. But, though its commanders may have shown timidity, the British force was not lacking in courage and resolution. The great enemy was the weather, which turned from rain to fog and to snow. The Division was caught on the fringe of the awful blizzard which was freezing men to death on Gallipoli. So grim were conditions

up in the mountains that, at the end of the month, after a week
of blinding snow, more than 1,500 men had to be brought back
to the base at Salonika in a state of collapse. Yet the 10th Division clung on to their positions in this savagely bleak countryside, until forced to fall back as part of the general retreat in
December.

Snow was falling, too, in central Serbia. There it had come even
earlier than usual, the first drifts checking invaders and defenders
alike on November 17th. As the blizzard swept in, the Serbs
were fighting desperately at Kosovo, where five hundred years
before the medieval kingdom had perished in one last magnificent stand against the Turks. Momentarily the snow was to prove
Serbia's salvation. For six weeks the Serbs had endured assault
by Austro-German forces from the north and west, and for one
week less from the two Bulgarian armies in the east. Twice Field
Marshal von Mackensen, who was in command of the joint
armies, believed he had manœuvred the Serbs into a trap, seeking to emulate that classic victory of the military textbooks,
Cannae. On both occasions, first at Kragujevac and again at
Blače, the Serbian chief of staff, Putnik, denied Mackensen the
mantle of Hannibal. Kragujevac was left burning, the Serbian
arsenal sending column after column of exploding munitions
high in the sky as the Austrians moved in. While the snow enveloped 'The Plain of Blackbirds', as Kosovo was called, the
Austrians and Bulgars were closing the last routes along which
the Serbs might escape. Four of the five roads were in enemy
hands. The remaining road, if such it can be called, led up to the
mountain bastion of Montenegro and Albania. The Adriatic
coast, where the Allies might at last link up with the Serbs, lay
over the mountains – far over the mountains. The Serbs could
either go down fighting in one last symbolic battle at Kosovo or
they could seek sanctuary on the inhospitable slopes. They chose
to retreat, reckoning that only thus could they return to liberate
their land; and at Prizren and at Peć funeral pyres were lit, the
last trucks and guns going up in smoke, as the shells had done
at Kragujevac four weeks earlier.

   The Serbian horde – it could hardly now be called an army –
took to the hills on November 23rd. The Serbs split into four
groups, each seeking a different way across the mountains.
Albanian tribesmen ambushed the fugitives. There were no
provisions to succour the famished men and the cold grew more

2*

intense with each mile that they trudged along the narrow defile between the mountain peaks. The snow, which had saved them at Kosovo, now claimed as many victims as a pitched battle. Twenty thousand of the refugees in one contingent died in the mountains. Moreover, this was no forced march of young and healthy recruits. Typhus continued to take a heavy toll, and many of the men who had rallied to the colours were septuagenarians (čiče, 'uncles', as they were called). The Serbian prime minister, Nikola Pašić, who accompanied the troops with his government, was over seventy, a patriarchal figure with a grey beard tapering down almost to his waist. Putnik himself was a veteran of sixty-eight whose health had been failing even before the war began; he was borne across the mountains in a sedan chair. King Peter was three years older than Putnik and had first fought in this wild terrain fifty years before, against the Turks; now, with the rest, he stumbled on beside his devoted soldiery. Prince Regent Alexander, Peter's son and Serbia's commander-in-chief, was only twenty-seven; but he, too, was a sick man, in agony from a stomach ulcer. Nor were all these refugees Serbian. Four medical units had been sent to Serbia from Edinburgh by the Scottish Women's Suffrage Federation and although most of the nurses stayed to tend the wounded in the occupied lands one group participated in the ghastly retreat, heroically championing a woman's right to pass judgment on the political folly of a man's world. Yet perhaps the most pitiable of all this human flotsam were the twenty thousand Austrian prisoners, captured in the fighting of the previous winter and now dragged with their captors away from salvation. Like Tolstoy's Pierre, who was carried back by the French as a prisoner in 1812, some may have 'learned that suffering and freedom have their limits and that these limits are very near together'; but many, like Pierre's companion Karataev, perished on the way.

The passage of the mountains took most of the Serbian contingents three weeks. Even when they reached the coast there was still a tragic delay. The Italians, who had been entrusted by the Allies with the task of ferrying food and medical supplies across the Adriatic, would not risk running their vessels so close to the Austrian naval base at Cattaro. Considerable political pressure had to be applied to the Italians by the other allies before they would aid the Serbs. Eventually, it was decided to evacuate the remaining Serbs from the Albanian coast to the Greek island of Corfu, which the French occupied early in

January, 1916, despite angry protests from Athens. Estimates of
the number of Serbs who reached Corfu vary; possibly it was as
many as 155,000, although the earliest reports put the figures
considerably lower. Yet so emaciated were these survivors that
nurses in Corfu were able to lift fully-grown men in their arms as
if they were babies. It seemed impossible that within eight
months they would again constitute a formidable fighting unit
in the Salonika Army.

As the Serbs were forced further and further back westwards
into the mountains the French troops in the Vardar valley became more and more exposed. Sarrail had sent the best part of
45,000 men into Serbia, retaining several thousand more on
Greek soil including a sizeable contingent grouped around his
headquarters outside Salonika. He had also moved much heavy
material across the frontier and beside each of the railway stations
were dumps of ammunition and packs of waggons gathered in
case it were possible to advance to Veleš. But, in fact, by the
middle of November it had become clear that the French would
not be able to press on up the Vardar. Paris advised withdrawal
with increasing urgency in each successive telegram but Sarrail
was reluctant to give the order. Not only did he wish to support
the Serbs for as long as possible, but his pride was effected.
Kitchener had come out to the Dardanelles and called at Salonika
in the third week of the month. It would ill become a patriot
Frenchman to order a retreat when the victor of Fashoda was
visiting his base. And then, too, there was the first party of
French journalists, anxious to see the *poilu* repelling the Bulgar;
no good political general would disappoint the Press.

    The decision was, as it happened, taken out of Sarrail's hands.
On November 20th a newly-arrived Bulgarian brigade occupied
high ground overlooking the advanced French position. The
commander of the 122nd Division, General de Lardemelle, knowing that Sarrail was contemplating a withdrawal, ordered his
men to fall back. The retreat was on, although another ten days
were to pass before it became general. Gradually the French
began pulling out, painfully slowly, one division covering only
four miles in twenty-four hours. In heavy snowfalls, broken now
and again by spells of fog, it became difficult to shift all the
material along the hard-pressed railway and the adjoining tracks,
deep in slush. To their right, on December 7th, the British were
forced to leave the positions they had occupied on the heights

beyond Lake Doiran. The Bulgars sent four divisions to harass
the Allied force; elated by their success against the Serbs, they
fought ferociously. The French beat off each assault but there
were moments when disaster seemed close at hand. Fortunately
they were spared concentrated shelling since the Bulgarian
artillery had come to rest in heavy snowdrifts. Otherwise few of
the French could have crossed back into Greece for the conges-
tion in the valley grew worse as waggons and carts and limbers
ploughed on through the mud and the slush. Yet despite Bulgars,
despite snow, despite flocks of sheep and goats straggling across
the cart-tracks and the derailment of a train on the vital railway,
it was 'a methodical and orderly retreat' – or so we are assured
by a French military commentator. The fiercest fighting took
place, not along the river, but over to the east where the British
10th Division, already under strength, was evacuating a group
of small villages on the mountain slopes north-west of Lake
Doiran. By December 12th all French and British troops had left
Serbian territory; one in ten of the Allied force was listed as a
casualty, killed or wounded or missing. It was a heavy price to
pay for taking pressure off the Serbs and few people back in
France and Britain appreciated what had been done. Bulgarian
casualties were even higher; but it was easy for the critics to point
out that not a German nor an Austrian nor a Turk had come
under the fire of Sarrail's or Mahon's men.

Sarrail had none the less conducted a masterly withdrawal,
bringing back almost all the guns and supplies which he had
sent up into the Balkan defiles. Yet one's admiration for his
administrative ability and unruffled tenacity is lessened by an
incident characteristic of the man and his policy. During the
retreat General de Lardemelle was superseded as commander of
the 122nd Division. He was dismissed because he had ordered
withdrawal on November 20th without waiting for authority from
Sarrail; and, having been rebuked by his commander, he had
attempted to clear his name, showing in Sarrail's own words, 'an
open lack of discipline'. If this were really the case, then Sarrail's
action was of course justified. But one wonders. It could be argued
that if Sarrail were determined to conduct operations from eighty-
five miles behind his advanced positions, he should have allowed
his subordinate on the spot greater independence of judgment.
For this episode was essentially a conflict of personalities. De
Lardemelle was no ordinary divisional commander. He had
earned his promotion, like some of the later war leaders, by his

skill as a colonel on the field of battle in France. As Franchet
d'Espérey's chief of staff he had helped prepare the plan for an
offensive on the Danube a year before. Balkan problems had
fascinated him and, in company with d'Espérey, he had pressed
his views on President Poincaré as late as June 17th, only a few
weeks before Sarrail's own dismissal from the Third Army.
Everything about de Lardemelle ran counter to Sarrail's predilec-
tions: he came from an aristocratic and Catholic family, his
political contacts were with the conservatively minded Poincaré
rather than with the radicals, he had been favoured by the
paladins of Chantilly. Sarrail may well have felt that he had been
imposed on the Salonika Army by Joffre as a potential successor.
At all events, General de Lardemelle was packed off to France.
He was not the last of Sarrail's senior commanders to be ousted
in this way.

At the time, there were more pressing problems than the eclipse
of a brilliant young divisional general. Would the Bulgars halt
on the old Greek frontier? Sarrail thought so, and he soon received confirmation of his belief from intelligence sources within
Bulgaria. From the Allied point of view, this was as well; for the
enemy forces were no more than six days march from the base
at Salonika and the defences around the town were incapable of
checking a determined adversary. The decision to halt on Serbian
soil was not Bulgaria's nor Austria's but Germany's, or more
correctly, General von Falkenhayn's. For discord had broken
out among the enemy commanders.
    Falkenhayn argued that Germany had undertaken the cam-
paign against Serbia to destroy the tiresome hornets' nest around
Belgrade and to ensure communications with Turkey. Both of
these objectives had been achieved. It would be simple enough
to throw the Allies into the Aegean, but was this strategically
desirable? Falkenhayn thought not. Better five divisions inactive
on the shores of the Aegean than swelling the Allied line in
France. And there were other considerations. Who would move
into Greece? Falkenhayn was a latter-day Bismarck despising the
Balkans from the depths of his Prussian soul: 'Not one German
soldier must be left to die of hunger and typhus in this inhospitable land', he declared. If not Germany, who then? The Austrian chief of staff, Conrad, had no doubt of the answer. The
Habsburg Monarchy had long coveted Salonika as a potential
Trieste on the Aegean: 'The most advanced gateway in the south-

east for the commerce of southern Austria and Hungary – our hope for the future'; thus an influential publicist in Vienna had described Salonika only eight years before. But the Bulgars had entered the war with only one objective – to gain what they felt was rightly theirs in Macedonia. It was inconceivable that Bulgaria would allow Austria-Hungary to take over Salonika; and it was equally inconceivable that Greece (at the moment, well-disposed towards the Germans) would permit either the Austrians or the Bulgars to annex land so recently added to the Greek Kingdom. Falkenhayn believed that by sanctioning the occupation of Salonika he might even lose one of the prime achievements of his campaign. The Bulgars and Austrians were already on bad terms. Once let the Salonika question be posed and there would be a complete breach. Bulgaria might easily go out of the war or even turn against Turkey; how, then, would Berlin keep open the line to Constantinople?

Austrian and Bulgarian writers have not spared Falkenhayn. Had he not vetoed a crossing of the frontier, they say, peace would have been restored in the Balkans and there would have been no Macedonian problem to nag Hindenburg and Ludendorff in the critical days of 1918. Even at the time, Falkenhayn had the greatest difficulty in imposing his will. Conrad charged him with betraying the Austro-German Alliance and was induced to write a letter of grudging apology only upon the insistence of Pan-Germans in Vienna who dreaded the effect of bad relations between the two General Staffs on the campaign in Russia. So Falkenhayn had his way, and, for the moment, his strategy seemed justified. The Bulgars, up in the mountains, kept guard over the passes, while below them in the malarial swamps around the estuary of the Struma the sick-list of the Allied Army grew longer and longer.

Falkenhayn's strategic logic was curiously similar to the reasoning of the staff officers in Whitehall. They had hated the Balkan venture from the start and their attitude hardened with every item of news which reached them from Salonika. And, now that Gallipoli had failed, their views carried more weight with the Government. It is true that one member of the cabinet, Carson, the Attorney-General, had resigned in disgust at the half-hearted way in which the Asquith Coalition had reacted to the Serbian crisis. But, in general, the politico-strategists were more inhibited than they had been earlier in the year. Only Lloyd

George and Bonar Law still accepted the need for a positive Balkan policy.

Salonika which, as we have seen, strained the relations between Germany and Austria-Hungary also led to tension between Britain and France. The crisis in the Entente came earlier, but lasted longer. On the last Friday evening in October (the 29th) Hankey strolled over from his office to 10 Downing Street. There seemed no reason to suppose that it would be anything but a quiet weekend. The Prime Minister was busy with the preparation of a major speech and all the military experts were at Chantilly conferring with Joffre and the French General Staff on the Balkans. Since Murray, the Chief of the Imperial General Staff, and Joffre had for months been restraining the Easterners in their respective capitals, it seemed hardly likely that they would fail to agree over Salonika. Indeed, Murray was confident that the French would accept the British view that no more troops should be sent to Greece. Yet when Hankey reached No. 10 that evening, he found Joffre himself closeted with the Prime Minister. A remarkable change had come over the French commander. Now he was persuasively championing the Macedonian project and had walked out of the Chantilly Conference because the British staff officers countered every French proposal to send fresh divisions eastwards. Joffre the imperturbable was rattled. His offensive at Loos had proved a costly failure and there was dismay and disappointment in Paris. Viviani's Government was breaking up and his own days as commander-in-chief seemed numbered.

The situation in Paris soon became clearer. Viviani resigned that very evening and Poincaré entrusted the formation of a new government to Briand. Back in January Briand had been as strong an advocate of the Balkan policy as Lloyd George. Now he also took over the portfolio of foreign affairs, which Delcassé had given up because of his disapproval of the Salonika venture, and appointed as Minister of War General Galliéni, another 'Balkaner' and a grand old soldier whose record rivalled Joffre's. Even before these appointments were announced, Joffre in London had not minimized the significance of the political crisis. As Hankey noted in his diary, 'It appeared . . . from private conversation, first, that his own position was at stake, and, second, that the alliance itself would be gravely endangered if we refused to co-operate. He was promised an answer on the following day'.

The Cabinet was not prepared to quarrel with the new French Government. It was agreed that the British would 'co-operate energetically' with Sarrail's force, but at the same time Kitchener was authorized to notify Joffre that if it proved impossible to re-open and maintain contact with the Serbs, the whole Allied force would be evacuated from Salonika 'to be used as circumstances may require'. Few in Whitehall welcomed the compromise and Murray continued to emphasize that the General Staff was utterly opposed to the whole venture.

Events in November only strengthened the antipathy of the staff officers. Four days after notifying Joffre of the British decision, Kitchener left London to see for himself what was happening at the Dardanelles and in the Aegean. By now his colleagues had come to regard Kitchener as an empty legend, an old warhorse needing the peace of green pastures. But as this frail Bucephalus scented battle some of his former energy returned. A couple of days on Gallipoli, a hurried trip to Salonika to consult Sarrail and Mahon, across to Mudros to umpire a contest in policy between the naval and military authorities, and down to the Piraeus to seek out King Constantine in his palace in Athens; by the end of the month, back to London – a formidable programme for a man of sixty-five before the era of air transport. Yet little enough was achieved. Evacuation of Gallipoli? Evacuation of Salonika? Evacuation of Gallipoli *and* Salonika? The questions were still being posed on Kitchener's return; and he would not give a clear answer. Only in Athens had he scored a success of a sort. There were fears that the Greeks might attempt to disarm British and French troops in Macedonia. Kitchener made it clear to Constantine that no such action would be tolerated. The King protested that there had been a breach of Greek neutrality; Kitchener asked for a pledge that Allied troops would not be interned. Constantine gave his word, assuring Kitchener that he personally did not favour the German cause. Five allied battleships and several cruisers were in Greek waters at the time. It was hardly a friendly interview. Kitchener had arrived at the Palace at midday; he was not invited to lunch.

Yet, though reluctant to admit it and prone to chop and change, Kitchener knew at heart that Gallipoli should be evacuated. His conflicting instincts were resolved by the General Staff in London. But the news of the Serbian retreat and of the failure of the Allies to reach Veleš made the staff officers go even further. Britain's course was clear: end both enterprises in the eastern Mediterranean and concentrate on the defence of Egypt.

Serbian cavalry in the Albanian retreat

The Serbian retreat, 1915: Voivode Putnik in a sedan chair

The Serbian retreat, 1915: climbing the Babuna Pass

General Sarrail and General Sir Bryan Mahon, April 1916

Transporting a motor boat across the mountains for service on
Lake Langaza

Serbian battle honours: troops dancing a traditional *Kolo* round a
cairn of stones carrying the names of their victories

Winter War: a Serb mounts guard near the Albanian frontier

The Government, still hesitant over Gallipoli, gave way over Salonika. The French were sent a stiff telegram on December 1st reminding them that the conditions of Kitchener's compromise with Joffre had not been fulfilled and insisting that the Allies should leave Greece. There was no response. A sharper message followed the next day; it was hinted that some of the B.E.F. might be recalled from the Western Front. This time Briand reacted. A conference was summoned for December 4th at Calais.

Asquith selected his party for Calais with great care. Only convinced Westerners were included; no Lloyd George, no Bonar Law. Briand assembled an impressive array of brass-hats. Galliéni was there and so too was Joffre, for the moment reconciled to each other since each believed himself to be the military constable of France. For, with characteristic ingenuity, Briand had avoided the odium of sacking Joffre while none the less clipping his wings. On paper he had even given Joffre greater responsibility. Two days before the conference Joffre had been created commander-in-chief of all the French armies in the field (including Sarrail's Army of the Orient) but Galliéni had been placated by the institution of a 'General Staff of the French Army', nominated by the War Minister, which would, Briand assured him, effectively control Joffre's actions. Joffre, for his part, went to Calais knowing that later in the week staff officers of all the allied armies would gather in Chantilly to determine strategy for 1916. If he was silent at Calais it is hardly surprising, for there was little doubt in Joffre's mind that he remained châtelain of Chantilly.

The British took a firm line at Calais. The French were informed that they had decided to withdraw from Salonika. Neither reproaches nor blandishments could shake Asquith's rare resolution of purpose. He read a formal statement to the conference:

'We give no opinion as to what new operations may be undertaken in the future in the Balkans or elsewhere, and we agree that there are questions which should be considered in concert by the Allies. But in the opinion of the military advisers of the British Government, the retention of the present force of 150,000 at Salonika is from a military point of view dangerous and likely to lead to a great disaster. They cannot therefore agree to its continued retention, and are of opinion that preparations should be made without delay for evacuation'.

The French bowed to this pronouncement, the British left and returned to Dover. It had been a grim conference and it was to be a grim sea-crossing; heavy seas, whipped up by a south-westerly gale, broke over the destroyer carrying the British party. But, even in the miseries of sea-sickness, they could take heart. At last a decision had been taken. No more sideshows; now the Allies could concentrate on defeating Germany.

The French rejected the whole arrangement within forty-eight hours. At the Chantilly conference the Italians, the Russians and the Serbs all supported the French policy of keeping open the Balkan Front. Lest there should still be doubt in London, a telegram was sent from the Tsar of Russia formally regretting the decision which Asquith had given at Calais. Britain had been manœuvred into invidious isolation. It was the turn of the Foreign Office to be alarmed. The Alliance must be held together at all costs.

Another hasty cross-channel journey, this time for Kitchener and Grey. Another conference with Briand and Joffre, less than a week after the meeting in Calais. Nothing was now said of evacuating Salonika, only of how best to employ the British divisions in defence of the base. Kitchener reported back to the War Committee that 'good feeling had been restored'. In those days appeasement was still a valid instrument of policy.

Everyone knew that it was easier to start a war than to end it. Now the statesmen and the soldiers and the sailors were to learn that it was easier to land in Greece than to leave it. But, at all events, the dispute with her allies had resolved one of Britain's problems. It was clearly impossible to maintain a force at Salonika and at the Dardanelles. By Christmas the War Committee had finally decided to evacuate Gallipoli. Within a fortnight the last British troops had been withdrawn. And at Salonika there were five British divisions (90,000 men) and three French (60,000). It was a development which few people in London had foreseen – and even fewer welcomed.

4 / 'The Greatest Internment Camp'

W HILE HIGH POLICY decisions were being taken – or
evaded – in Calais and Chantilly, the men of the Salonika
Army were busy with spades and wire. For Sarrail and Mahon had
agreed that Salonika must be converted into an entrenched camp
capable of repelling any attack. The Greeks, under protest, retired from some of the surrounding countryside, although retaining garrisons in the city and the forts commanding the mouth of
the Vardar and the entry to the Gulf of Salonika. And, as the
Greeks watched with ill-concealed derision, the Allies prepared
for an attack which never came.

Sarrail planned to establish a defensive line from Lake Langaza,
six miles north-east of the port, along a ridge which ran north-
westwards for eleven miles up to the railway (known sometimes as
the 'Seres Line' and at moments of optimism as the 'Constantinople Line'). To the west of the railway line the land was flat and
marshy, but protected by the Vardar itself. East of Lake Langaza
lay a valley some seven miles long which opened out into another
lake, Beshik. And beyond Beshik was the Rendina Gorge, running
down to the Gulf of Orfano. An arc of French reconnaissance
posts was set up twenty miles out towards the frontier. The whole
fortified position, from the village of Skala Stavros on the Gulf of
Orfano to the Vardar marshes, was slightly over seventy miles
long. It was manned in the centre and east by five British divisions, supported by a Royal Marine brigade and naval units (to
patrol the two lakes), and in the west by the three French divisions. A cruiser and a monitor lent support in the Gulf of Orfano
and a naval squadron, which included battleships, was based on
Salonika itself.

By the end of January 1916 the entrenched camp already
contained a remarkable concentration of Allied military and
naval power. Rather more than 160,000 men were confined in an
area about twice the size of the Isle of Wight, four-fifths of the
force within a twenty mile radius of the port. The nearest Bulgarian posts were twenty-five miles from the fortified line, along

the old Greco-Serbian frontier. Between the Bulgars and the
Allies lay a no-man's land which, apart from the Vardar valley
and the wooded slopes around Lake Doiran, was bare and mountainous. Occasionally there would be a cavalry skirmish between
reconnaissance groups or an exchange of artillery fire, but for days
on end there was no contact with the enemy – only the monotony
of digging and filling sandbags or the tedium of training exercises.

Construction of fortifications went on for four months, until the
first signs of the Aegean Spring began to shame the ugliness of the
wire and the gashes of trenches. Winter was harsh. Snow fell
heavily through January and every now and again a strong, icy
wind would sweep down the funnel of the Vardar cutting through
the goatskin jackets of the men as they hacked away at the rocky
ground. Near the city there was heavy work to be done. New
jetties were erected in the harbour, for there were far too many
lighters and small craft for the cramped quays. Roads had to be
made to link outlying posts and light railways to enable supplies to
get through more easily. Local civilian labour was used as much
as possible for work of this type, under the direction of officers who
were alleged to speak Greek, but there were far too many spies in
the city for the inhabitants to be employed on the actual fortifications. All along the inner defence line were machine-gun emplacements, dug-outs and wire entanglements. The French, in the
tradition of Vauban, excelled at military engineering of this kind;
but it was no easy task to sink concrete positions along the banks
of the Vardar, especially when the river began to flood with melt-
ing snow. Often the soil was treacherous; a lorry would creep
tentatively forward like a cautious bather taking the first dip of
the year and suddenly start to subside, and a weary detachment
of swearing soldiery would sling ropes around its muddy axle,
hoping that a second vehicle could haul it out. One French civil
engineer sought to offset this difficulty by adding a caterpillar
tread to the rear wheels – but established practice frowned on such
far-sighted eccentricity. The British, too, had problems of a
specialized nature. How, for example, were the naval patrol boats
to reach Lake Langaza and Lake Beshik? There seemed only one
way: hoist them to the quay and load them on to pontoon waggons. But it took a waggon train a whole day to shift its load three
miles under these conditions. In both the British and French
sectors it was slow and tedious work.

Yet, by April 1915, Salonika had been transformed into one of
the best fortified cities in the world. The base was now an Aegean

Verdun; it was an impressive achievement. Nevertheless, in retrospect, it must be admitted that the scale of these defensive preparations seems out of all proportion to the danger of an enemy
attack. The commanding officer of the engineer detachments in
one of the British divisions calculated that in the first four weeks
of the operation his unit alone put up 245 miles of wire. By then
he was one-tenth of the way through his assignment. It was never
completed; to carry out his instructions fully he would have required enough wire to run a double line to Berlin in one direction
and to Constantinople in the other.

The enemy was kept well informed of these preparations.
Agents attached to the German, Turkish, Bulgarian and Austrian
consulates were to be seen on the quays, complete with notebooks
in which to record details of units and their equipment. Until the
end of 1915 a train actually ran daily from Salonika across the
Turkish frontier, enabling privileged diplomatic mail to be conveyed to Constantinople in a matter of hours. Sarrail did not
object to the enemy knowing that Salonika was becoming a
formidable base provided that this information deterred the
Germans and Bulgars from launching an attack. Indeed, the
Allies appear to have conducted a Greek general around the
defences with every intention that a report on their impregnable
character should be forwarded from Athens to Berlin and Sofia –
as it was.

Yet, clearly enough, if the Salonika Army were ever to break
out of its self-constructed 'birdcage' and go over to the offensive,
representatives of enemy powers could not be allowed such freedom of movement. The British, natural sticklers for security, had
found this situation irksome from the start, and Mahon began
pressing Sarrail to seize the Consulates as soon as the troops fell
back from the frontier. The French, however, decided to act only
after German aircraft had bombed the city, aided, so it was
alleged, by signals from the Consulates. This first air raid took
place early in the morning of December 30th 1915, killing a Greek
shepherd on the outskirts of the city but otherwise causing no
casualties and doing little damage. But it was enough for Sarrail.
At three o'clock that afternoon French and British detachments
entered the four Consulates and arrested twenty Austrians, seventeen Turks, twelve Bulgars and five Germans. Five more 'enemy
aliens' were subsequently rounded up in the city. With information obtained from the archives of the Consulates, the British and
French military police were able to gather in many of the

spies from the old quarter of the town. As the German Official History says, 'An essential source of information was thus lost.'

The mutual hostility of the Greek and Allied authorities eased a little in December, once Sarrail and Mahon had received a Greek staff officer sent by the General Staff in Athens to regularize the position of Greek units around the city. But now, at the end of the month, it flared up again. Sarrail evidently hoped that the air raid would mute Greek protests at his own action against the consuls. He reported to Paris, with undisguised satisfaction, that one bomb had fallen near a squadron of cavalry which was commanded by the King's brother, Prince Andrew (who, six years later, was to become the father of the present Duke of Edinburgh). Yet if Sarrail really believed that Greek susceptibilities would be assuaged by this inadvertent affront to dynastic dignity, he was swiftly disillusioned. That very evening the Greek Government complained of the arrest of accredited diplomatic representatives and requested Sarrail to hand them over to the civil authorities. Not unnaturally, he refused and shipped off all 53 men and 9 women to France, whence they were eventually repatriated. The Greek Press thereupon unleashed a tirade of abuse against the Allies, and Sarrail hardened himself for further measures. A fortnight later he sent a small force up the railway towards Constantinople in order to destroy the iron-bridge across the river Struma at Demir Hissar. This was an obvious act of self-defence, for the bridge covered a key position in the Rupel Gorge, the natural route of advance for an enemy moving against Salonika. Nevertheless, the Greeks were once again indignant and the Athenian Press howled at Allied disregard of the niceties of formal neutrality. It was clear that Sarrail was gradually assuming responsibility for the civil administration of the port and its hinterland, although for the moment the French Government refused to allow him to proclaim a formal state of siege in Salonika.

All this while, twelve miles to the south, the Greeks continued to man the batteries on the promontory of Karaburun, a fort which covered both the estuary of the Vardar and the main seaway into the anchorage of Salonika. From a captive balloon British naval observers kept an anxious eye on Karaburun, noting in particular the new gun emplacements which were going up with disturbing rapidity. Reports seeped through to Allied Intelligence that armour-piercing shells were being stacked in the capacious magazines, and there was the usual crop of rumours of flashing lights signalling to unobserved submarines. The Allies had already asked the Greeks to hand over Karaburun on two occasions but King Constantine had indignantly refused. 'I will not be treated as if I were a native chieftain', he had said with some heat when the matter was first broached. Mahon, for his part, still hoped that in time the Greeks would pull out of their own accord. He feared that if the Allies had to storm the fort the whole of the Greek Army in Macedonia would move against the Allied positions and pose a problem which would be, at the best, embarrassing and potentially disastrous. Mahon was convinced that it was better to wait; but for how long would Sarrail be content to leave the Greeks in control of the guns?

Sarrail's mind was made up by an incident early in the New Year. On January 22nd the British troop-carrier *Norseman*, with the equipment of the 26th Division on board, was torpedoed off Karaburun Point as she was ending her voyage from Marseilles. The *Norseman* was beached, all the men and women aboard her were saved (and so, even, were 500 of the mules she was carrying) but the destruction of the *Norseman* finally convinced the French that some of the Greek officers were in league with the Germans. Without consulting Mahon, Sarrail determined to evict the Greeks from Karaburun and its outlying defences without delay.

Ironically, this action against a contingent of 250 Greeks, technically non-belligerent, was the best planned inter-allied naval and military operation of the Macedonian campaign. Sarrail was taking no chances. He began to move some three thousand men southward through the entrenched camp on the Wednesday morning, January 26th, but it was not until the following evening that he informed Mahon of his intentions and asked for British co-operation. Under protest Mahon agreed to help. Twelve hours later, as dawn broke on the Friday morning, all was ready. British, French and Italian cruisers patrolled the Gulf; and the twelve-inch guns of the twenty-years old battleship *Albion* were trained on Karaburun as they had been trained on the forts of the Dardanelles ten months before. There was, too, another Dardanelles veteran, of even greater antiquity – the 'Packet of Woodbines', the Russian cruiser *Askold*, with its five tall funnels emitting filthy smoke from inferior coal. On land, a hundred British marines advanced on the outlying forts while, from the direction of the city, French infantry crept cautiously towards Karaburun with three aeroplanes circling over them and a squadron of cavalry in support. Would the Greek guns open fire on the naval vessels or the troops? If they did, it was anyone's guess what would happen in Salonika.

In the event, not a shot was fired. The whole operation ended in anticlimax. Plenipotentiaries negotiated the surrender of the fort; the Greeks withdrew, quietly enough; and the French manned the guns. The naval squadron dispersed, the troops returned to their encampment. It was then discovered that one of the senior Greek officers had been so little disturbed by the Allied movements that, while Sarrail was manœuvring his men into position, he had driven through their lines to begin a long weekend leave. Perhaps it is hardly surprising that the occupation of Karaburun receives no more than a sentence in the official French military history of the campaign. It remains one of the oddest displays of force in the whole war; Palmerston himself could hardly have done better.

Meanwhile, apart from the occasional air-raid, all was quiet from Salonika to Doiran and the Vardar. This inactivity was, however, to the liking of neither the French nor the German High Commands. By now there was an odd similarity in the way Joffre and Falkenhayn regarded the Balkan theatre of war. Both wished to keep the Macedonian Front on the boil; both tended to minimize difficulties of climate and terrain; both hoped that their respective allies would effectively menace the enemy in this part of Europe; and both found their allies reluctant to make any move.

At Chantilly Joffre still believed in the supreme importance of the Western Front. He rejected, with some impatience, a Russian proposal that 400,000 French and British troops should be poured into Macedonia in order to rendezvous later in the year in Budapest with a Russian Army of the Danube (which, as it happened, did not yet exist). And when Sarrail asked for two divisions, a cavalry regiment and some additional artillery, he was sent the horses and the guns but the two divisions remained in the Argonne. Yet Joffre had no intention of dismissing the Salonika venture from his mind. He was convinced that the Tommies rather than the *poilus* should play the leading rôle in the Balkans – although preferably under a French commander-in-chief. He could not induce Sir William Robertson, the new Chief of the Imperial General Staff, to send a single additional regiment to reinforce Mahon; but he did at least succeed in gaining British consent to the appointment of Sarrail as joint commander of all the allied forces defending Salonika, even though the British contingent was larger than the French. This was, in its way, a momentous concession on the part of the British; had not Kitchener cautioned Asquith, 'Never let your troops come under French command'? It was, none the less, made plain to the French that Sarrail's powers were limited to the actual maintenance of the entrenched camp; another six months were to elapse before conditional assent was given for the British divisions to participate in *offensive* operations under Sarrail's command.

The truth was that to Joffre, no less than to Robertson, Salonika was a sideshow – but he was determined (and in this he differed from the British) that it should, at any rate, be a sideshow in which there was a performance. Accordingly, on January 28th, the very day that the Allied force was arrayed against Karaburun, Joffre sent a despatch to Sarrail ordering him to prepare an operation which would lead the Germans and Bulgars to believe that an offensive might, in due course, be launched from the entrenched camp. By this means he hoped that some German forces would be sent eastwards away from the dangerous concentration gathering before Verdun.

There was, as it happened, little enough that Sarrail could do in the bitter wintry conditions. Two French colonial regiments were pushed up to the old Greek frontier in February and plans were made for a more general advance once spring had come. The Bulgars were duly reminded that they were still at war; but the German units, whose presence was reported to Sarrail, had come for another purpose rather than in response to the French move.

For the Germans, too, were prodding their allies; and it looked for a time as if they would be more successful in hotting up the war in the Balkans. Falkenhayn, who six weeks earlier had been strongly opposed to carrying the war over the Greek frontier, suddenly reversed his policy. He was busy planning what he hoped would be his master-stroke, the offensive against Verdun and, with a logic similar to Joffre's, he contended that if a Bulgarian Army, with German backing, moved against Salonika it would draw British and French divisions away from the Western Front. Unfortunately for Falkenhayn, the Bulgars were in no position to launch an attack. They were short of food, they had caught typhus from the Serbs and, having been held back when their morale was high, they had lost interest in the whole affair. A Bulgarian general had already blandly informed his German liaison officer, 'For us Bulgars the war is really over. We have all we want.' Moreover, the French had systematically destroyed the railway to the frontier as they withdrew in December, and there was little hope that supplies could be sent along it until the spring. The Bulgars did not want an offensive, and there were many Germans who agreed with them. Two of the finest brains in the German officer corps thought that Falkenhayn was courting disaster. General Groener, who was probably the staff officer most versed in transport problems in any army, warned Falkenhayn that his railhead would have to be sixty miles from the front-line. General von Seeckt, chief of staff to the Army in the East, insisted that if the attack were not to prove a fiasco, the Germans must supply 56 batteries of heavy artillery – an argument which, on the eve of Verdun, might have been expected in itself to silence Falkenhayn.

But Falkenhayn was obdurate. General von Gallwitz, the senior German commander in the Balkans, was ordered to prepare for an immediate attack across the frontier on January 26th, just two days before Joffre counselled Sarrail to simulate an offensive. Ignoring the Bulgarian protest that nothing could be done until the middle of March, von Gallwitz went ahead with his plans. Ammunition waggons were sent by road to Veleš to await the arrival of shells at the railhead. But, as Groener had foreseen, the railway could not stand the strain. It was carrying goods not only from Belgrade but from Sofia as well: coal, winter clothing, food and fodder, material for repairing the line south of Veleš – all this activity on a single track. As the days turned into weeks the ammunition waggons remained empty at Veleš; and von Gallwitz lost what little enthusiasm he had for the projected offensive.

Hence, while German Headquarters were making the last dispositions for the assult on Verdun, a tale of woe came in from the Balkan Front. The Bulgars could not move their troops into the Struma Valley; the wintry conditions were impossible; there were no mountain guns. When the first shells fell on the citadel of Verdun on February 20th, von Gallwitz was still without the leavening of German troops for which he had asked. They reached him a week later – two second-rate divisions, under strength and so short of food that they were promptly put on half-rations. Von Gallwitz was desperate; he begged for a postponement and, to his great relief, Falkenhayn gave way. On March 9th Falkenhayn ordered him to drop the whole idea and to establish a defensive line around Doiran and in the Vardar valley. The German High Command had discovered that it was not possible to meet the demands of a campaign in the Balkans except at the expense of operations in France. And, of its own accord, the war in the Balkans would not boil.

The Allied command had still to learn this lesson. In London the War Office continued to regard Salonika as a tiresome diversion of effort. Sir William Robertson, the bluff ex-ranker who had become Chief of the Imperial General Staff, obstinately refused to take the expedition seriously and he succeeded in winning over Kitchener to his point of view. For administrative purposes the British Salonika Army was subordinated to the Levant Command (which was actually a greater distance from Macedonia, as the crow flies, than London). This was in itself a cumbersome arrangement but it was made even worse by a peculiar division of responsibility between the British base at Alexandria and General Headquarters at Ismailia, midway along the Suez Canal. There have been few systems better suited to the avoidance of decision. With normal luck any problem might lead to a triangular correspondence lasting several weeks, but, if bumbledom were really triumphant, a question could be referred back to London, and the weeks would become months. The woollen underclothing which the British troops needed in the bitter winter reached Macedonia at the same time as the hot weather; and correspondence on the advisability of issuing sun-helmets, begun with admirable foresight in February, was still continuing in June as the shade temperature crept into the nineties. The official British Military History records that a request for fire-extinguishers met the bland response, 'Why are fire-extinguishers required?' – an absurd reply to a demand from an over-crowded city of predominantly wooden buildings anticipating a dry summer (and, it may be added, a demand which was proved to be fully justified). It is hard to avoid the conclusion that the supply services had learned nothing since the legendary blunders of Crimean maladministration.

The truth was that in Egypt it was assumed that Mahon's troops would soon be withdrawn and that accordingly nothing was to be gained by meeting their requirements. That there was some ground for the attitude of the authorities in Ismailia and Alexandria is shown by the record of the gathering of Allied leaders in Paris at the end of March, 1916. For there Robertson and Kitchener formally demanded that one British division should immediately be released from the Salonika Front for the British line in France, the others following it later in the summer. Joffre, hard-pressed though he was at Verdun, was furious at the suggestion. It had been agreed at an inter-allied conference in Chantilly less than a fortnight previously that there would be no

withdrawal of forces from Macedonia, and only two days before
the meeting Joffre had sent instructions to Sarrail on the re-deploy-
ment of the Allied forces for mountain warfare. Indeed the French
were already advancing out of the entrenched camp to face the
Bulgars and the Germans along the frontier and Sarrail was
counting on Mahon to relieve his cavalry in front of Lake Doiran.
Now it looked as if the British were going back on plans which
were already being put into operation. With ill-concealed dis-
pleasure, Robertson withdrew his demand. For the time being,
Mahon's five divisions remained in Macedonia; but the incident
only confirmed Joffre's conviction that he needed other Allied
contingents in the Balkans as speedily as possible. Where were
they to be found?

Joffre had hopes of an Italian division, of a Russian brigade,
perhaps even of the full Roumanian Army opening up yet another
front against both Bulgaria and the Dual Monarchy. But, for the
moment, there was one obvious source. Ever since the battered
Serbian detachments had reached Corfu, they had been anxious
to get into action once again. And, even though sickness was
carrying off the Serbs at the rate of 450 a week in the hospitals of
Corfu, the Serbian representative at the Chantilly conference
maintained that, provided France would equip them, Serbia
could put into the field an army of 120,000 men, organized in six
divisions. The deputy chief of the Serbian General Staff announced
that this force would be ready to be moved on April 1st.

There remained, however, the problem of transportation. The
obvious route was by sea to Patras, by rail through Athens to
Larissa and thence by forced marches, or by sea again, to the
Allied base at Salonika. But on April 3rd the Greeks categorically
refused an Allied request to use the Greek railways for the transference of the army of Greece's old ally. The French and the
British had, in consequence, to improvise convoys of troop-ships
to carry the Serbs round the Peloponnese and through the sub-
marine-infested waters of the Cyclades. Embarkation began on
April 11th and the convoys continued to make the four day voyage
for the next six weeks. Not a single attack was made on the ships
and by the end of May 112,000 Serbs (with more than 8,000
horses) had been brought to Salonika, where they joined several
thousand Serbs already in camp at Mikra, ten miles south-east
of the city. At the same time, some seventeen hundred Bosnians,
who were technically subjects of the Austro-Hungarian Empire
but had been fighting with the Montenegrins, were formed into

a South Slav ('Yugoslav') battalion within the French Army.

French observers, and even more the British, looked askance at this latest reinforcement. There was no panache about this army of veterans; and, it was suspected, very little discipline. The officers, deeply resentful of the French patronage which they knew to be inevitable, gave themselves airs; and before long they won for themselves an unenviable reputation for political intrigue and petty corruption. Moreover, there was a strange distribution of ages; the two campaigns which the Serbs had already fought and the horrors of the retreat had taken a toll of the most ex-perienced officers and of the younger men. Hence the Serbian Army in Macedonia comprised, for the most part, officers who were relatively young, or unusually old, but 'other ranks' with an average age of between thirty-five and forty. It was anyone's guess how this motley force would respond to the challenge of battle.

As the short spring passed into summer, it seemed that battle could not long be delayed. By the last week of April each of the four French divisions had passed out of the 'entranched camp' and advanced to the frontier, and a couple of British brigades took up positions astride the railway south of Lake Doiran. This move enabled the British, for the first time in this theatre of war, to make contact with specifically German units, a sharp cavalry skirmish taking place between two troops of Uhlans and the Sherwood Rangers on April 10th. Morale was higher – partly because the hardship of winter was over, but also because the proximity of the Germans suggested a purpose for being in this odd corner of Europe. The destruction of a Zeppelin by naval gunners on May 5th in full view of the people of Salonika also raised the spirits of the troops, especially among the British con-tingent for their families at home had already been subjected to raids of this type and it was to be another four months before the first Zeppelin was shot down on English soil. Throughout the Salonika base, there was an air of expectancy.

Back at Chantilly, Joffre had at last definitely committed him-self to the idea of an offensive in Macedonia. Once the Serbs reached the front, Sarrail would have under his command fifteen divisions – certainly equal to, and probably stronger than, the enemy forces who were facing him. It was unlikely that the 'Army of the Orient' had the equipment to break through to Sofia or to penetrate up the Vardar, but it was reasonable to expect it to dislodge the enemy from his positions. Accordingly, on April 25th Joffre wrote to Robertson proposing that the Salonika Army could have 'no other task but to attack the enemy with all its forces on the Greek frontier immediately it had received the reinforcement of the Serbian Army'. He maintained that a successful assault might bring Roumania and Greece into the field against the Central Powers and that, since the Bulgars were already half-hearted in prosecuting the war, a local victory in Macedonia would have a relatively greater effect on general strategy than one on any other front. Above all, any offensive would prevent enemy troops being moved from the Balkans to other fronts and might relieve pressure on the Allies in France and in Russia by attracting German or Austrian reinforcements to strengthen the Bulgars.

Joffre's argument made such sound sense that it might have been expected to win British approval from the first. The enemy was already making propaganda capital out of the French and British divisions enclosed within a wire-cage of their construction – 'the greatest internment camp in the world', as German commentators called it, with heavy-handed irony – and to keep the troops immobile would merely heighten the scorn in which the expedition was held by western and neutral observers. Underlying Joffre's assessment was one basic fact: by the end of May 1916, there would be 300,000 Allied troops in Salonika; why, then, should they remain inactive? It was a fair question to ask.

Robertson, however, was reluctant to accept any of Joffre's contentions. Never once modifying his conviction that 'strategically the right course was to bring the whole of the troops away', he began to mobilize opinion in the War Committee against any extension of British commitments in Macedonia. Joffre received a brief, and unpromising, acknowledgment of his letter on May 3rd and further criticisms a week later but, with over a fortnight passing without a full reply, the French went ahead with their dispositions. Eventually, on May 14th, Joffre forwarded his plan for an offensive to the British, at the same time asking for two further divisions to be sent to Salonika.

The British responded to this proposal with alacrity – and with indignation. On May 17th the War Committee rejected the whole concept of a Macedonian offensive. Joffre was informed that the British considered it unlikely Greece or Roumania would enter the war at this stage; that, anyhow, the Greek Army would require to be re-equipped, as it was in bad shape, and the British

had no ships for such an operation; that the Bulgars were re-
nowned warriors who would fight desperately to defend their own
country, while the Serbs were not yet a force in whom the British
could repose any confidence; and that an offensive on the Macedonian Front would not effect the other theatres of war since the
Bulgars had no intention of fighting elsewhere and the Germans,
Austrians and Turks would not send sizeable reinforcements to
the Balkans unless the Allies breached the formidable defences
between Doiran and Sofia, an undertaking beyond their present
resources. The British were short of horses and mules and lacked
both heavy artillery and mountain guns; there was no obvious
source from which these deficiencies could be made up, even if the
shipping could be found to convey them to Salonika, a difficult
problem in itself. It was far better, the British felt, to fall back on
to the defensive and to limit the Salonika Army to units capable
of defending the city and thus to prevent it from becoming a
potential base for enemy submarines operating in the eastern
Mediterranean.

This indictment of Joffre's plan laid bare the prejudices and
pre-occupations of the British – distaste for an enterprise in a part
of Europe beyond the range of Britain's traditional interests;
distrust of Serbia, contempt for Greece, and a partiality for
Bulgaria; and a peculiar evaluation of the shipping problem by
which, while no vessels could be found for sending men and equipment to Salonika, it was apparently possible to find them if the
troops were to be moved from Salonika to other fronts. After a
meeting between Joffre and Robertson on May 26th, the breach
between the two governments appeared to be so wide that it was
agreed there should be a full discussion of Balkan problems by
the allied leaders in London a fortnight later.

Briand, accompanied by Joffre and by his Minister of War,
arrived at Downing Street on June 9th to find the atmosphere
cool. The War Committee had discovered that Sarrail was going
ahead with preparations for an offensive, even though Robertson
had withheld British consent. All the War Committee was present
and some members of the cabinet as well. The two sides re-stated
their points of view, but there were two significant variations on
the forthright correspondence of the previous month. The French
now insisted that an offensive in the Balkans was desired by both
the Russians and the Italians, both of whom were sending detachments to Salonika. Yet, as a debating point, this plea of inter-
allied solidarity failed to convince the British for, in the middle of

the conference, a telegram was handed to Robertson from the Italian commander-in-chief indicating that, since he had no knowledge of Balkan requirements, he would be happy to accept the advice of the British on all questions relating to this theatre of operations. For their part, the British maintained that they were not opposed, in principle, to an offensive in Macedonia – provided that one determined thrust could end in final victory. As the conference proceeded the French appeared less and less enthusiastic, perhaps because, at heart, they were still concerned with the crisis on the Western Front. Joffre spoke with his customary forcefulness but, in the eyes of that astute judge, Lloyd George;

'It was difficult to believe that he was convinced even by his own eloquence. He was urging an attack with forces devoid of the armament necessary to achieve their purpose, and he made no suggestion that the equipment should be strengthened up to the point of effectiveness. It was one of the most cynical performances I have ever listened to.'

Hence, at this stage, even the critics of the convinced westerners opposed an advance from Salonika. It was agreed that the British would concentrate their efforts on the Somme; but not a man nor a gun was to be moved away from the Balkan Front.

Thus, once more, a decision on the future of the Salonika force had been avoided. When, three weeks later, the British Expeditionary Force in France was thrown against the heavily fortified positions along the Somme, their brothers in Macedonia were encamped among the swamps of another river, their chief enemy the malaria-bearing mosquito. Morale was beginning to fall again.

But affairs in Salonika were not quite the same. The knowledge that in April the French had countenanced an offensive induced the British to authorize a change in command. A stronger man was needed to stand up to Sarrail. On May 9th General Mahon left Greece to fill a vacant appointment in Egypt (which, as it happened, he never took up as he fell seriously ill with sunstroke on arrival at Alexandria and was invalided home). His successor at Salonika was Lieutenant-General G. F. Milne, who had come out from France with the 27th Division in the previous January and had immediately assumed command of XVI Corps, setting up his headquarters in the hills five miles to the east of the harbour.

General George Milne was forty-nine when he succeeded Mahon, his senior by some five years. He was the son of a bank-manager in Aberdeen and had been commissioned in the Royal Artillery in 1885. Like Mahon, he had been one of Kitchener's men, allegedly first attracting his attention at the battle of Omdurman in 1898 when Milne's battery had scored a direct hit on the Mahdi's tomb in Khartoum. He had served as an intelligence officer on Kitchener's staff in South Africa but, when war came in 1914, he was back with the gunners and fought at Le Cateau, on the Marne and at Ypres. He was a strict, but not unsympathetic disciplinarian whose shrewd eyes reflected his keen intellect and dry wit. An Italian liaison officer later described him as 'A fine-looking man, a great lover of sport, a hard worker, a gentleman in every sense of the word'. And among his attributes were two which he would need in full measure, tact and firmness of will. Mahon had co-operated as best he could with Sarrail – and is one of the few commanders to win praise in the vitriol spattered pages of the Frenchman's memoirs – but Sarrail, who had always been secretive, was becoming more and more inclined to pursue a policy that was independent of Paris, of Chantilly, and, it goes without saying, of British Salonika Headquarters in the suburb of Kalamaria. It was hoped that Milne, who had been in Macedonia long enough to accustom himself to Sarrail's impulsiveness, would have the strength of personality to restrain him. He was soon to be put to the test.

Relations between the Allies and the Greeks had remained coldly formal since the seizure of Karaburun. In February Sarrail went to Athens, met King Constantine and Skouloudis (who had become prime minister early in November, 1915) and lunched with some of the leading Greek staff officers. He also, rather pointedly, visited Venizelos whose very name was, at that time, anathema to the Greek General Staff. Sarrail returned to Salonika with few illusions and reported to Paris that Skouloudis and the General Staff 'were, are and will continue to be pro-German' but that the King wished to remain neutral and avoid incidents. There was, perhaps, a slight detente between France and Greece in the spring for, when the Allies advanced out of the entrenched camp, they were able to move through the Greek battalions encamped along the roadside without encountering any opposition. Indeed, in some places on the western sector of the new line, the Greeks were prepared to share guard duties with the Allies on the bridges.

3

But all co-operation between Constantine's Greece and the Allies virtually ended on May 26th. Fifty miles to the north-east of Salonika and seven miles south of the Greco-Bulgarian frontier, the Greeks had constructed an impressive military obstacle, Fort Rupel. It was sited some 300 feet above the river Struma and commanded the best road – the use of the superlative is relative – from Bulgaria proper into eastern Macedonia. On the morning of May 26th a column of Bulgarian infantry, with German officers attached, advanced along the road beside the Struma and appeared before the Fort. The Greek defenders opened fire with rifles and artillery and the column of invaders withdrew. The Greeks were well pleased; it would need a far more serious military operation than this to dislodge them from such a position. But the Greek Government had no intention of offering resistance. In the late afternoon orders reached the garrison commander at Rupel from his divisional headquarters at Seres that the General Staff had decided to evacuate the Fort and hand it over to the Bulgars. Hence when the invading column returned, the Greeks retired and left this key defensive pivot in the hands of the Bulgarian Seventh Infantry Division. The Greeks also withdrew from three villages on the southern slopes of the mountain barrier which had formed the Greco-Bulgarian frontier and the Bulgars were thus able to establish a defensive line ten miles within Greek territory overlooking the Seres railway and on the Salonika side of Demir Hissar, where Sarrail had destroyed the bridge four months previously in the hope of checking just such an incursion.

The surrender of Fort Rupel startled the Entente Powers, and there were open accusations of treachery. But the Greeks had repeatedly made it clear that if any of the Central Powers sent a force across the frontier they would not impede its advance. Moreover, it was Sarrail himself who, at Karaburun, had set the Bulgars a precedent. None the less, Sarrail was now beside himself with rage. He was determined to mount a summer offensive against the Bulgars as soon as possible and, suspicious of the attitude of the other Greek forces in Macedonia, wished to assume complete responsibility for the administration of Salonika and the whole area occupied by Allied troops.

Milne was thus faced with a double dilemma. He had already been reminded by Robertson that the British were subordinate to Sarrail's command only for the defence of Salonika itself and that the Imperial General Staff was resolutely opposed to any assault

being launched against the Bulgars; and on June 3rd fresh instructions were telegraphed to him by which he was ordered not
to be drawn into any offensive operations. He personally felt that,
through his intransigent republicanism, Sarrail had allowed himself to become tangled in the web of Greek politics. Once Sarrail
was permitted to intimidate the Greek authorities he would provoke a revulsion of feeling against the French and British which
would offset the propaganda value to be gained from the handing
over of a Greek fortress to a traditional enemy of the Greek people.
In two trying interviews, Milne counselled moderation: but
Sarrail knew that Joffre, who had previously restrained him, was
no less indignant than he over the surrender of Rupel and was
exasperated by what he considered to be the persistent prevarication of the British. Accordingly Sarrail bluntly informed Milne
that he would attack the Bulgars with British support, if it were
forthcoming, if not, with the French and Serbs alone. A lesser
commander than Milne might have been cajoled into action for
fear that the British would otherwise incur the odium of leaving
an ally in the lurch; but Milne kept his head and obeyed the
letter of his instructions. The British forces were disengaged and
established themselves in new positions in the southern Struma
Valley. The French, moving into the line vacated by the British,
continued their preparations for an offensive – which Sarrail was
now hoping to launch on August 1st.

Milne was, however, not able to prevent Sarrail from proclaiming a state of siege in Salonika. June 3rd was, as it happened, the
'name-day' of King Constantine and the people of Salonika had
determined to celebrate the occasion by a torch-light procession
in honour of the King who, as Crown Prince, had commanded the
army which liberated them from the Turk. Sarrail, who had
received permission to establish a state of siege two days previously, seized the opportunity to prohibit a demonstration which
was naturally repugnant to 'the best republican in the French
Army'. At the same time, the French gendarmerie took over the
railway installations, all postal and telegraph services and established a censorship of the newspapers published in Salonika.
Milne, unwilling to advertise his disapproval of Sarrail's action,
put units of the British military police under the command of the
French gendarmerie.

Salonika thus became an occupied city as effectively under
alien military administration as Brussels or Warsaw or Belgrade;
and, not unnaturally, there were demonstrations against the

Entente Powers in Athens. But the French had not yet finished chastening the Greeks for the Rupel incident. A blockade was imposed on all the Greek ports and a squadron of Allied warships, under a French admiral and with one of Sarrail's brigades aboard, sailed from Salonika for the Cyclades to put pressure on the government in Athens. The French and British demanded demobilization of the Greek Army, the replacement of the allegedly pro-German Government of Skouloudis by a 'neutral' ministry, new elections, and the dismissal of police officials who had tolerated insults to the Allied diplomatic representatives. With battleships and cruisers anchored in the bay of Milos and thus able to appear off Athens at eight hours' notice, the Greeks gave in. Skouloudis made way for the less heavily committed Zaimis, who formed a government pledged to carry out the Allied demands. The blockade was lifted (apart from the port of Kavalla, which was within a few miles of the Bulgarian border) and the naval squadron withdrawn. It was an incident of which neither the French nor the British could feel proud; and, as the Germans did not fail to point out, it made any claim that the Entente was championing the rights of the smaller nations sound distinctly hollow.

The British and French had by now been in Salonika for more than eight months and, in a material sense, had left their mark on the city and its hinterland: new roads and new quays, a mushroom crop of bell tents, a harvest of barbed wire. They had brought employment to refugee labourers, enabled property owners to push up their rents twelve times over and were lining the pockets of the café proprietors with as many drachmae in a week as they had been accustomed to take in a year. There were cabarets and music halls and cinemas; and a brass band to play stirring marches in the main square. Journalism, too, was flourishing – two French dailies, one English, one Serbian and the customary library of Greek newspapers. The town was packed, and vulgarly prosperous. The Athenians might protest at the way in which Sarrail had usurped authority in Greece's second city; but the people of Salonika found the burden of such an occupation tolerable, and the profits from a war in which they did not have to fight not displeasing.

But it could be argued that the Salonika expedition had, as yet, made little contribution to the winning of the war. It had not saved Serbia, it had drawn no German troops away from Verdun, it had remained immobile while Brussilov's Russians were gaining a striking victory in Austrian-held Galicia. On the credit side it could list one (non-belligerent) fort occupied, one (non-belligerent) government overthrown, and several (non-belligerent) harbours denied to enemy U-boats. To Robertson and his fellow westerners in London, Salonika had become a vast, insatiable and useless mouth, rapacious of men, material and munitions. And by now, overshadowed though it was by the glory and misery of Verdun, there were plenty of critics of the expedition in Paris as well – parliamentarians suspicious of Joffre, veteran deputies fretful at the squandering of resources on distant fronts, and a handful of radicals still clamouring for the return of France's banished saviour, Maurice Sarrail.

At last, in mid-June, the French Government reluctantly permitted the Chamber of Deputies to hold its first secret session of the war. For four days Briand defended Joffre's general strategy on the Western Front; but the debate went further than Verdun. On June 20th Briand gave a long and able survey of his policy in the Balkans, ending with an assurance that conditions for a Macedonian offensive were becoming better and better. It was a good speech, and with the rhetorical question, 'Who would be occupying the Balkan stage now, if we had deserted it?', Briand received lively applause. But he was followed by Delcassé, a deputy with more experience of foreign affairs than anybody else in the Chamber, and Delcassé had no illusions about the Salonika venture. He now revealed, for the first time, that he had resigned from the Government shortly after the French landed at Salonika because 'the prospect of sending French soldiers overseas when the enemy was on French soil filled me with anxiety'. And he went on:

'I have heard it said that if we were not in Salonika, the Germans would be there at this moment. Everyone must speak his thoughts; I am here to say mine. And I say I wish to heaven they were there! And not just 200,000 or |250,000 of them, as our army is, but 400,000 or 500,000. For, gentlemen, then at least we would not find them at this moment on the Front in France.'

The presence of French troops at Salonika had, he maintained, made it easier for the Germans to launch their assault on Verdun; Serbia, no less than Belgium, could be restored only through victory in France. Delcassé had delivered an out and out statement of the westerner's philosophy of war; and it made a

considerable impression on the Chamber. Briand received a vote
of confidence with a majority of more than 300; but when
deputies looked back on the Balkan debate, it was not his speech
they remembered.

Delcassé had spoken in the closed camera of parliament,
and the French people did not know of his attack. But there
was a far more formidable critic, one who was inhibited only
by the demands of military censorship and adept at evading
even that obstacle; it was hard to shackle Georges Clemenceau.
Thirty years ago Clemenceau had destroyed the political career
of the great radical Jules Ferry because he had preferred to
wage colonial wars rather than prepare for the next struggle
with Germany. Now the Franco-German conflict had at last
been resumed and Clemenceau was in his element. Each day
his newspaper reminded its readers, 'The Germans are at Noyon'.
It was hardly likely that he would give his backing to an enterprise on the fringe of the Balkans. Others might condemn it on
grounds of strategy; but Clemenceau's weapon was ridicule.
What were Sarrail's men doing? Digging! Then let them be
known to France and to Europe as 'The gardeners of Salonika'.
Like most of Clemenceau's jibes it was a cruel caricature but a
telling phrase. It was high time that something was achieved
in Salonika to confound the critics. When would the war in
the Balkans boil?

*In reading the following chapter, the maps on pp. 188 and 198 and the first end-paper
map will be found helpful.*

5 / The Battle for Monastir

THREE HUNDRED MILES to the north-east of Salonika, beyond the Balkan Mountains and the broad sweep of the Danube, lies Bucharest which, in the early summer of 1916, was the capital of the one country in eastern Europe still untouched by war. Not that Roumania's neutrality sprang from principle. As the one land link between Russia and Serbia, she had been wooed by her eastern neighbour ever since the guns opened up in front of Belgrade and promised the rich prize of Transylvania if she entered the war on the side of the Entente. But the Roumanian prime minister, Ion Bratianu, who had no small opinion of his country's military worth, avoided committing himself, confident that with each overture from Petrograd or Paris, he could raise his price higher and higher. And, indeed, after twelve months of haggling, he was asking for so much territory that Roumania would have more than doubled her size and acquired, not merely a large Hungarian minority, but districts predominantly Serbian in character as well. The Entente Powers were willing to concede even this demand if it enabled the Russians, Serbs and Roumanians to establish a joint front along the Danube; but, before the negotiations got as far as a draft treaty, the military situation changed for the worse and, once Serbia was overrun and Bulgaria a belligerent, Bratianu chose to remain ostentatiously uncommitted – a happy state which gave him an opportunity to see if the Central Powers would make a higher bid than the Entente. They would not.

This situation was drastically changed by a series of Russian victories just north of the Roumanian frontier. On June 4th 1916 General Brussilov launched an offensive against five Austrian Armies on a sixty-mile front along the Dniester. The Russians covered twenty miles in the first week and for ten days carried all before them, the Austrians surrendering in their thousands. By mid-July they stood at the foot of the Carpathians; the Allies had enjoyed no comparable success on any other front in Europe. There was excitement, not only in the Entente capitals, but in Bucharest as well. Bratianu's political rivals encouraged a mass agitation for a march into Transylvania to 'liberate' the three million Roumanians living within the Dual Monarchy. Bratianu, who had a marked distaste for quick decisions, was alarmed; suppose Austria-Hungary collapsed, under the impact of the Russian attack, before the Roumanians could stake their claim. It was clearly necessary to sound out the Allies once more. On July 4th Bratianu informed the French Minister in Bucharest that he was prepared to enter the war provided that Roumania was offered the same terms as in the previous year, that the Russians continued their offensive and co-operated with the Roumanian Army, and that the Bulgars were engaged by a full scale offensive from Salonika. Negotiations thereupon began for the signing of a formal military alliance.

The prospect of having Roumania's army of half a million men added to the list of allied combatants induced the War Committee in London to think again about British participation in a Macedonian offensive. On July 10th the French were informed, in a somewhat grudging message, that, provided Roumania entered the war, the British were willing to co-operate in an offensive from Salonika 'on a scale commensurate with the strength and equipment of their force'. The French were duly warned that the British would not participate in any attack before the Roumanians had definitely committed themselves to entering the war by singing a military convention – a proviso that was to cause Milne considerable embarrassment in the weeks ahead. The British, under pressure of events, were beginning to accept the principle of a unified command, but they still had qualms of doubt.

A fortnight later Robertson telegraphed instructions to Milne to clarify the position of the British force. As commander-in-chief at Salonika, Sarrail had been ordered to consult Milne over the employment of British troops, but Milne was to meet Sarrail's requirements for the disposition of his units. He was reminded that the allied armies had the double task of covering the mobilization of the Roumanian Army by engaging 'the maximum number of Bulgarian troops' and of subsequently co-operating with the Russian and Roumanian Armies for the destruction of the enemy forces in south-eastern Europe. He was also notified that it was hoped to open the offensive on August 1st – exactly one week after Robertson's message reached him.

After months of virtual inactivity, the Salonika Army was to be thrown into battle at short notice.

Sarrail had, however, completed his plan of operations by the middle of July and his troops were moving into the positions he had assigned to them before Milne received Robertson's instructions. There was a flurry of activity around the port and along the main roads from Seres and from the Vardar, which met on the edge of the city. The Serbs, whom Sarrail planned would form the spearhead of his initial assault, began to move westward on July 17th in order to take over sixty miles of the front from the French well beyond the Vardar and facing the mountain peaks which marked the old frontier of their land. As the Serbs had been encamped ten miles south-east of Salonika, it was necessary for them to be brought through the outskirts of the town. There was little transport available; they marched along, chanting interminable patriotic ballads as they went, and all could see that the Serbian Army was resurrected. A chain of enemy agents, recruited from the peasantry of the Struma Valley and the high land east of Salonika, spread the news up to the Bulgarian lines, and Sofia knew that the Serbs were moving to the front long before they reached their new positions.

There were other items for the agents to report as well, if they knew their business; intensive training by British units along the Struma and by the French guarding the route of the Vardar, machine-gun companies arriving for the British divisions, a squadron of the Royal Flying Corps disembarking from Alexandria. It was, however, at the very end of July that the most impressive arrivals of all reached Salonika – a brigade of Russians, five thousand strong. There was, as yet, no sign of the malaise of defeatism which was to sap the Tsar's army before many months were past. Physically these men seemed giants, a magnificent sight as they marched eight abreast through the city, gleaming bayonets on long rifles, a moving forest of steel. And, along the quays, rumours spoke of further vessels on their way – the artillery park was awaiting howitzers and anti-aircraft guns, a camp was being prepared for fresh engineer units, eight hundred Albanian partisans were in training near Naples, a division of Italians was expected any day (and, indeed, arrived on August 11th, to be followed by the hair-raising incursion of Albanians in another Italian warship a week later). It was clear to all Salonika that an offensive was coming.

3*

Yet by August 1st, when it had been hoped that Sarrail would open his attack, he was far from ready. The fault was hardly his. From the marshes of the Struma to the distant mountains around Koritsa his motley army was extended along a front of one hundred and seventy miles, as far as Exeter from London, or, to use an analogy from the Western Front, as the battefields of the Somme from the fortress of Verdun. It would take longer than a fortnight to deploy a force over such a vast area. It is true that some sectors of the line, particularly in the far west, were manned by outposts of little more than a handful of men; for the terrain was so barren and broken that it would have been imprudent for either side to undertake serious operations in such an isolated and unrewarding corner of Europe. But there were problems, too, in the very centre of the front. Despite all the preparations of the previous months, the villages were still ill-served by roads and the troops reached their new dispositions with painful slowness under a scorching sun and clouds of dust. Moreover, Sarrail was hampered by other difficulties: the French Government had belatedly – and of its own accord – decided to ease his burden of responsibility by sending out a new commander for the four French divisions in the field, General Cordonnier, and he could not reach Salonika until August 11th; and Milne was still reluctant to permit his divisions to participate in a general offensive as the Roumanians seemed in no hurry to conclude a binding agreement.

As it became clear that war was coming to Macedonia in earnest, each side began to probe the other's line: the Bulgars moved in to a couple of deserted Greek villages between Monastir and Florina before the Serbs, who were to have defended them, had established themselves; and the French began an attack on Bulgarian hill positions around Lake Doiran with support from British infantry attached to the 22nd Division.

By the middle of August Sarrail was ready. Cordonnier was at his headquarters, reconnaissance patrols were out in force, the Italians and the Russians constituted a tactical reserve, the Serbs had reached their sector. There were some 320,000 men of five nations under his command. All that he wanted was news from Bucharest. It came in the afternoon of August 18th. Bratianu had duly signed the convention shortly before noon on the previous day: Roumania would declare war on Austria-Hungary on August 28th, provided that by then Sarrail's force had, for at least three days, been conducting an offensive against the

Bulgars, and that the Russians had sent 50,000 men to help
Roumania check a Bulgarian advance across her own frontier.
But by the time this information reached Sarrail, it had lost
much of its significance. The Bulgars had stolen a march on him;
for, on the very morning that the convention was signed, their
troops launched an offensive on both flanks of the Salonika
Army.

The Bulgars and the Germans were well informed of Allied
plans and had made their dispositions accordingly. One of
Falkenhayn's last acts as chief of the General Staff – he was
edged out at the end of August by the formidable combination
of Hindenburg and Ludendorff – was to authorize the reinforcement of the Bulgarian Army on the Greek frontier by two German
divisions of nine battalions each, one of which was brought
from a quiet sector of the Western Front, the Vosges. The centre
of the enemy line, from Doiran astride the Vardar, was accordingly put under General von Winckler, who had relieved
Gallwitz as commander of the German Eleventh Army early
in August. But, since the main German and Austrian forces
would be engaged on the Roumanian Front, the overall command was entrusted to the Bulgars, and it was Bulgarian troops
who were expected to launch the attack, the main assault being
made by the First Army under General Bojadiev on the left
flank of the Entente forces, in the very area in which Sarrail had
hoped the Serbs would open his own offensive. The Bulgarian
Second Army was, at the same time, to advance southwards
from Rupel so as to drive a wedge across eastern Macedonia.
The High Command did not believe that the Bulgars would
capture Salonika itself, and indeed had no desire to test the
defensive ring around the port. They knew, however, that the
occupation of eastern Macedonia would provide the Bulgarian
people with a tangible reward for their efforts; and they calculated that, if the First Army could break through to the plains
below Vodena, Sarrail's force would be besieged within the entrenched camp. In such circumstances, would the Entente Governments have been prepared to continue the Salonika venture?
The odds seemed against it.
   At two in the morning on August 17th a column of Bulgarian
infantry with light artillery trundling behind, set out along
half-forgotten hill tracks on the western fringe of the Kenali
Valley, which led from Monastir to Florina. Shortly afterwards

a second infantry regiment began a parallel advance on the opposite side of the valley. By dawn they had overpowered the Serbian outposts and, by the time that news of the attack had reached Sarrail eighty miles away in Salonika, the Bulgars had captured the station of Florina and were in a position to cut off the town, which lay three miles west of the railway. By the following morning the Bulgars had rushed 18,000 men through the gap and outnumbered the Serbs who opposed them by two to one. Throughout that day and the next there was fierce fighting along the road into Greece, the Serbs falling back from one ridge to the next, each unit seeking to find shelter behind parapets of hard stone, for it was impossible to dig trenches in the sun-baked rocks. In haste, British transport units rushed lorry loads of Serbs from the reserve camps to the west of Lake Ostrovo, for if the Bulgars penetrated around the lake the whole of the left of the Allied front could easily have crumbled.

The Bulgars were exhilarated by their success; 'We shall be in Salonika in a week', they boasted. And in Athens, more than three hundred miles to the south, a curious panic seized the Venizelist sympathizers with the Entente; they were convinced that a German cavalry squadron would suddenly canter into Syntagma Square and carry them off to the hills. A senior official of the Greek Foreign Office was sufficiently impressed by this picturesque notion to assure the Russian Minister, 'German pickets are outside Larissa'; and the Russian was so alarmed that he cancelled a journey he was to have made to the north. The situation was, of course, not yet so catastrophic; but it was serious enough. For by now, the Serbian Third Army, which had borne the brunt of the attack seemed exhausted and its commander – a septuagenarian martinet who had fought beside the Prussians in 1870 – was no longer capable of rallying his troops.

On August 20th Sarrail convened a conference of the senior officers of the five Allied contingents. The news from the eastern sector was little better than from the western ; a French column had been pushed back across the Struma before Seres with heavy casualties, and, further east still, Bulgarian patrols were on the outskirts of Kavalla. Sarrail, convinced that attack was the best defence, determined to mount a counter-offensive as soon as possible and the Allied commanders accepted his plan. The British were to destroy the bridges along the Struma and stand on the defensive while every effort was to be made to seize key positions on the hills around Doiran. Sarrail abandoned his

earlier plan for a major assault along the Vardar; but the main
attack was still to come in the west, as he had always intended.
The Italians were to relieve a French division in the extreme
north-east of the front, 4,000 feet up in the Belasica Mountains
on the old Greco-Bulgarian frontier, while the French, with the
Russian brigade, would be hurried across to Lake Ostrovo.
As the Italians had been in Salonika for little more than a week,
there was some risk attached to this manœuvre but the Italian
troops had a fine record from skirmishes in the Alps and it was
assumed, rightly, that they would have little difficulty in establishing themselves among the mountain peaks. At the same time,
the Serbian chief-of-staff, Bojović, agreed to replace the commander of his Third Army by a younger man, for he was eager
for the Serbs to be given a chance to redeem their reputation.

The Bulgars, meanwhile, continued to claim a great victory
and German propaganda, still anxious to prevent the Roumanians
from marching, puffed up this local success into a spectacular
triumph. But the Bulgarian First Army fell victim to its own
elation. On August 17th it had advanced with craft and circum-
spection; on August 22nd it threw caution to the winds and sent
column after column against the reinforced Serbian position west
of Ostrovo. Five times the Bulgars stormed the ridge beyond the
lake and five times they were beaten back with heavy losses, but
on the following day they took one last Serbian position. It was
the limit of their advance. By August 26th the Serbs were holding
firm. For four more days there was sporadic gunfire as rival
batteries opened up on each other's positions, but gradually
the fighting died down and, by the end of the month, all was
quiet.

Over a hundred miles to the east of this battle, the British
had responded quickly to the initial task Sarrail assigned to them
at the staff conference on August 20th. A force of infantry, with
platoons of armed cyclists and of engineers, crossed the Struma
near its mouth and penetrated more than twenty miles up the
valley of a small tributary to blow up two bridges on the railway
linking Seres with Drama and the Bulgarian coastal region.
Two nights later a similar raid destroyed road bridges in the same
region. The Bulgars showed no desire to attack the British positions but were content to dig in along the left bank of the Struma.
Further east still, beyond the area covered by allied troops, they
pressed on towards Kavalla; and, on August 24th, the commander of the Greek Fourth Army Corps handed over the forts

north of the town to the Bulgars without offering any resistance, but the port itself was not occupied until September 12th.

Sarrail completed his revised plan for an offensive on September 5th, one week before he hoped it would be launched. The governing consideration behind his strategic assessment was the strength of the enemy positions to his north, along the mountain chain which ran from the Vardar, through Doiran, to the Rupel Pass. British and French reconnaissance raids early in August had met heavy resistance in this sector (which was manned, in part, by a German division). Not only did this formidable obstacle exclude an advance along the 'natural' route into Serbia, the Vardar valley; it also reduced the value of an offensive from the line of the Struma into eastern Macedonia since, quite apart from the appalling state of the roads, there was always the danger that the Bulgars would thrust forward from their northern wall down the Rupel Pass and cut off the advancing British forces. Accordingly, Sarrail continued to stake everything on his western front, even though the Serbs had already been forced back there by the Bulgars. The Serbs themselves wished to liberate a corner of their land and capture Monastir, a town which, in normal times, had some 60,000 inhabitants; but other considerations lay behind Sarrail's choice of this area as the main field of battle. From Monastir, two valleys ran north-eastwards to the upper Vardar: one, a difficult route, followed a mountain stream known as the Crna and rejoined the Vardar slightly north of the furthest point reached by the French in their abortive advance of the previous year; the other led, over the Babuna Pass, to the town of Veleš. Reach either of these objectives and the Vardar defences would be turned. And, looking further ahead, the way would be open to Skopje and old Serbia, in the north-west, or, continuing north-eastwards up further valleys, to the mountains around Sofia itself, a hundred miles distant, midway between Veleš and the new Roumanian Front on the lower Danube. There was much to commend Sarrail's grand design – provided that the enemy defences in front of Monastir could be broken before the onset of the autumnal rainstorms. Sarrail himself was already thinking in terms of a resounding victory, with the Serbs carrying the main frontal assault and the French, under Cordonnier, achieving a brilliant enveloping movement. For the moment, all that he asked of his Italian and British colleagues was that they should relieve as many French divisions as they could on the Doiran and Struma sectors and

pin down the Germans and Bulgars to prevent them transferring units westwards. This rôle, unrewarding though it seemed,
both Milne and the Italian commander, General Pettiti, were
prepared to fulfil. And, in the event, it was the two British
Corps which made the first move, one sending down a heavy
artillery barrage on the German-Bulgarian positions at Doiran,
and the other despatching a strong raiding force across the
Struma.

At six in the morning of September 12th the French and Serbian
artillery opened up around Lake Ostrovo, the mountain wall
behind the Bulgarian positions throwing back the sound of the
guns so that the roar of each barrage fell on the awaiting infantry
with ominous iteration. Before the Serbs towered the twin summits of the Kajmakcalan (or 'butter-churn'), a mountain crowned
by a ridge 1,500 yards long, which separated an eastern peak
7,700 feet above sea level from a western peak five hundred feet
higher still and which, indeed, formed the Greco-Serbian frontier. The Bulgars had mountain artillery well above the lower
slopes and observation posts on each summit, looking out over
the lesser hills beyond Ostrovo and down to the plain beyond.
Behind the 'butter-churn' lay the defiles through which the
Crna had cut its circuitous route and westward was Monastir,
its white minarets shimmering in the heat haze of the valley. So
long as the Kajmakcalan was in enemy hands, there could be no
advance. But to storm the Kajmakcalan the Serbs would have to
scale a peak twice as high as Ben Nevis. There had been no
assault of this character at such an altitude on any other front,
not even in the Italian Alps.

The commander of the Serbian First Army, General Mišić,
victorious veteran of the Danubian campaign and of the Balkan
Wars, had no doubt that the Kajmakcalan would be taken. His
battle-orders rang with romantic inspiration, as great a contrast
to the business-like prose of the French staff officers as the Serb
infantrymen were to the *poilus*: 'Our aim is to throw back the
enemy to the far side of the Crna and to pursue him. The valour,
skill and fighting qualities which you have already shown bear
you up in this battle also . . . Our cause is just. Go forward with
confidence, brave fighters, filled with hope in God'. The Serbs
are a deeply religious people; and, in the camp at the railhead,
the priests invoked the aid of the warrior saints who had won
medieval Serbia its brief epoch of glory. For had not Stephen

Dušan himself, Stephen the Mighty, 'Emperor of the Serbs, Greeks, Bulgars and Albanians', gained a famous victory in these very mountains five and a half centuries before?

But it needed more than a blood-stained legend to carry the Kajmakcalan. The foothills were taken easily enough, but by September 14th the going had become difficult. A precipitous road clung to the lower slopes as far as the village of Batachin, and for three more days the Serbs pushed relentlessly ahead under successive artillery barrages. But beyond Batachin the guns were of little use; a belt of beech forest shielded the tracks up to the summit, giving good cover for attackers and defenders alike until the bayonets had finished their grim task. And once the forest was cleared, there was nothing above but the bare face of the mountain, with each natural gully and cleft manned by the defenders as though it were a rock-hewn trench. From head-quarters down in the valley, General Mišić could, through his field-glasses, watch his troops creep forward, tracing their pro-gress by the white puffs of exploding mortar-bombs swept across the rockface by a bitter wind that never seemed to drop. He could not, however, see them reach the summit for it was in the early hours of September 19th that the Drina Division fought their way to the Bulgarian eyrie and sent back to Batachin fifty prisoners as testimony to their achievement. Below them the Serbs could see that the Bulgars had not yet accepted the loss of the Kajmakcalan. Such a key bastion could never be lightly abandoned; but, for the moment, the Serbian flag flew once more over a few hundred yards of Serbian soil.

For nearly a week each side prepared to renew this extra-ordinary battle on the rooftop of the Balkans. The Bulgars, despite pressure from the British on the central sector of the front, moved five regiments west of the Vardar. The Serbs hauled up mountain guns to the old Bulgarian observation posts on the ridge between the twin peaks. The counter-attack came on September 26th and it was as fierce a combat as any. The Drina Division fell back, down that last expanse of bare rock up which it had struggled only a few days before. But Mišić rallied the defenders: 'To fall back is treason', he declared uncom-promisingly. The Serbs stood fast as the Bulgars launched new attacks; and on September 30th once again they fought their way forward, seeking such cover as they could get from the shattered outcrops of rock, until the whole summit was in their hands. And this time, pressed hard at the foot of the mountain by other

Serb divisions which had advanced across the foothills, the
Bulgars retired, away from the 'butter-churn' for ever.

Meanwhile General Cordonnier, who had been entrusted with
two French divisions and a Russian brigade in order to turn the
Bulgarian right flank, was making slow progress. The offensive
had begun on September 12th, on the same morning as the
Serbs moved forward north of Ostrovo, after some preliminary
skirmishing two days earlier. The first objective was the town
of Florina, which stood on a ridge commanding the valley from
Ostrovo to Monastir. Sarrail had hoped that it would fall within
hours of the initial assault, but, each evening as Cordonnier sent
his report back to Salonika, all he could say was, 'Our troops
moved forward towards Florina'. Miles behind the fighting line,
Sarrail was beside himself with rage. The fault was as much his
as Cordonnier's – and it is reasonable to suppose that he knew it.
It was, after all, Sarrail who insisted on bringing the French
troops up to the line from other sectors of his front, imposing
long marches on them so that they arrived at Cordonnier's headquarters foot-sore and weary. But Sarrail was not the man to
admit a mistake. A flood of peremptory telegrams issued forth
from Salonika: 'Press forward with all your forces'; 'Go forward
on your flank. I count on it'; 'March ahead. March ahead. March
ahead'. And, though the morale of his troops was low and the
supplies for his guns uncertain, Cordonnier 'marched ahead',
slowly.

On the evening of September 16th, Cordonnier reached the
village of Boresnica, which stands on the railway four miles east
of Florina. To the surprise of its inhabitants, the French made a
grand entry, with regimental band playing and the General himself riding at the head of a company of infantry. Cordonnier
was eager to raise the spirits of his troops by giving them the
feeling of victory. But Sarrail put a very different interpretation
on the episode when he heard of it: 'Cordonnier entered Boresnica believing it to be Florina', he subsequently wrote in his
memoirs. The unfortunate General sank even lower in his estimate. And when, on the following afternoon, Florina was at last
occupied, Sarrail noted with approval that it had fallen to the
mixed brigades of General Leblois who, in the previous winter,
through strict attention to Sarrail's written word, had stage-
managed the retreat from the Vardar after the disgrace of
General de Lardemelle. It was common talk among the Allied

liaison officers in Salonika that Cordonnier's days were already numbered. If you came with an untarnished record from the Western Front, you had to be a paragon of all the military virtues to win the confidence of the ex-commander of the Third Army. For Sarrail, good republican though he was, had all the pettiness of a dispossessed Bourbon: he had learned nothing and forgotten nothing; and his capacity for resentment remained unassuaged.

But, for the moment, Cordonnier was still in command of the Franco-Russian Army, as it was impressively called in Salonika. The detailed injunctions continued to hum along the telegraph wires: 'Keep up the advance towards Monastir. There is no doubt of your numerical superiority: the Bulgars have 20 battalions to the French 31. Exploit your advantage without delay'. But to Cordonnier in Florina such logistical mathematics seemed academic. The plain fact was that the Bulgars were ensconced in the monastery of St Mark on a hill above the town and until they could be prised out, Monastir, although only fourteen miles away, might as well have been as far as Salonika. And even when the monastery was captured, on October 2nd, the French and Russian troops had to wheel into new positions, for Monastir lay almost due north and they had been advancing north-westwards to take the Florina defences.

Today, tourists seeking to enter Greece from Yugoslavia by the alternative route to the Vardar Valley, drive from Monastir (now called Bitolja) to Florina Station in little more than half an hour down a tolerably good road. Apart from the customs-posts on the frontier at Kenali there is little to be seen except isolated farmhouses. On both sides of the valley the mountains rise in magnificent splendour although less precipitous in the west than in the east, but between them the plain itself is a broad avenue of green grass with no natural obstacles, apart from an occasional copse of trees. Yet in 1916 it took the Allied troops six weeks to make their way along this corridor to Monastir; for, around Kenali, the Bulgars had dug three lines of trenches, constructed as carefully as any works along the Somme or at Ypres, and climbing a sandstone ridge in the east to the village of Brod, which lay in the path of the Serbs. Before this valley was cleared, the position cost the Allies over two thousand lives – and General Cordonnier his command.

The French reached the Bulgarian outposts in front of Kenali even before the fall of St Mark's monastery. As soon as he realized the strength of the defences, Cordonnier paused. Instinct and experience alike rejected the thought of throwing tired divisions against such an obstacle without careful preparation and while the enemy still commanded his left flank from the monastery walls. He conferred with a Russian brigadier; and the Eastern Front veteran liked the prospect no more than his colleague from the Western Front. They would await reinforcements and study the terrain. Sarrail would have none of it. 'The attack will be launched along the whole front from the Kajmakcalan to the left of the Franco-Russian Army on September 30th at seven in the morning', came the relentless order from headquarters. 'It will be pushed home with vigour'.

It was folly to attack so soon, and Cordonnier knew it. He was still awaiting three colonial regiments which had been promised to him. Patiently he wrote two long letters to Sarrail outlining his plans and detailing his difficulties; and he sent a staff officer down to Salonika to deliver them to Sarrail in person. 'By September 30th', wrote Cordonnier, 'there is no possibility of my destroying the enemy's defensive preparations. The organization of our artillery will not be completed and our left flank will not be established. . . . Success is scarcely likely and would certainly prove costly. However, if you hold to your orders, we will go ahead with them'.

Sarrail was furious at having his plan of battle questioned in this way. He flatly refused to discuss Cordonnier's problems. The most that he would concede was postponement for three days. 'The Serbs and Roumanians are counting on the French', wrote Sarrail in reply, 'Consequently I order you to attack with your infantry on October 3rd. If you do not think yourself able to do so or if you are unwilling, pray inform me so that I may give instructions to General Leblois and put yourself at the disposal of the Ministry'.

The implied rebuke and the veiled threat stung Cordonnier. At the end of yet another letter describing his preparations, he wrote: 'Anxious to see the difficulties of the enemy along the Florina Armensko road, I went with two officers and two men up to Armensko under fire. My horse was wounded and several times the bullets whistled past my ears. I am not one to fear battle. We are willing to die on the day you wish, but the enemy will not be beaten until the Russians can play their part nor without the aid of the colonial division'. Such plain speaking was enough to bring Sarrail hurrying up to the front, at last. On the Sunday morning (October 1st) the two Generals had a frigid meeting at Banica Station: Cordonnier came in for some harsh words from Sarrail, but the attack on the Kenali lines was, at any rate, postponed until St Mark's monastery was fully in French hands.

Cordonnier was, as we have said, able to report the fall of the monastery on the Monday. Three days later, with what was in 1916 novel enterprise in a senior officer, Cordonnier flew over the battlefield as observer in a French reconnaissance plane. From the air he could see clearly enough the snare of trench-works against which he was expected to pit his men; and he could also see, just as plainly, that it would be possible to find a way around the defences through the foothills to the west and the offshoots of the Kajmakcalan, where the Serbs were already in strength. He had, however, no chance of putting this strategy to the test, for when he returned to his headquarters he found that at three o'clock in the afternoon a peremptory order had arrived from Sarrail demanding a frontal assault on the Kenali lines on the following day 'to profit from the moral depression which had fallen on the enemy' after the capture of the monastery. So sure was Sarrail of success, that he appended instructions on harrying the retreat of the Bulgars to Prilep once they had evacuated Monastir.

At two o'clock on the Friday afternoon, the guns opened up and the French and Russian infantry advanced on the first Bulgarian trenches. There was bitter fighting with grenades and bayonets, but not a hundred yards was gained. The Allied force fell back, with heavy losses, especially among the Russians. The attack had been as disastrous as Cordonnier had feared. But still Sarrail persisted. Reinforcements reached Cordonnier over the following weekend, and on the Saturday of the following week (October 14th) the Allies attacked again. It was a ghastly shambles. Meeting uncut wire, the French and Russians came to a halt and, as they tried to hack their way through, the Bulgarian machine-guns opened up on them. In one afternoon the French lost nearly 1,500 men and the Russians 600. And still the Bulgarian lines remained inviolate. On the extreme right of the valley, the burning village of Brod showed that the Serbs, at any rate, had fulfilled their mission.

Cordonnier had had enough of this butchery. He ordered a reconnaissance in force of the hill positions, intending to put into effect the plan he had worked out high above the lines. Once again he was prevented from putting it into practice. For to

Sarrail this new design, so sensible to the men on the spot, sounded like rank disobedience. On October 16th he telegraphed to Joffre for permission to relieve Cordonnier of his duties; and four days later Cordonnier was ordered to hand over his command to Leblois and return to France. He had been in the Balkans exactly 69 days.

Sarrail's treatment of Cordonnier scandalized a considerable section of the French officer corps, and a fierce debate began which was to subside only with Sarrail's own death in 1929. The whole tragic episode showed Sarrail's character at its worst – his obstinacy, resentment, suspicion, imperiousness and lack of good faith. It damned him with the other Allied commanders, each of whom found an excuse, in October, to complain to his government of the cavalier way in which he, too, had been treated on various occasions by Sarrail. It fetched the French Minister of War in person out to Salonika in November to see this intractable commander-in-chief for himself. It would, with any other general and any other government, have been the end of Sarrail's career. But his protectors were still strong in the Senate and the Chamber, and Briand's Ministry was too weak to dismiss him. So Sarrail survived in Salonika for thirteen more months, until greater scandals nearer home unleashed the Tiger.

Yet hard though it is to defend Sarrail's handling of Cordonnier, it must be remembered that from G.H.Q., Salonika, he could see the operations at Kenali in perspective, against the background of the whole Balkan campaign and, to some extent, of the general balance between the antagonists throughout Europe. Back in July, before Roumania had struck her bargain or the Allies had approved a joint offensive, he had been convinced that Monastir was the most profitable objective for his troops and nothing that had happened subsequently on any other sector had caused him to change his mind. The British, for example, had fought two sharp engagements, one on the Vardar and the other across the Struma. In the first, five infantry battalions had come up against a German regiment dug in to well planned positions on the crest of a hill overlooking the village of Machukovo; and had lost almost half of their effective strength without dislodging the Germans. And in the second action, which lasted for five days at the beginning of October, the British had, indeed, captured three villages south-west of Seres but they had lacked the reserve divisions to follow up this success by advancing on the Rupel Pass. Pressure of this type might, in time, wear down the enemy; but casualties had been relatively heavy and Milne certainly had no desire to see the Machukovo incident repeated. The Balkans were not the place for a war of attrition; the number of men available was limited and the incidence of sickness too high. Everything seemed to indicate the need for a determined thrust at a strategic point. Intelligence reports convinced Sarrail – and, indeed, Milne as well – that the Bulgars were finding it difficult to meet the demands of a long front in Macedonia and an invasion of Roumania at the same time. If they could only be hit hard enough at the pivot of their defences, they might well crumble. If they did not, then at least they could be saved only by German aid, and the more the Germans were committed to fighting in Macedonia, the fewer troops they would have in France or Russia or Roumania. Hence, time and time again, as he looked at the map, Sarrail's eye came back to Monastir and the sweep of the Crna.

Sarrail was, in fact, not far out in his assessment of the situation in the enemy High Command. The great Hindenburg-Ludendorff partnership had, characteristically, begun by relegating Macedonia to the bottom of its list of priorities. 'The last man who can be spared from the East and West must be sent against Roumania', said Hindenburg on the day he took over at Pless. The Bulgars could take care of Sarrail and Milne. The carefully prepared Austro-German invasion of Roumania began in the third week of September and seemed, at first, to be carrying all before it. But at the very moment when the Germans reached the Roumanian line of prepared defences and resistance stiffened, disquieting messages started to reach German Headquarters from Sofia. The morale of the Bulgarian First Army was low and there had been a minor mutiny in a battalion on the Crna. The Germans had withdrawn one regiment from Macedonia for service in Roumania, leaving only six German battalions (and auxiliary services) to bolster up the Bulgars on the Greek frontier: now the Bulgarian Staff wanted the German regiment back again. The master minds at Pless thought the situation could be saved by administrative changes. General von Winckler with the so-called German Eleventh Army was ordered to assume responsibility for the defence of Monastir from General Bojadiev on September 26th. But to Hindenburg's surprise, Winckler too needed support. Clearly another change in command was called for. Winckler retained his responsibilities but was subordinated to General von Below, who in the first week of October established an Army Group Headquarters for the whole Macedonian Front in Skopje. And, lest von Below proved importunate, he was firmly told that the Macedonian Front must be content with small forces until Roumania was defeated, 'when the Balkan question would be as good as solved and the Bulgarian troops would liquidate Sarrail easily enough'.

The first message that greeted Below in Skopje told him of the repulse of Cordonnier's initial assult on the Kenali lines. So far so good; but, as a precaution, two German infantry battalions were moved across from the Vardar section on October 10th, another one following them a few days later. Yet this, it seemed, was not enough. The Bulgars were faltering and had no reserves left. On the very day that Cordonnier was dismissed, Below sent an urgent message direct to Berlin. Scratch battalions were collected from Champagne, from the Vosges, from Poland and hurriedly entrained for the Balkans. Even batteries of heavy-artillery were moved eastwards from France to prevent the Bulgarian line cracking in front of Monastir.

Sarrail's persistence was beginning to reap its reward. Carefully the General sifted the intelligence reports, letting Chantilly know each time a new German unit was identified. He had, however, another concern by now. The weather had broken at the end of October. Violent storms flooded the trenches and turned the railhead into an impassable morass. The Kenali valley looked like a huge rice-field, and each day the snow-line was creeping lower and lower down the mountains. The railway to Banica, never the most reliable of routes, became blocked and congested; and lorries failed to make the gradient on the primitive roads. It took the Italian brigade three weeks to move across the front from its old positions in the mountains east of Doiran to Florina. As day after day Leblois sent reports of rain and floods and snow back to Salonika, Sarrail began to wonder if it would be possible to resume the offensive against Monastir before the spring.

All this while, the Serbs were keeping up their pressure on the enemy forces in the bend of the Crna. It was this sector which seemed to Winckler the most vulnerable part of the whole line of defence and he sought to plug it by bringing in eight German battalions. Sarrail, too, had perceived its importance and withdrew an infantry division with artillery support from Leblois's force in the valley and put it under the command of

Mišić for operations beyond the Crna. At the same time he moved other French units westwards, where they linked up with irregular bands of Albanians who were harrying the Bulgarian positions south of Lake Prespa. Subsequently, when it at last reached the front, the Italian brigade was moved into line between this western group and the main Kenali position. By thus re-grouping his forces so as to put greater emphasis on the two mountain flanks Sarrail was adopting a strategy which bore a close resemblance to the proposals Cordonnier had vainly put forward on the eve of his dismissal.

It was along the Crna, despite the irregular terrain and the appalling weather, that the offensive was first resumed after the heavy rain had ended. On November 10th and November 11th two Serbian divisions and a regiment of French Zouaves captured more than a thousand prisoners, the majority of them Germans who complained that they had been deserted by their Bulgarian ally. But again the weather deteriorated, the chief obstacle this time being fog, which blanketed the Crna region throughout the morning of November 13th, silencing the artillery and forcing both allied and enemy patrols to lose their sense of direction and stumble against each other as they moved in circles between the opposing lines. But when suddenly, at three in the afternoon, the fog lifted the Serbs broke through the German position, sending more than six hundred of them, sick and dispirited, back to the prison-camps around Salonika. So horrified were Winckler and Below at the failure of their battalions to repulse the Franco-Serbian force that they telegraphed for yet more reinforcements, the majority of whom were fetched from the Western Front.

The French pushed forward against the Kenali lines once more on November 14th. The fighting was as grim as ever, but yard by yard the Bulgars were pushed back to their final trenches. Then, at night, the fog came down again and the attackers crept back disconsolate. Their persistence had not been in vain; the enemy command now concluded that the time had come to shorten the front and, during the night, the Bulgars pulled out of the defensive positions in the valley which they had held for six weeks. Kenali was at last in French hands.

Sarrail saw that Monastir, as well as Kenali, was now within his grasp. Yet conditions grew rose rather than better. Supplies from base were held up, not merely the equipment of war but bread for the men and fodder for the horses. Ox-carts were pressed into service, lumbering along painfully slowly past lorries that had slipped into the deep ruts beside the road. A fierce wind was blowing the snow relentlessly along the icy banks of the Crna, and when, down in the valley, the artillery sought to move up from Florina, the wheels of the guns sank lower and lower in the mud and slush. The Italians, who were by now in the hills towards Prespa, were exposed to the full blast of the blizzard, the temperature falling at night to 1° Fahrenheit. But the fury of the winter fell no less cruelly on the defenders, making it impossible for them to throw up adequate defences on the outskirts of Monastir and stranding the newly arrived German regiments on the icy road across the Babuna Pass. The battle had become a struggle between two armies of exhausted and half-frozen men, plagued as much by sickness and disease as by the ravages of war. And, given one day free from blizzard or fog, victory must go to the side with the greater number of guns and rifles, the Allies.

On November 17th the dawn was bright and clear, the white contours of the mountains and the roofs of Monastir standing out sharply in the frozen air. The indomitable Serbs stormed two nameless hills due east of the town while the French and Italians and Russians moved slowly forward from one tiny hamlet to another all that day and most of the night. During the following afternoon the Serbs reported that a convoy of waggons were moving along the Monastir–Prilep road beneath them. The Bulgars were salvaging what they could from the doomed town, but the Allies were too weary to hamper their retreat. That night the enveloping troops watched as the sky above Monastir turned orange; the enemy had set fire to the quarters they had occupied. Patrols approached the trenches which the Bulgars had tried to dig in the previous week; they were empty. A few hours later, a young cavalry officer, leading his troop of mounted scouts cautiously forward, was just in time to see the last battery of German guns pulling out of the town. His name was Murat; by a fortuitous piece of historical symbolism, a descendant of the captor of Moscow was about to lead a Franco-Russian division to its first conquest. By noon on November 19th the French and Russians and Serbs had all entered the silent and shuttered town. After nine weeks of hard campaigning, Monastir had fallen.

The capture of Monastir was rightly celebrated as a major

triumph throughout the Salonika base. Welcome news at any time, it came now to raise morale when it was at a particularly low ebb: reports from Roumania were gloomy; and the British, striving to engage the Bulgars in the waterlogged valley of the Struma, had run into stiff resistance around two heavily fortified farmhouses. Sarrail claimed, with some justification, that Monastir represented the first victory of French arms since the Marne, more than two years before. But in his Order of the Day he remembered to congratulate all the national units under his joint command, including those who, like the British, had been given the thankless task of mounting costly diversions far from the field of glory.

Yet it was, of course, the Serbs who were most elated by the success at Monastir. The town had fallen four years to the day after its capture by other Serbian divisions from the Turk in the first Balkan War. And, just as victory then had presaged the liberation of the old Serbian lands, so now they were convinced that, with four hundred square miles freed from the hated Bulgar, they would go forward in the spring to Skopje and Niš and Belgrade. Within two days, Prince-Regent Alexander had been welcomed in Monastir as if the war were nearly over; while on Mount Athos, the Serbian monks, improbably informed of the victory by a British Member of Parliament, unfurled the green silk banner of Stephen Dušan and sang a solemn *Te Deum*.

The Bulgarian front had been broken; but the enemy was only a few miles north of the town, which remained within range of his artillery throughout the winter. Even while the celebrations were going on, occasional shells were lobbed into its crowded streets, and one of these seriously wounded General Pettiti, the Italian commander, as he was visiting the old Italian consulate. Sarrail had hoped to pursue the Germans and Bulgars to Prilep, and for another three weeks the joint armies sought to move forward. But battle and sickness had taken their toll – one Serbian Army was reduced from 30,000 to 6,000 – and, in the heavy snow, it was impossible to make progress. Moreover, it could be argued that the offensive had served its immediate purpose. It had relieved pressure on the Roumanians, although it is true that the German Command had preferred to send reinforcements from France rather than from beyond the Danube. By the beginning of December, however, Roumanian resistance had virtually collapsed: Bucharest was occu-

pied by the Germans on December 5th and the Ploesti oilfields
a day later. On the Macedonian Front the important task
now was to safeguard what had been gained until the snows
melted and fresh divisions reached the battle-line. Hence, on
December 11th, Joffre ordered Sarrail 'to suspend all operations for the time being'. For the weary divisions up above the
snowline, the order came not a day too soon.

6 / Politics and Knavish Tricks

WHILE THE ARMY of the Orient was fighting its way up to Monastir, the struggle for supremacy in Greece and the activities of General Sarrail and the French Admiral in the Aegean had posed questions for which neither London nor Paris could find an easy answer. Within months Monastir was little more than a name from the past, another battle-honour on tattered banners, as remote as a victory in the Crimea. But the political problems which plagued the Macedonian campaign in the last months of 1916 remained unresolved even when the fighting was over and the last allied troops had returned to their homeland. In no other venture in the war did local feuds exert such an influence upon the military command. Not least among the burdens borne by the ordinary soldiers in the Salonika Army was the conviction of its leaders that politics was much too serious a business to be left to the statesmen.

Throughout his life Maurice Sarrail possessed an insatiable appetite for political intrigue. He found plenty to feed on in Salonika. For centuries the town had been a centre of rebellion and unrest, the second city of the Byzantine Empire when Athens was little more than a ruined village; and, more recently, it had nurtured the 'Young Turk' movement which forced Sultan Abdul Hamid to summon a parliament in 1908. By now the Turkish officers seemed as distant as their Byzantine predecessors, but Salonika, with its waterfront harbouring the flotsam of many nationalities, retained its lurid reputation as a cradle of conspiracy. With Greece divided between the rival champions of the King and Venizelos, Sarrail had every opportunity to exercise his talent for meddling in political affairs. And by the autumn of 1916 his British allies had become firmly convinced that he was permitting his devotion to republican principles to warp his judgment and distract him from military matters.

There was, moreover, another aspect of Salonika's past which lingered on amid the present muddle and confusion. The city had flourished as a trading community, a western outpost of the Levant, lacking the oligarchic traditions of Venice or Ragusa but no less alive than the independent republics to the wealth that Asia could bring to Europe. If, in 1916, the political sympathies of its many races were fickle and uncertain, there was no doubting the willingness of its merchants to back whatever régime brought business to the town and prosperity to their own enterprises.

The French, too, were concerned with these matters. Before the Balkan Wars France had been second only to Germany in the amount of foreign capital invested in Turkish concerns: a Frenchman was Inspector-General of Finance and another controlled the tobacco monopoly; the Director-Generalship of the Imperial Ottoman Bank alternated between the French and the British; and all the bank's financial operations were controlled from Paris, even if its headquarters were in Constantinople. The Societé Immobiliere Ottoman, the Societé Génèrale d'Enterprise des Routes, the Societé Nationale de Commerce, d'Industrie et d'Agriculture may have had their main concessions in Syria but their hold was also strong on European Turkey. A French company had been responsible for modernizing the harbour facilities of Salonika at the turn of the century. By virtually destroying Turkey-in-Europe the settlement which followed the Balkan Wars had challenged France's commercial position in the East. French bond-holders already had considerable investments in Serbia and Roumania, but far less in Greece (where, indeed, Britain's pre-war trade was double that of France). It is, accordingly, small wonder that Sarrail proved not uninterested in the economic well-being of Salonika and its hinterland; for there were influential backers on the Paris Bourse who warmly welcomed his activity. By the autumn of 1916 an efficient commercial bureau was operating in the port under the auspices of the French command. And before long the other allies were complaining that merchants who sent orders to France were favoured at the expense of those who turned elsewhere. The loudest protests came from the Italians; but one feels that their moral indignation at Sarrail's business ethics was not unalloyed, for Rome, too, had interests in the commerce of the Levant.

This suspicion that Sarrail aimed at becoming satrap of a Greek republic backed by French capital underlies much of

the political manœuvring in the last months of 1916, not only
among the Allies but among the Greeks themselves. Yet it is,
of course, no more the whole truth about Sarrail than the black
and white caricatures of the time were the whole truth about
the King or the greatest of Greek statesmen. For Constantine
was not a two-faced traitor willing to sell Greece to his German
brother-in-law; nor was Venizelos a farsighted idealist unfurling
the banner of liberal democracy. Sarrail, for all his petty pre-
occupations, never forgot that he had been entrusted with waging
a military campaign against Germany and her allies; and by
encouraging a Greek revolt he did at all events ensure that a
quarter of a million Greek soldiers were fighting beside the French
and the British in the final victorious offensive. No character
comes well out of the Greek tragedy of 1916; but those who
were in Athens or Salonika at least had the excuse that they
were so deeply involved in events from day to day that they
failed to appreciate broader questions of principle. It is harder
to justify the self-righteous evasiveness of London and Paris.

The Bulgars had, as we have seen, crossed into Greek Macedonia in force on August 17th. Their advance caused such
elation in Royalist circles in Athens that it was suspected the
General Staff had prior knowledge of the invasion. In Salonika,
on the other hand, there were many Greeks from villages now
overrun by a traditional enemy and the city was soon full of
rumours of atrocities committed by the Bulgars as they moved
forward. There was little love lost between the Greek-speaking
and Bulgar-speaking population of Macedonia, and the decision
of the invaders to arm the Bulgarian (and Turkish) villagers
inevitably led to a renewal of old feuds. Reports came in of
Greek homes burnt, of Greek men and women with their throats
cut. The failure of the Greek Government to protect its newest
citizens rankled in Salonika. Irate patriots, genuine liberals and
a handful of café-terrace demagogues set up a 'League for
National Defence' to voice the general will of the Macedonian
Greeks. With unconscious irony, the League established its headquarters in the same building from which the Young Turks
had set out to revitalize the Ottoman Empire nine years ago.
A 'Committee of Public Safety' came into being – a gesture
which Sarrail, the friend of Danton's most enthusiastic biographer, no doubt appreciated. All the talk in the town was of
revolution. As a British officer noted in his diary; 'Another

scorching day, but we forgot the heat in the excitement of the Revolution'.

Yet, for a time, it seemed as if the revolution would progress little further than the talking stage. Enthusiastic proclamations appeared in the streets, and meetings of protest were held in Eleutherios, the square known to the Allies as 'the Place de la Liberté'; but nobody seemed inclined, in those torrid days, to storm the Bastille of King Constantine's soldiery. Then, on the last Sunday in August, an excited crowd followed Colonel Zymbrakakis, a hero of the Balkan Wars, to Sarrail's headquarters and pledged support to the Entente Powers: *'Zito Ghallia'* ('Long live France'), they had shouted, adding for good measure, *'Zito Venizelos'*. A few hours later, once darkness cooled the streets and liquor warmed their spirits, the revolutionaries prepared to attack the Royal barracks in the centre of the town. There was shooting, and three of the insurgents fell dead. Sarrail stood aside no longer. The French artillery was moved up and the Royalist troops surrendered. Any who were reluctant to serve in a revolutionary army were marched through the streets under French escort to an internment camp. Salonika had cut its links with Athens; but the sword which made the break was French.

The leader whose name the mob had invoked was still more than three hundred miles away. Venizelos was far too astute to commit himself irreparably to the proclamation of a provisional government until he could be certain that it would have some genuine independence; the old Cretan rebel would never sit as dummy for a French ventriloquist. In June Sarrail had proposed that he should escape to Salonika but Venizelos had shown little enthusiasm for the suggestion and had remained at his home in Athens despite the constant intimidation of his supporters and the formal anathema of the Orthodox Metropolitan. Yet, defying the authorities, more than 55,000 demonstrators heard him pledge himself, on August 27th, to support any government prepared to associate Greece with the Entente Powers and throw the Bulgars out of eastern Macedonia. There was, perhaps, at that moment, some prospect of reconciliation between the King and the liberals. On August 30th Sir Francis Elliott, the British Minister in Athens, reported that the King, his prime minister and the chief of staff had all indicated the possibility that Greece might shortly become a belligerent on the side of Britain and France. Not without hope, he informed Grey that he was to have an audience with Constantine on the morning of September 1st.

But by noon on that day watchers on the Acropolis could see the tripod masts and heavy funnels of Dreadnoughts manœuvring in the waters off Salamis, where the triremes had fought in another September long ago. The threat of French field-guns had sufficed at Salonika; Athens, it seemed, required the presence of the commander-in-chief of the French Mediterranean Fleet with a battle squadron nearly as large as the one which had tried to force the Dardanelles: ten battleships, three cruisers, three monitors, sixteen destroyers and thirty-eight supporting vessels. 'It is time that we finished with these diplomats', remarked the French naval attaché to a British colleague, Captain Compton Mackenzie R.M. The Admiral was to seize Austrian and German merchantmen interned at Eleusis and the Piraeus, and support the French Government's demand for the expulsion of German agents and the right to supervise postal and telegraph services. The battle squadron achieved its immediate purpose: the enemy vessels were duly surrendered and the Greek Government formally agreed to carry out the other requirements; but, for the time being, the fleet remained off Salamis.

The British Government was alarmed at the way affairs were going in Greece. The French appeared to have lost all sense of proportion. Sarrail had actually embarked a brigade of troops which were to have been landed in Athens but, partly because of British protests and partly because of the needs of the Florina counter-attack, the men were sent back to camp without ever having left the harbour of Salonika. The Foreign Secretary and the British Ambassador in Paris sought to restrain Briand (who was being harassed by his Minister of Marine, a member of a family of ship-owners). Yet the British were unwilling to allow a Balkan issue to precipitate a political crisis in France; they had no wish to see Briand forced out of office at the height of the battles on the Somme. Hence, while deploring drastic action in Athens, the War Committee had weakly accepted the need for a naval demonstration. One in four of the vessels off Salamis flew the White Ensign.

It was, however, not only the politicians who were perturbed in London. King George V, with his strict sense of constitutional propriety, rarely intervened in the foreign policy of Grey or, indeed, of his successors. But the Greek situation so troubled him that, on September 4th, he sent an unusually strong letter to Asquith. After deploring the extent to which the Allies had intervened in a 'neutral and friendly country', the King continued:

'I cannot help feeling that in this Greek question we have allowed France too much to dictate a policy, and that as a Republic she may be somewhat intolerant of, if not anxious to abolish, the monarchy in Greece. But this is *not* the policy of my Government. Nor is it that of the Emperor of Russia, who, writing to me a few days ago said:

"I feel rather anxious about the internal affairs in Greece. It seems to me the protecting Powers, in trying to safeguard our interests concerning Greece's neutrality, are gradually immersing themselves too much in her internal home affairs to the detriment of the King."

I cannot refrain from expressing my astonishment and regret at General Sarrail's arbitrary conduct towards those troops who, loyal to their King and Government, refused to join the Revolutionary movement at Salonika. Could not a protest of some kind be sent to the French Government against General Sarrail's proceedings? . . . Public opinion in Greece, as well as the opinion of the King, is evidently changing and if the Allies would treat her kindly and not, if I may say so, in a bullying spirit, she will in all probability join them.'

Throughout the following weeks, King and Tsar remained suspicious of French policy in general and Sarrail's in particular. Constantine, for his part, made every appeal that he could to monarchical solidarity: Prince Andrew was despatched to London, Prince Nicholas to Petrograd. And in Paris, Princess George – whose husband was an old enemy of Venizelos from Cretan days – used all her charms on the not unsusceptible Aristide Briand. Good republicans had no monopoly of intrigue.

As darkness fell over Athens on September 25th a bearded man with spectacles slipped out of a house in Patission, the long road north past the National Museum. With hat turned down and coat collar turned up, he moved off towards the centre of the town, shaking police trailers off down side-streets as he went, the epitome of conspiracy. Near the old parliament buildings a French car waited, tricolour flag flying on the bonnet.

4

Venizelos stepped in, and the car sped down the Piraeus Road to the coast. At the Plato Restaurant in Phaleron he was joined by Admiral Koundouriotis, a member of a famous and wealthy sea-faring family from Hydra, and in his own right a hero of the Balkan Wars and former Minister of Marine. By dawn the next morning they were on their way to Crete, escorted by French patrol-boats. Once in Canea they received an enthusiastic reception and called on the Greek people to continue the fight to free Greek territory from the invaders. 'We claim the support of every Greek citizen who feels that further toleration of disaster and humiliation would mean the death of the nation', declared Venizelos.

In escaping to Crete rather than to Salonika, Venizelos was once again showing his political wisdom. The French military attaché had been pressing him to go north ever since the setting up of the Committee of Public Safety. Had he done so, he would have taken over a movement which owed everything to the peculiar powers enjoyed by Sarrail. Instead he chose to go to an island where the head of every family of importance was his supporter and where the people were proud of leading Greece rather than of following the example of the mainland. Moreover in Crete and the islands the resistance to Constantine's policy had been encouraged, not so much by the French, as by the British. Venizelos was thus, to some extent, able to counteract the excessive influence of France, which had troubled him already in Athens and was patently obvious in Macedonia.

To have chosen Salonika and not his birthplace as his first sanctuary would, in fact, have done Venizelos' reputation irreparable harm. As it was, Crete became a natural centre of defiance. He was soon joined by other prominent figures. General Danglis, a pocket-sized Army commander whose following among the soldiery was as great as Koundouriotis's among the seamen, crossed to Canea within a few days. A cruiser, a destroyer and a torpedo-boat slipped off from Phaleron to lend their support to the movement. The islands of the Sporades followed the example of Crete; and the people of Chios and Samos and Lesbos welcomed Venizelos with hardly less enthusiasm than he had received in Canea. In all he spent little more than a week in Crete, but they were days full of portent for the future of the Greek State.

When, on October 9th, Venizelos at last landed at Salonika and Sarrail came forward to greet him on the quayside, he had more to offer the general than his name. There had been a possibility that the Salonika Revolution would be exploited by Macedonian separatists. Conceivably this might have benefited France; it must have infuriated the other Allies, particularly the Serbs. But Venizelos had some claim to speak for 'Greater Greece'. His followers in Athens were, at that very moment, suffering considerable hardship at the hands of a right wing organization, 'The League of Reserve Officers'; but each day hundreds were escaping to the islands which had already pledged him their support. Once in Salonika Venizelos did not hesitate to establish a Provisional Government, which was headed by a Triumvirate of Koundouriotis, Danglis and himself. He appointed as Foreign Minister an experienced diplomat, Politis, and wisely left commercial affairs to the leading Greek shipowner of those days, Embeirikos, whose attachment to the Venizelist cause was received with mixed feelings by the French. For the moment neither the British nor the French recognized the Provisional Government, but at least there was an administration with some semblance of support from the Greek people to act in their name in Salonika.

This was just as well, for the six weeks which followed the Salonika 'Revolution' had hardly been happy ones and the Committee of Public Safety proved remarkably inept. Colonel Zymbrakakis had committed himself to the creation of a 'National Army' to fight for the honour and interests of Greece. That was an admirable sentiment, certain to win cheers from the populace. Enthusiasm swiftly evaporated, however, when it was realized that the people of Salonika would themselves have to constitute the National Army. Zymbrakakis had a nucleus in his own regiment and these were soon joined by two thousand men from the Greek Seventh Division (who had escaped from Kavalla when the town was surrendered to the Bulgarians) and by some ex-royalist 'volunteers'. But the Committee required hundreds of recruits, and it must be admitted that the methods used to swell the ranks had more in common with Falstaff than with Kitchener. A heavy hand fell on townsfolk and villagers alike. Among the least fortunate were some of the wealthier citizens of Salonika who, anxious to escape the Committee's net, induced boatmen to convey them from small harbours further along the coast to places of refuge in the outer islands; but the boatmen, either from motives of patriotism or the knowledge that they would thus get a further payment, brought them back, after miserable hours at sea, to areas where Zymbrakakis and his men were in firm control.

It would, of course, be misleading to suggest that with the coming of Venizelos such practices ceased. Intimidation continued, both in Salonika and other regions which proved a little slow to rally round the 'National' standard. Nevertheless, ship-loads of genuine volunteers began to arrive from Crete and even from Athens; at the end of October one such vessel, the *Angheliki*, was attacked and severely damaged, apparently by a German U-boat. But the reinforcements got through to Salonika and, at the same time, the people of the town and the surrounding countryside began to show a little more enthusiasm for the National Army. A powerful incentive to recruitment was the news that the Bulgars had handed over a section of the front around Kavalla to the Turks and that Moslem divisions were being raised in eastern Macedonia to recover the lands lost by the Crescent in 1912. The Church authorities, who at first had looked askance at the excommunicated Venizelos, began to have second thoughts.

By the middle of November three battalions of the National Army were serving under British command along the Struma and fought well in an attack on one of the fortified farmhouses. Later they were moved to the mountains east of Monastir, where they again distinguished themselves. Venizelos was able to inform Sarrail as early as November 18th that the National Army had over 23,000 men in its ranks. So many volunteers wished to join the army in the islands that recruiting had to be slowed down through shortage of equipment. The islanders proved to be much better soldiers than the people from the mainland, partly because of the difference in the way in which they had been 'called to the colours'. This was shown clearly enough in January 1917 when a thousand men from the peninsula of Khalkidike, who had been pressed into service in the early days of the 'Revolution', walked out of camp with their rifles on being ordered to the Vardar Front. For some weeks the whole of southern Khalkidike was in a state of anarchy, until Milne was forced to send in a regiment of Nottinghamshire yeomanry to restore order and protect his communications. By contrast, the Cretans had by then aroused the admiration of all the Allied commanders.

Meanwhile, throughout the autumn and into the first months

of winter the battle squadron lay off Salamis, a flotilla of destroyers occasionally slipping away to hunt a U-boat, or a capital
ship to Malta for supplies and replenishments. For a few days
an Italian or a Russian cruiser would moor behind the anti-
submarine nets to preserve the fiction of inter-allied solidarity.
But all these weeks the command remained in the hands of
the French Admiral, Dartige du Fournet, a man thus thrust into
a prominence unwarranted by his abilities.

Vice-Admiral Dartige du Fournet appears in his memoirs
as a weak and obstinate meddler, ignorant of Greek politics
but pathetically eager to play a part in history worthy of the
dignity of his name. Suspicious of the British, resenting the
initiative of even his own country's diplomats and easily charmed
by the honeyed words of the King, the Admiral stumbled on
for three months until, in the humiliation of near-disaster, he
was beleatedly recalled to France. Not all the errors of policy
were his; but as we picture him surveying the Acropolis from
above the ten thirteen inch guns of his flagship, he cuts a singu-
larly unsympathetic figure. It must, however, be said in all
fairness that the Admiral was under considerable pressure from
the Ministry of Marine, a traditionally Anglophobe section of
the French administration.

For the first month after the squadron's arrival there was
little enough for it to do. Once again Constantine's representatives in the Allied capitals were holding out the possibility that
Greece might yet range herself on the side of the angels, and,
while the telegrams were passing between London and Paris,
the Admiral remained inactive, apart from sending a party of
marines to guard the French Legation. But suddenly at the beginning of October the Ministry of Marine ordered the Admiral
to put new demands on the Greek authorities which would have
put the Greek fleet and the railway services under French control. The Admiral blandly informed the Allied Ministers that
he intended to land 300 marines. The British protested: Grey
sent a tart message that 'The presence of the French fleet did
not entitle the Admiral to act as he liked'. It had no effect;
on October 9th Dartige du Fournet was instructed to disregard
the reluctance of the diplomats. He thereupon ordered the
Greeks to surrender their naval vessels at the Piraeus and hand
over the shore batteries by the afternoon of October 11th. When
at eleven o'clock that morning a Greek officer arrived on the
French flagship to negotiate with Dartige du Fournet, he found

the gun crews already at action stations. The Greek fleet was duly seized, an incident which, the Admiral writes, 'afforded him neither pleasure nor pride'. By the end of the week, patrols had been landed in the Piraeus, a company of marines had been sent into Athens and railway transport around the capital was controlled by the French. Demands were now made for the expulsion from Athens not only of German intelligence agents, but of the whole staff of the enemy Legations; and in due course they sailed for Kavalla past the guns of Dartige du Fournet's fleet.

These activities of the French were of highly questionable validity in international law. They were also a sad blow to the Entente's sympathizers in Greece. The swing among the naval officers to Venizelos and Koundouriotis was sharply arrested; and the British, for their part, were furious. The Greek fleet had been turned into a modern fighting force by serving officers of the Royal Navy and a solemn protest was made by the Rear-Admiral who had headed the naval mission to the Admiralty. Logically the British units in the Allied squadron should have been withdrawn from Salamis. But with lamentable weakness the British shrank from a public breach with their French ally. The battleships *Exmouth* and *Duncan*, with attendant cruisers and destroyers, remained under the orders of Dartige du Fournet.

There followed a curious incident which was to prove tragic in its consequences. While the question of expelling the enemy diplomats from Athens was still under discussion a young French Deputy named Bénazet arrived in the city on his way back to Paris from an official visit to Salonika. Bénazet, a confidant of the leading French royalists, had for almost two years been an enthusiastic supporter of a vigorous Balkan Front and had, indeed, been responsible for passing on Franchet d'Espérey's plan for an offensive in south-eastern Europe to President Poincaré. Now that he had re-assured himself about the activities of the 'red republican' in Salonika, Bénazet sought, and obtained, an audience with King Constantine at the end of October. He returned from the palace convinced that the King intended no harm to the Allied cause. Sarrail and Milne were at this time alarmed by the massing of Constantine's troops in Thessaly, on the southern flank of the Macedonian Army. Bénazet considered that he had overcome this obstacle without difficulty; the King agreed to withdraw two Army Corps from Thessaly to the Morea. Indeed, Constantine was prepared to go further; he

even suggested that if the Allies were to ask for mountain batteries to compensate them for the equipment handed over to
the Bulgarians in Macedonia, the King would surrender the
guns with only a formal protest. Believing that he could heal
the breach between 'official' Greece and the Entente, Bénazet
visited Admiral Dartige du Fournet and it was arranged that
the Admiral, too, should have an audience with Constantine.

The Admiral welcomed Bénazet's attempt at mediation, but
before he met the King he was determined to put forward a
written proposal embodying some of the King's ideas. Accordingly he sent a note to the Greek Prime Minister which was
mild in tone but extraordinary in content. It expressed the
appreciation of the French for the withdrawal of troops from
Thessaly but went on to stipulate the amount of war material
which it was hoped the Greeks would hand over as compen-
sation. The full list was a long one but the French made it clear
that they would not press immediately for every item. 'The
French Government', the note concluded, 'demands as an
earnest of the goodwill of the Greek Government that 10 mountain batteries should be immediately handed over to me. . . .
The material must be placed in the Thessaly railway-station in
Athens, whence it will be transported to Salonika at our charge'.
No immediate reply was forthcoming from the Greeks.

It is possible that at this moment the French were contemplating the abandonment of Venizelos, who persisted in showing
a tiresome spirit of independence, in order to throw their support
behind the King. If this were, indeed, the case, they were a
long way ahead of their allies. The British remained highly
sceptical about the King's offer to give the Allies mountain
batteries; they knew their Constantine better than the French –
or, perhaps, they were more familiar with their *Aeneid*. Yet,
once again, they did little enough to assert their policy, contenting themselves with urging caution on the Admiral.

The King received the Admiral in audience on November
19th. Although he made it clear that he could not hand over
the weapons as the French wished, for fear that they might
fall into the hands of Venizelists, the Admiral was hardly less
pleased with the King than Bénazet had been. He was confident
that he would reach an agreement in the end. Constantine
seemed unmoved by the impending departure of the enemy
diplomats and appeared reconciled to the hoisting of the tricolour flag over his vessels at the Piraeus. His most bitter com-

plaint was at the lack of understanding shown towards his policy by the British Press. And in this the Admiral was prepared to agree with him; for when pressed by importunate journalists Dartige du Fournet habitually retreated behind a wall of impeccably good breeding.

Unfortunately, the Greek Government proved less accommodating than the King. On November 21st it rejected the Admiral's note. Irritated, and surprised, the Admiral despatched a virtual ultimatum. If the guns were not handed over by December 1st he would send some 3,000 men into Athens to seize what arms they could. Again he sought a royal audience, which was granted to him on November 27th. Again he was well satisfied by the King's attitude. Constantine was as full of goodwill as ever. He had assured the Admiral – or so the Frenchman believed – that, although his royal dignity would not permit him to hand over the guns, he would order his troops not to fire first if it proved necessary for the Admiral to send detachments into Athens.

The Admiral returned to his squadron and, it is said, began to reflect on the etiquette for inviting his royal friend to lunch on the flagship. These pleasant thoughts were interrupted by disquieting news: Greek reservists were flocking to their barracks and ominous daubs of red had been painted on the shopfronts of avowed Venizelists. But the Admiral was not disturbed by this information; clearly the intelligence agents were in league with the revolutionaries. 'I don't give a damn for intelligence reports', he told the British Minister. And, still trusting in the King's word, he went ahead with his plans.

A cloud of uncertainty hangs heavily over the events of December 1st 1916 even now. There is no lack of evidence. We have the Admiral's account; we have Compton Mackenzie's; we have a report by a British major and telegrams sent by the French military attaché; we even have the version which the Queen of Greece forwarded to her brother, the Kaiser. The basic facts seem incontrovertible. We know that French sailors and British marines were landed in the small hours of the morning; that they advanced unmolested to the exhibition hall called the Zappeion and to other points between the Acropolis and Phaleron; that at eleven o'clock there was a fusillade on Philopappos hill; and that fighting continued for much of the afternoon. We also know that the Admiral, cut off at the Zappeion, signalled to his fleet to shell the Stadium, which lies some 1,200 yards to the east of the Parthenon. And we find that the British and French lost 212 officers and men killed or wounded, and that the sole benefit to the Allies of this bloodshed and destruction was the surrender by Constantine of six mountain batteries.

It is not, then, difficult to construct a synopsis of the tragedy. But the questions remain. What was this handful of men strung out along the slopes of a hill and the gardens of a public park expected to accomplish deep in a capital city? Who began the shooting, the Greeks, all of whose units opened fire at the same hour as if to a concerted plan, or the French, alarmed by the black hatred of the Athenians facing them? Most accounts blame the Greeks; but what are we to make of the British major who writes that, before eleven o'clock, 'The French were firing blank to frighten the crowd back'? And what cruel fate determined that the heaviest casualties should have fallen on the British marines, the reluctant force drawn into a conflict which its government disliked but was too timid to forestall? There are answers to some of these questions, but not to all. If the movements of the protagonists are clear enough throughout the day, the encounters of man with more than man continue to elude us as in a Sophoclean myth and we begin to feel that these scenes are enacted on the wrong stage; for Thebes, the only appropriate setting for a drama of such irony, lies some fifty miles to the north.

When the British and French withdrew to their ships, this strange contest seemed ended; but there was no peace within Athens. That night and all the following day the Athenian Chorus, which had witnessed these events with traditional submissiveness, became actors in the play. The shops of leading liberals were looted, the offices of the Venizelist press were ransacked, the homes of known sympathizers with the Entente attacked. The purpose of those sinister red paint marks became all too clear. Opponents of the army leaders were murdered or cast into prison. And while murder and arson filled the streets, King Constantine himself issued an order of the day congratulating his troops on their forbearance, loyalty and spirit of self-sacrifice.

The allied squadron was still at its moorings in Phaleron Bay. One last problem remained for Admiral Dartige du Fournet: should he avenge the dead by swinging the guns of his fleet on

4*

to the rioting city? He hesitated; and the French Minister
begged him to spare Athens from a general bombardment.
In 1687 Venetian cannons had blown up the Parthenon. In
1916 Athens escaped the destructive power of a modern fleet.
It was as well; the good name of the Entente had sunk low, but
it was spared the shame of a crime for which there could be no
retribution.

Constantine remains, even today, an enigma. It would be false
to assume that he had deliberately enticed Dartige du Fournet
to send the marines and the sailors into Athens in order that
they should be ambushed in a treacherous attack. Naturally
this was the reaction of public opinion in both Britain and
France. Yet Constantine genuinely believed that his troops had
not fired first. He may even have thought that the Venizelists
would take advantage of the presence of an Allied force to
begin a revolution in the capital which would have depended
for its success on Dartige du Fournet just as Zymbrakakis' insurrection in Salonika had relied upon Sarrail. That, at any rate,
was the explanation which he hastened to send to King George V,
and there is no reason to suppose that it was an excuse intended
solely for foreign consumption.

But the shooting around the Zappeion had destroyed the last
vestiges of respect for Constantine in both London and Paris.
Now no one believed him, not even his royal cousin. King
George sent an icy reply to Constantine's message: 'I am unaware of the conspiracy to which you refer', he wrote with
studied coolness, 'but I know that no agents of the Allied Powers
were connected with anything of the kind. The Allied Powers
have, from the outset, confined their demands upon Greece to
the observance of a benevolent neutrality. Unfortunately this
condition has not been observed'. All of Constantine's excuses
were rejected out of hand; and the Greek Government was
forced to make reparation for the attack and give an assurance
that it would never be repeated.

The immediate consequences of the events of December 1st
are hardly surprising. Dartige du Fournet was relieved of his
command and disappears from the arena in which he had made
such a disastrous appearance. At the same time, the British and
French determined to give official backing to Venizelos. Their
Ministers withdrew from Athens, and on December 19th Venizelos' Triumvirate was recognized as a Provisional Government,

a British 'diplomatic agent' being accredited to it in Salonika early in the New Year. None the less, the Allies still sought to prevent the spread of civil war in Greece. They took pains to maintain a neutral barrier across northern Thessaly in order to make it impossible for the Venizelists and the Royalists to fight each other in the rear of the Macedonian Army. For the moment, Constantine remained on his throne; but in the eyes of the British and French public – and more especially in the columns of their newspapers – he was a figure hardly less despicable than his imperial brother-in-law in Berlin. Paradoxically Dartige du Fournet, with his aristocratic indulgence towards a crowned head, had dealt the concept of monarchy a more grievous blow than it suffered from any intrigue of the 'red republican' in Salonika. The gunshots around the Zappeion continued to echo across Europe for many years yet; perhaps they can still be heard faintly even now.

In reading the following chapter, the first end-paper map and the maps on pp. 198 and 207 will be found helpful.

7 / Spring Offensive

THE FINAL WEEKS of 1916, which in Greece witnessed the running down of the Monastir offensive and the tragic blunder at the Zappeion, were dominated in Britain and France by a crisis of leadership. On December 5th Asquith's resignation made way for Lloyd George and a policy of total commitment. A week later in Paris Briand survived as premier only by drastically reconstructing his whole government. The British public, reassured by the powerful Unionist element in Lloyd George's Coalition Cabinet, accepted the change as a political redeployment for victory. But the French, weary of twenty-eight months of 'blood and mud', wanted more than a general post among the Deputies. By the end of the year Joffre had retired with the dignity of Marshal of France, and command of the army on the Western Front was entrusted to the dashing cavalryman, Robert Nivelle. The war machine at Chantilly was dismantled: Nivelle, whose powers were strictly limited to metropolitan France, set up headquarters at Beauvais (moving later on to Compiègne); and the overall responsibility for the French military effort was thereafter exercised by the Ministry of War in the Rue St Dominique, Paris.

Sarrail, who had long chafed at the restrictions imposed by Chantilly, rejoiced at the eclipse of Joffre. Believing that he would now enjoy greater independence of command, he at once asked for permission to attack the Greek Army around Larissa. It was, he insisted, a menace to his left flank. He was, indeed, still genuinely alarmed by the possibility that this wing of his army might be trapped between Bulgars and Germans, in the north, and Greeks, in the south. He also thought that the 'Army of the Orient' was not powerful enough to occupy and control the whole of Greece as well as fighting the common enemy. Hence at the same time that he requested freedom to deal with the Greek Royalists, he renewed earlier pleas for reinforcements; and he warned Paris that he might otherwise be forced to order a withdrawal to a new defensive line, even if this entailed the abandonment of Monastir itself.

Briand could not ignore these demands. Quite apart from the news from Athens, he dared not risk offending Sarrail at this moment, for he had only recently been severely mauled by the radicals in a secret session of the Chamber. If his new Ministry were to survive, it must retain the support of those tiresome Deputies who still looked on Sarrail as a republican Maid of Orleans. Yet Briand could see, clearly enough, that all the experience of the previous weeks was against precipitate action in the Balkans. Characteristically, he sought to evade a decision. On December 26th he sent a strong French delegation to London, primarily to discuss American peace moves, but with instructions to sound out the new British Government on Sarrail's proposals and to urge the immediate despatch to Salonika of two more British divisions.

Lloyd George, too, was in an embarrassing position. Already distrusted by the General Staff and physically exhausted by the manœuvres of the camarilla which had brought him to power, he had no wish to pit himself at this stage against the soldiery; and Robertson was still as hostile as ever to any ventures in the Balkans. He could point out, with some justice, that only three weeks before, the 60th (London) Division had reached Salonika from the Somme; and that Sarrail had immediately despatched one of its brigade groups to watch the Greek royalists from the foothills of Olympus, where there were plenty of birds to shoot but no Bulgars within seventy miles. To the British War Office such a deployment seemed a reckless luxury.

All Lloyd George's political instincts favoured an accommodation with the General Staff, but there were difficulties: neither he nor they could forget that for more than two years he had preached the need to seek a decision elsewhere than the Western Front. So, like Briand, he played for time. The meeting with the French dragged on for three days; it satisfied nobody and solved nothing. But, shortly before the delegation returned to Paris, Lloyd George came out with a master stroke. A top level conference should be held with the Italians and with the commanders at Salonika in order to prepare for a combined inter-allied offensive in 1917 in Italy and/or the Balkans. So that Sarrail and Milne might attend, it was agreed that the conference should meet in Rome. Thither on the first day of 1917 departed Lloyd George and Robertson and Hankey, travelling from Paris on the same train as Briand and his new War Minister, General Lyautey.

As recognition of the need for a unified strategy, the Rome conference was a significant innovation and a portent: as a means of securing a unified strategy it was little more than a fiasco. The conference was not even a full gathering of the allies; despite Lloyd George's intention of raising Balkan issues, there was no spokesman for Roumania, nor for Serbia, nor for Venizelist Greece, and Imperial Russia herself was represented only by an ambassador and a military attaché. Convened too speedily for effective staff work and attended by delegates divided among themselves, the conference shelved all major decisions, contenting itself with patchwork solutions of the most pressing problems. While the political chiefs, especially Briand, struck fine attitudes over rhetorical platitudes, their military and civilian aides vied with each other in seeking out the Italian commanders so as to win them for their own point of view. Were they 'Easterners' or 'Westerners'? To officers whose battle front lay northward it seemed a curiously irrelevant question, probably unposed in Rome since the rivalry of Augustus and Antony. But, from the most patriotic motives, they had little doubt of the answer. Convinced that the military might of France and Britain could best be deployed well away from the Mediterranean – and more especially from Albania – the Italian General Staff were Westerners to a man. They would keep their division in Macedonia to watch Sarrail's activities on the Albanian frontier, but they knew that a decisive victory in the Balkans would raise the stock of the Venizelists and the Serbs: this was a development which no ambitious Italian could wish. When Lloyd George pressed the Italians, as the Allied Power nearest to Salonika, to send reinforcements to Sarrail, his appeal was met with obstinate silence.

Nothing was settled at Rome about the future line of battle against the Bulgars: the British and Italian military advisers thought Monastir should be evacuated and the front shortened; the French (and the Russian military attaché) maintained that the 'highest interests of the allied coalition' forbade any withdrawal and required the immediate despatch of one British and two Italian divisions. If Monastir were abandoned, argued the French, the Serbs might well seek terms from the Austrians and Bulgars, a contingency which, as Milne had already warned the British, was not improbable. In the event, the Monastir line was held; but the British, who were seriously alarmed by German submarine activity in the Mediterranean, sent as their reinforcement only three batteries of heavy artillery; and the Italians did not move a man. They did, however, reluctantly agree to assist in the construction of a road from the Monastir Front to Santi Quaranta, a tiny harbour on the Albanian coast which was held by the Italians and was no further across the Adriatic from Brindisi than Le Havre from Southampton.

The most valuable result of the conference was the contact established between the political leaders in the West and the field commanders, Milne and Sarrail. Nine weeks earlier, when the battle for Monastir was going badly, Milne had sent a closely reasoned assessment to the War Office suggesting that, while the Army of the Orient was only capable of waging limited offensives, these attacks 'might at any moment cause a breakup in the Bulgarian Army'. He maintained this moderate optimism throughout his days in Rome. His quiet confidence, which was in such striking contrast to the habitual attitude of the British senior officers towards the Balkans, was a valuable corrective and considerably enhanced his prestige. It is significant that, on his return to Macedonia, 'Army Headquarters in Salonika' was raised in status to 'General Headquarters of the Salonika Army', while Milne himself was officially described as 'commander-in-chief' rather than as 'General Officer Commanding', his title for the previous eight months.

Unexpectedly, the conference was an even greater personal triumph for Sarrail. 'I have presented myself in Rome to clear my name', he told a friend on his arrival. His reputation had preceded him: the Ladarmelle and Cordonnier affairs, the apparent slights to the Allied commanders, the mounting evidence of political ambition – there was little about his career to make him a sympathetic figure with the British and Italians, nor indeed with many of his compatriots. As Lloyd George wrote twenty years later, with ironic meiosis, 'I was not quite prepared for the attractive and magnetic personality to whom I was introduced at the Rome Conference'. And even Hankey, who was by nature so much less impressionable than his chief, described Sarrail in his diary as 'a man of quite exceptional charm'. Only that incorrigible Westerner, Robertson, was unconvinced. To him, Sarrail was 'a fine looking, handsome man of the swashbuckler type. . . . In my opinion he is a man who may one day pull off a good coup, but he is quite as likely, perhaps even more so, to do the reverse and to land us into difficulties'. It was a shrewd assessment; but not, at that moment, a popular one.

Sarrail and Lloyd George found that they understood each other. The General arrived at the British Embassy early on the third morning of the conference and frankly admitted that 'all he asked was for the British and French Governments to shut their eyes or turn their heads for a fortnight' while he dealt with the Greek royalists. If the Greeks conducted a guerrilla war against him, he would shoot all whom he captured. It was an uncompromising start to a conversation. But when Lloyd George, asserting that he had always befriended the Salonika expedition, suggested that drastic action of this type would harm the Allied cause in the eyes of the neutrals (and especially in the U.S.A.), Sarrail calmed down and came round to the British point of view. A bargain was struck, sealed by a dramatic handshake: the Greek royalists would be summoned to withdraw their forces to the Peloponnese; Sarrail would not move southwards without British permission; and Lloyd George, for his part, would see that Sarrail received 'fair play'. It was, perhaps, a curious interview for a British prime minister and a French subordinate general; but it had the effect of making Sarrail appear a far more reliable person, convinced of the importance of his mission and yet amenable to rational argument. 'It is on record', wrote Lloyd George' that the favourable impression he made upon me was shared by all those who took part in the Rome Conference'. It was agreed that Sarrail should henceforth serve as 'Commander-in-Chief of the Allied Army of the Orient', with all the national commanders accepting his orders for military operations but retaining a right of reference to their own government.

Sarrail had won a vote of confidence. Little enough had been said of the threat from the Bulgars; and yet there seemed some hope of a successful offensive in the Balkans under his direction. But it had to come soon if Sarrail were to retain Lloyd George's sympathy, for already his imagination was stirred by thoughts of an advance into Palestine; and, on the Western Front, General Nivelle was most persuasive.

As if to demonstrate their determination to persevere in the Balkans, the French (who had already sent two colonial divisions to Salonika in December) despatched another two divisions to Sarrail within a fortnight of the Rome Conference. But, for the moment, there was little enough that he or any other general

Albania: part of Essad Bey's private army

Annamites in Salonika: French colonial infantry from Indo-China

Russian troops disembarking, Salonika, 1916

Russian troops moving up to the front

The Voivode Mišić and General Sir George Milne

Serbian infantry, adequately
re-equipped

The liberation of Monastir:
Russian troops entering the
town

could do. Day after day through January and into February
grey clouds swept over the grey rocks of the mountains. In the
east, the British units waded through flooded trenches short of
food and supplies, for the heavy rain had swept away the Seres
Road in several places and lorries could only cover two-thirds
of the distance from Salonika, coming to a halt on the Beshik
Dagh ridge, the edge of the Struma Valley itself. For the last
fourteen miles everything had to be conveyed by mules, slithering
down what had been a serpentine road from one mud hole to
another until they reached the comfortless and inundated plain.
Yet despite the snow and the rain and the mud, patrols made
raids against both the Bulgarian and the Turkish positions;
there was never a complete lull in the fighting.

Conditions were no better elsewhere along the front. Water
coursed down the steep inclines of the hills around Doiran; and,
to the west, blizzards continued to claw into the veterans in
Monastir and the broad loop of the Crna River. There was,
however, bitter fighting here in the second half of February
when German battalions launched a surprise attack on the
Italian division which, after falling back from 'Hill 1050', recovered most of their trenches at heavy cost. Further west still,
the Austrians (whose intelligence services had acquired details
of the Rome Conference) advanced against the thinly held Italian
positions on the Albanian frontier in order to prevent the opening
of the projected route to Santi Quaranta. Sarrail responded
promptly. The Austrians were ejected by a French force which
established contact with the Italians around Valona, two hundred miles from Salonika overlooking the Adriatic. The Italians
were particularly sensitive about this area and regarded the
alacrity with which Sarrail had intervened as highly suspicious.

All these operations were, however, secondary in importance
to the plan which Sarrail and his staff began to evolve after the
conference. For a few weeks the Salonika staff officers believed
that they had captured the interest of Paris and London. Much
more than Sarrail's military reputation was at stake; now was
the chance to nail the 'gardeners' jibe for all time. The staff
worked as a team. They seemed, in those rain-swept February
days, to have confidence in their commander.

Sarrail knew, by the second week of February, what he wished
to do. The Army of the Orient would attack at five different
points along its front: the main assault by the Serbs in the Moglena Mountains to the east of the Crna loop would aim at taking

the Bulgarian defences along the Vardar in the rear; to the
west, French units would advance between Lakes Prespa and
Ochrid, also moving eastwards so as to link up with a Franco-
Italian group advancing along the upper Crna between Monastir
and Prilep. At the same time the British 28th Division would
lead a fourth attack against the Belasica Mountains across the
valley between Doiran and the Rupel Pass; and beyond the
Struma the British 10th and 27th Divisions would occupy the town
of Seres. If all went well, the French, Serbian and Italian
contingents would advance on Sofia through Kumanovo or
Stip; and the British would wheel northwards and seize the
Rupel Pass, from which there was a direct route up the Struma
to Sofia, one hundred and twenty miles away. Although he did
not think it would be possible to begin the full offensive before
the middle of April, Sarrail saw no reason why he should not
start probing the Prespa area early in March. Much depended
on the weather.

On paper, it was a good plan, far more ambitious than in the
previous summer and covering a greater area. But was it realis-
tic? At the end of October Milne had written to Robertson
declaring that, with 20 divisions, it would be possible to make a
general attack with limited objectives, but a major offensive
along the whole Front would require 29 divisions. In February
Sarrail had nothing like this number in his army. Including the
Venizelist contingent, he had the equivalent of 21 divisions;
and intelligence reports suggested that he was opposed by a
slightly larger enemy force of 240 battalions, 198 of whom were
Bulgarian and 18 Turkish. Although the enemy was strongly
entrenched and favoured by the terrain – which, on every
sector except the Struma Valley, necessitated a slow advance
up rising ground – there was a good prospect that if the line
were once broken it would be difficult for him to move troops
rapidly along the mountain chain in order to plug the gap.
Sarrail had learnt much from the autumn campaign. By mounting an offensive in the spring, he would have time to halt, if
necessary, and regroup for a further thrust towards Sofia before
the onrush of winter. He now had a field commander of the
French force whom he liked and trusted, General Grossetti;
he found it possible to work with him as he had never done
with Lardamelle or Cordonnier. Reserves of ammunition had
accumulated over the winter period and, in the French sector,
there had been some remarkable engineering achievements,

including the construction in three weeks of a fine road to supply the forces in the Crna loop and, in the same wild and in-hospitable country, improvements to the over-strained railway line.

Of course, Sarrail had his worries: he was still awaiting aircraft, which he had been promised, but for which there appeared to be no transports; he needed more heavy artillery for the initial assault; and he had an exaggerated fear of the Greek royalists down in Athens. Inevitably, there were risks in the plan, the most serious of which was the numerical inferiority of the force at his disposal. But, given good weather and close cohesion between the commanders of the six national contin-gents involved, there was no reason why Sarrail should not gain an even greater victory than at Monastir.

General Lyautey, at the Ministry of War, gave his blessing to the project on February 21st. In the intervening fortnight, there had however been a modification of momentous impor-tance. The British had been cast in a far more important rôle. Milne had no wish for his main forces to be engaged around Seres: road communications with Salonika remained grim; the town itself, like Monastir, was backed by steep hills from which it would be difficult to dislodge the enemy; and, above all, the whole Struma area became a malarial swamp in summer and it was therefore courting disaster to make it the centre of a campaign which might be protracted for several months. Ac-cordingly, on Milne's suggestion, the principal British attack was to be made, not on the Struma (where there would be only a feint) but on the key position in the whole Bulgarian defence line, the hills between the Vardar and Lake Doiran. Although this region was heavily fortified, it was easier to approach from Salonika and gave the best access to southern Serbia and southern Bulgaria.

Milne thus committed the British to as vital a part in the projected offensive as the Serbs had played in the previous autumn. His men had already suffered heavy casualties in seizing 'Horsehoe Hill', south of the lake, in August 1916; but he instinctively sensed that Doiran had more than a military value to the enemy. For this oval lake, five miles long and four miles wide, which had been divided between the Greeks and the Serbs after the Balkan Wars, was to the Bulgars an almost mystic symbol of their will to dominate Macedonia; it was a Balkan Ypres or Verdun in reverse. A British victory at Doiran,

if it could be attained, might decide the whole campaign; but
it was a stern test of command and endurance.

There followed, at the end of February, a curious incident.
With the gift of hindsight we can say that it boded ill for the
whole operation; but, at the time, it was seen in Salonika as a
rueful illustration of the extent to which both the British and
French high commands were obsessed by the needs of the
Western Front.

On February 26th a stormy conference between the British
and French political and military leaders opened at Calais.
After many hours of wrangling over a French demand for the
B.E.F. to be put under Nivelle's command, the delegates (shortly
before lunch on the second day) turned to the Salonika question;
but, as a British liaison officer wrote, 'that vexatious problem
was not allowed to keep them long from the hors-d'œuvres'.
The conference formally declared 'that, for the present, the
decisive defeat of the Bulgarian Army is not a practical objective, and that the mission of the Allied forces at Salonika is to
keep in the front the enemy forces now there, and to take advantage of striking at the enemy if opportunity offers'.

The French did not notify Sarrail of this pontifical ambiguity,
probably because they had no idea what it meant. But Robertson telegraphed the decision of the conference to Milne: he
made no reference to Sarrail's plan of operations but concluded
with the cryptic instruction, 'It is for you and Sarrail to act in
accordance with the policy given'. As soon as Milne received
Robertson's message – by then it was March 4th and only
seven days before Sarrail intended to send his 76th Division
forward around Lake Prespa – he waited on Sarrail to ask if
the offensive had been countermanded. Sarrail, puzzled, telegraphed back to Paris and, after a further five day delay, received the details of the Calais decision with the additional
information, 'Your plan of operations, presented to the British
War Council, was approved. In consequence, you retain full
liberty to initiate operations when you consider the moment
favourable'. Such casual treatment showed clearly enough that
Nivelle was now the man of the hour. Sarrail's triumph at
Rome had been short-lived: out of sight, out of mind. It was
hardly encouraging.

Thereafter the preparations for the offensive were plagued by
misadventure. The early movement around Lake Prespa was

checked by a sudden blizzard, which swept down unusually
late in the year; no attacks could prise the Bulgars and the
Germans out of the hills above Monastir; a rising of 8,000
Serb irregulars in the heart of old Serbia south of Niš, broke
out too soon to assist Sarrail and was ruthlessly suppressed;
and on the Doiran Front in the third week of March the Bulgars
laid down a heavy barrage of gas shells which, as they had never
been used before in the Balkans, took the British by surprise.
Even more disturbing were the activities of a German bomber
squadron which made three highly successful raids on the
Salonika base itself, the most serious of them on February 27th.

Perhaps Sarrail ought, at this stage, to have called off the
offensive, especially as Paris was urging him – although it was
hardly necessary to do so – to take action against King Constantine. But there were sound political reasons for prodding the
enemy in as many places as possible in the spring of 1917; and
Sarrail was not one to stand inactive while his fellow generals
were on the move.

Milne, for his part, continued with his preparations. Respi-
rators were rushed up to the front from G.H.Q. in a matter of
hours. The Naval Air Service lent a fighter squadron and a
bomber squadron to join the R.F.C. in meeting the German
menace from the skies. Gas shells were requested from England
and in due course arrived, too late for the offensive and too few
to be effective, less than a third of the rounds he had demanded
and the majority of them defective, anyhow. The brigade group
which had been happily shooting woodcock on Olympus began
a seventy mile march up the Vardar; and all along the British
sector raids were made to probe the enemy defences. By April 8th,
a week before the date fixed by the French War Ministry for the
start of the offensive, the British XIIth Corps was ready in front
of Doiran; but up in the Moglena Mountains, the snow was
still swirling down and Sarrail postponed his general attack
until April 26th, with Milne committed to send the British
forward two days earlier.

At this moment, as the XIIth Corps waited, the allied leaders
were in conference yet again. There had been a further change
of government in France: bad relations between Lyautey and
the Chamber of Deputies led, at the end of March, to the final
resignation of Briand; and Lloyd George was anxious to confer
with the new premier, Ribot, and Lyautey's successor, the
Republican Socialist deputy Paul Painlevé. The British, French

and Italian leaders met in a train at St Jean-de-Maurienne, beneath Mt Cenis.

There was, in fact, at this meeting far more to worry about than the intentions of the latest French Government. Since the Rome Conference, and even since the stormy session at Calais, the rhythm of the war had quickened everywhere except Macedonia. That April the eyes of the western world focused on Arras and on Gaza where fierce battles were already waging; or peered anxiously out over the grey waters of the Atlantic for the hidden menace of the U-boat. In Petrograd a dynasty had fallen; and in Washington the greatest of all republics had entered the war against Germany. Who, at such a time, could care about the Balkans? Certainly not Lloyd George.

The British prime minister, never the most consistent of men, had become disenchanted with the Balkan imbroglio. Now Lloyd George and Robertson, divided though they were on so many issues, stood together against the Salonika expedition. 'It had no military justification', declared Robertson uncompromisingly in a cabinet paper, and 'had been a failure from the first'; the British contingent should be withdrawn, preferably to the Western Front but otherwise to Palestine where Robertson insisted that it was 'likely to contribute far more to winning the war' than in Macedonia. Lloyd George's views were not dissimilar. At St Jean-de-Maurienne he was obsessed by the thought of taking Jerusalem and Damascus as though he were some latter-day crusader; he could see Milne's men only as a means of keeping Turkish reinforcements from being sent to Palestine. Why were Turkish troops allowed to slip away from the Struma lines? Why had Sarrail postponed his attack even though Milne was ready? This, Lloyd George insisted, must be the Army of the Orient's last chance. Unless a substantial victory were won now in Macedonia, the British would have to pull some of their divisions out of the Balkans. Perhaps it was as well that the men of the XIIth Corps, calmly digging support trenches in full view of the enemy, knew nothing of the conference's deliberations.

Lieutenant-General Sir Henry Maitland Wilson, who commanded the XIIth Corps, had his headquarters at Yanesh, a village with that rare luxury in Macedonia, an hotel with a bathroom – and, indeed, two baths. Yanesh (which is now called Metallikon and was then more frequently known as 'Janes') is thirty-five miles north of Salonika, a little way back

from the Seres Railway, where it begins to climb up from the
marshy Gallikos Valley. It was a pleasant enough place, with
a mineral spring, a fountain beneath cypress trees and a little
church. The village itself was a cluster of sepia walls and sagging
roofs which glowed purple as the fading evening light mellowed
the dusty plain to the west and the scent of charcoal braziers
drifted across the tiny stream: long after the fighting, men
remembered those sunsets at Yanesh. But, for the moment, the
attraction of Yanesh was its position on the map. It was no more
than two and a half hours from Salonika along a road newly
gashed into the hillside and yet it was within twelve miles of the
Doiran trenches: in the sharp air, the crest of the Bulgarian
position on a ridge above the lake could be clearly seen on the
horizon. Yanesh was, in many ways, a natural site for a headquarters; and for almost two years General Wilson and his staff
anxiously waited there beside the field telephones or stood
listening on the ochre plateia, seeking to anticipate each change
of fortune from the muffled noise of battle echoing in the folds
of the mountains.

On the morning of April 24th, with only twelve hours to go
before the attack, disturbing news reached Yanesh. A prisoner
had been brought in by a wire-cutting patrol in the small hours
and had volunteered the information that the Bulgars had received reinforcements and, what was more serious, that his regiment had been told to stand on the alert that evening at eight
as a British attack was expected after dusk. General Wilson
hurried off to consult Milne, who had driven up to Yanesh to
await the battle: should the plan be changed? Milne thought
not: there had never been much chance of surprise; but it was,
none the less, disturbing to find that the enemy was expecting
an attack at night rather than at dawn. Had Milne also learnt
that, in the ten miles separating Doiran from the Vardar, the
Bulgars and Germans had concentrated 33 searchlights, he
might have been even more concerned; for it was essential that
the first assault in the exposed stretch of no man's land before
Doiran town should be launched while the British parapets
were, to the defenders, no more than an irregular smudge against
the shadows of the hills.

The Corps Operation Order was a simple one, deceptively so.
The 26th Division was to attack over a front a mile and a half
wide, westward from the shore of the lake, and the 22nd Division
was to support its left flank for another 2,000 yards; the 60th

Division was to relieve pressure on the main attackers by raiding Bulgarian positions in the Machukovo Salient, some two miles east of the Vardar. During the evening of April 24th the Hampshires, Devons and Wiltshires of the 79th Brigade (26th Division) assembled in the gullies to the south of the lake. Before then was the hillock known as the Petit Couronné which, with its western offshoots, was the first line of the Bulgarian defences and therefore formed the immediate objective. Half a mile back lay another ridge, no less heavily fortified; and behind and above this second line, some two miles from the British positions, was the greatest obstacle of all – the bare-topped hump which the French, nearly eighteen months before, had named the Grand Couronné, after a similar natural fortress in Lorraine. Even this was not the end of the defensive position, for the Grand Couronné was itself overlooked by 'Pip Ridge', long and steep and tapering to a razor's edge crest.

Yet it was the Grand Couronné which dominated the whole area. With its summit at less than 2,000 feet, it was not strictly speaking a mountain – the Kajmakcalan was four times its height – but it loomed over the British force as Achi Baba had done at the Dardanelles and as Monte Cassino was to do in Italy in 1944, mercilessly omnipresent, a warder prying into the cells of an imprisoned army, seeing all, hearing all, noting all. For from the Grand Couronné an observation post, sunk deep into the rock and protected by twelve feet of solid concrete, enabled the Bulgars to survey the trenches, peer down the road to the railhead and Yanesh, and sometimes even catch a glimpse of the sun-gripped scimitar of the Gulf itself, with the transports riding at their moorings. It was an intelligence computer of which the Bulgars were justly proud: 'The arrival and departure of trains, the number of waggons reaching Kilindir Station, were listed on special comparative tables which gave a precise idea of movements in the rear of the enemy', wrote a Bulgarian officer, 'We could deduce where we must expect an attack and what, roughly, would be the timing of the operation'. The British soldiers, who could pick out the narrow slit of the observation post as a black dot on the bare hilltop and through binoculars see the steel grille which protected its occupants, called it 'The Devil's Eye'; and watched hopefully as the gunners planted shell after shell on the rocky summit. But, if the face was bruised, the Eye remained; and so long as it was there, it seemed prudent for the two British divisions to attack at night.

For the front ever to move beyond Doiran, the Devil had to lose his Eye; which meant, in more prosaic terms, that sooner or later the Grand Couronné must be scaled.

But first it was necessary to take the little Demon at the Devil's foot, and that was task enough. As the Wiltshires and the Devons crouched in their trenches, Bulgarian howitzers and a battery of German naval guns pounded the boulders around them. There was a lull in the barrage in the early evening, and from the lakeside a waiting officer heard a familiar sound – the croak of hundreds of frogs, adding a touch of Aristophanic mockery to the irony of war. It was no more than a brief respite. Soon the shells were lobbing down once more; and the gullies became caverns of dead and wounded even before the hour of advance.

At 9.45, with the relentless barrage unabated, they pressed forward, down to the bottom of the smoke-filled Jumeaux Ravine and across a swift-flowing stream. And when they emerged from the hell of the ravine, two powerful searchlights threw their beams across the open ground, exposing the attackers to a withering cross-fire: few reached the Bulgarian trenches. The tragic pattern was to be repeated in other ravines and ridges throughout the night. Within half an hour the Berkshires and the Worcesters of the 78th Brigade, who were coming on the Jumeaux Ravine from the south-west, had been swept by a similar hurricane of gun fire; and, although some battalions captured the enemy outposts and two of the Devon companies reached the inner line of trenches on the Petit Couronné, there was confusion in the centre. The Bulgars counter-attacked, and about four in the morning, when it was clear that there was no reasonable chance of making headway, the 26th Division was ordered back to its lines, exhausted and sadly depleted.

Meanwhile, on the left of the front, the 22nd Division had had more success and fewer casualties, mainly because the Bulgarian artillery could not rake the gullies in this sector and it was therefore possible to find covered approaches to their outposts. The 22nd Division reached their first objective and held it against five counter-attacks, but the costly failure on their right prohibited any further advance up the hills behind Doiran as they would then have come under strong enfilade fire from the unassailed Bulgarian positions. Still further westward the 60th Division raid at Machukovo had started well; but, with searchlights once again silhouetting the attackers against the night sky, it was not possible for them to get beyond the first line of Bulgarian trenches.

By the morning of April 26th, it had become clear down at Yanesh that, apart from the tenuous foothold gained by the 22nd Division, the attack had failed. And, with mixed feelings, Milne heard at the same time that bad weather to the west of the Vardar had led Sarrail to postpone the general offensive, which should have begun that day. Hence, while the postponement gave the British another opportunity of seizing the Bulgarian lines, it also meant that the disastrous meleé two nights before had been unncessary. Supposing it had succeeded, would the British have been left to take on all the enemy forces because snow was falling in the Moglena Mountains? It was a disturbing thought that the British might have moved forward in isolation. Some of the old distrust between the allied commanders began to show itself again. And, back in Whitehall, the General Staff seemed confirmed in its worst suspicions: the French were notified that early in June the 60th Division and two cavalry brigades would be withdrawn from the British Salonika Army for service in Palestine. The St Jean-de-Maurienne pronouncement was to be implemented.

Yet Milne personally was as convinced as ever that resolute action might well destroy the Bulgarian Army. On May 2nd he sent a letter to the commander of the XVIth Corps which shows both his hopes and his sense of frustration: 'Had a synchronized attack by the Allies taken place', he wrote, 'and been pressed home with vigour, it was possible that the Bulgarian forces would have been driven back all along the line from the Doiran Lake to Monastir'. Now Sarrail had informed him that he had no intention of continuing the offensive (when it came) into the hot weather and his primary objective 'was to clear the enemy from the immediate vicinity of Monastir'. The February plan, with its fine talk of a joint advance on Sofia, had become an historical curiosity before the spring offensive had even begun. It is hard to escape the conclusion that in May 1917 the one commander with faith in ultimate victory in Macedonia was General Milne – and by now he knew that there was no one at home to back him up. He was in an unenviable position.

But Milne's immediate concern was to ensure that when Sarrail ordered the resumption of operations, the XIIth Corps would be able to redeem the reputation of the British infantry after the failures of April 24th. Again he consulted Wilson:

should the new attack be made at dawn? It was a difficult decision; but, fearing counter-attacks in full daylight before the advancing troops had established themselves, the two Generals were against it. Some changes were, however, essential in the Operation Order: the artillery preparation was to be of shorter duration but greater concentration, with particular attention given to the enemy gun positions; and the troops were to avoid, as far as possible, the death trap of Jumeaux Ravine by attacking in the first instance nearest to the lake, where there was a shorter gully, Patty Ravine, which turned inwards towards the British lines and thus afforded some measure of protection. But otherwise the pattern of the attack was ominously familiar; a main assult on the Petit Couronné at 10 p.m. by the 26th Division, with diversionary actions further west.

At dusk on May 8th the British artillery thundered out once again over Doiran Town. The Bulgarian batteries replied, and all the southern end of the lake was lit by a cascade of fire and flame so that it seemed as if lightning were striking each knoll again and again in some freak storm. For several days there had been intermittent rain, but the night was finer and milder, and from the lake a mist drifted in which, mingling with the smoke of explosives, lay over the gullies like a reeking cloud. As if to emphasize the weirdness of the scene on the narrow front, a good moon shone down on all the surrounding area, picking out the tumbledown houses of the town and the contours of Pip Ridge and the Grand Couronné brooding over the lake. At ten minutes to ten, two companies of the Scottish Rifles moved forwards on the right flank across the Patty Ravine, but soon they were enveloped by the fog and for four hours even the battalion commander had no news of them. As other companies crept towards the Bulgarian trenches, seeking for a gap where the wire had been cut, from each of the brigade headquarters senior officers peered out, trying to discover what was happening in the smoke. Optimistic at first – for in the glare of the searchlights figures were momentarily seen scrambling into the enemy trenches – the 78th Brigade sent forward supporting companies, three of which actually crossed Jumeaux Ravine with few casualties and reached the lower slopes of Petit Couronné three-quarters of an hour before they were due to scale the hill. For twenty minutes they remained immobile under heavy trench mortar fire. Their position was desperate: 'Am going through in ten minutes', signalled their commander. But it was too soon:

the men came under fire from the British artillery as well as the Bulgarians; and few of the officers remained unwounded. Throughout the night, with magnificent courage, they clung on to a sector of the Bulgarian trenches, some fifty yards up the hill.

Meanwhile the brigade commanders had discovered that things were going wrong elsewhere along the line. They now knew that, from the start, there had been confusion in the swirling smoke of no man's land and they could see that disorder had spread to the support positions. The communication trenches, which were painfully few and under intensive bombardment, were choked with units seeking to move in opposite directions. It became almost impossible to obtain accurate news of the battle, for telephone wires had been destroyed and, in the murk of action, visual signalling was out of the question.

The corps commander was baffled. What on earth was happening down by the lakeside? Anxiously he sought to fit the contradictory reports which came to him into a coherent whole. The information was fragmentary; but he feared the worst. As the first faint streaks of dawn were reflected in the lake, the right flank was ordered to withdraw. As it happened, at that very moment, a detachment of the Gloucesters was in possession of a middle sector of the Bulgarian trench system above the Patty Ravine and some 1,000 yards from the lake. Now, with murderous fire coming at them from the Bulgarian positions on their left and their right, they pulled wearily back across the deep scar of no man's land.

The diversionary attacks to the west had once more been successful and half a dozen hillocks had been seized by the 22nd Division and the 60th Division. Even in the blood-soaked mile between Petit Couronné and the lake, more yards had been gained than a fortnight before, and some of the trenches were still in British hands after the sun came up. Hence when, that morning, Milne's chief of staff reported the battle situation to Sarrail he still held out some hope. Throughout the morning the British kept their grip on the lowest works of the Petit Couronné, but continuous cross-fire made it impossible to seize the crest, although several platoons of infantry reached the summit. There was no chance of retaining the trenches so long as the Bulgarians were above and around them; and by noon it had become clear that the British could not dislodge the enemy under present circumstances. Slowly, through the afternoon, the British forward troops were brought back, in parties of twelve.

And, twenty-four hours after the action began, all the survivors of the main attack were once more in the British lines.

The 26th Division alone had lost in this one action 1,700 dead, wounded or missing: this was as high a casualty rate as a fortnight before. The total number killed or incapacitated in both these operations was more than 5,000. These two, largely abortive, night attacks of April 24th and May 8th (and the subsequent counter-attacks) accounted for almost a quarter of the battle casualties for the British Salonika Army in the whole three years of the Macedonian campaign. Not a single Allied soldier had come within two miles of the Grand Couronné, the central keep of the Devil's citadel; from its ramparts the Eye would stand sentinel for another sixteen months, watching and counting and waiting.

Meanwhile, sixty miles west of Doiran, the weather had improved sufficiently for Grossetti to launch Sarrail's long-heralded Spring Offensive. At dawn on Wednesday, May 9th, just eight and a half hours after the resumed British attack, the French 16th Colonial Division moved forward in the centre of the Crna loop supported by the Russian Second Brigade on the right and the Italian 35th Division to the left. At the same time, further east, in the Moglena Mountains the Serbian Second Army, under General Stepanović, assaulted hill positions south of the Dobropolje, a limestone wall little more than half as high as the Kajmakcalan but far steeper. Around Monastir each side threw hundreds of rounds of high explosive across the valleys, but, apart from patrol activity, the infantry remained in their trenches; and all remained quiet in the outposts between Lake Prespa and Lake Ochrid. Right across the front on the banks of the Struma, the British XVIth Corps was moving its field artillery into position intending to delay action until the end of the week, when it was hoped that the Bulgars would be heavily engaged elsewhere and consequently thrown into confusion by a diversionary attack on yet another sector. The whole project was far less ambitious than Sarrail had originally planned; but, at all events, in one point after another the Army of the Orient was moving into action.

In the Crna loop all went well for the first hour. Unexpectedly it was the Russians who stole the show. The Second Brigade began brilliantly. Advancing behind a hail of hand grenades, they swept over the first trenches and one battalion even occupied the village of Orle, on a mountain spur more than a mile behind the enemy line. But the momentum of their assault had carried them too far and no one followed them up. By noon these fine troops, trapped on an isolated hillock, were faced by the alternative of death or imprisonment. They held on grimly until nightfall, when a few even crept back to the Allied lines, but in the course of the day German cross-fire accounted for half of the men who had seized the trenches that morning and most of the others were captured. In its combination of valour and ineptitude this little known incident on a forgotten front was almost an epitome of the tragedy of the old Russian Army.

The French were more circumspect. The 16th Colonials advanced cautiously and ran into stiffer resistance; but they captured the first of the three positions assigned to them. The 17th Colonials, who were on the Russian Brigade's right, could make little progress: they met what was virtually a wall of shell fire, for a failure in communications had led their own gunners to lay a barrage over the same area as the enemy was bombarding. The Italians had gone into the attack less sanguine than their neighbours; for Sarrail had vetoed the proposals of their own commander and, after a casual one hour inspection of the terrain, had ordered them to conform to the general plan laid down by his staff. Yet even if they had little faith in their task, the leading Italian battalion carried the hill facing them and killed many of its defenders in the trenches; but as they reached the crest and were outlined against the sky, machine guns began to pick them off like clay pigeons in a fair; and the reserve battalions remained in the first line of defences.

After three hours of heavy fighting that Wednesday morning, the position was not unlike that in front of Doiran at the same time. There remained a possibility that the enemy would be dislodged and at 9.30 both the French and the Italians launched further assaults. But this time no progress at all was made. The Monastir-Moglena sector of the enemy line was under the control of the German Eleventh Army and, although it contained six times as many Bulgarian battalions as German, it was the Germans who formed the Headquarters' staff and, as the Allied attack mounted, German regiments, which had been held in reserve, were hurriedly moved forward to meet the challenge. As in the Monastir battle, the Germans put a backbone of steel into the wavering Bulgars.

On the Thursday morning there was a disastrous breakdown

in the Allied system of command. Sarrail had ordered a resumption of the attack at eight in the morning. And, at that hour, an Italian regiment and three companies of French infantry valiantly rushed forward and seized the German trenches. But nobody supported them. At 7.30 the attack had been cancelled, because not all the French units were in position. French headquarters had failed to inform the Italians and were apparently unable to reach one of their own colonial battalions as the enemy bombardment had shot away the telephone wires. It was a ghastly shambles; and an error for which the Italians, already fretting at Sarrail's exercise of authority, never forgave the French command.

Next day the postponed attack duly took place but, with the Germans forewarned, it met with no success. The weather worsened at the weekend, with heavy rain followed by a clammy mist. A mood of bitterness and even despair settled on the Allied troops. On the following Thursday (May 17th) one final attempt was made and, at the same time, the infantry advanced north of Monastir; but in both sectors there was bitterly cruel fighting with grenade and bayonet. Over 1,100 men were lost and hardly a yard was gained. It was stalemate.

The situation was little better up on the Moglena. There, too, on May 9th all had at first gone well but by noon the attackers had been halted. Throughout Wednesday night and Thursday the Serbs held on desperately to the hill they had taken, although the initiative had passed to the Germans and Bulgars who remained entrenched above them. The whole action became a formless artillery duel – in which the Serbs were supported by five French batteries and, more curiously, by two old 4·7 naval guns, manned by the British and brought up by rail a fortnight before, still labelled with an earlier destination, 'Ladysmith'. The infantry tried again on the Friday: Stepanović sent the Sumadija Division up the steep approaches to the Dobropolje. The Serbs, too, broke off the action on the Sunday when fog swirled over the valley, but on the Monday evening (May 14th) they took two spurs within a mile of the summit. It was the limit of their achievement. Thereafter they awaited orders to advance which never came.

The only real success to Allied arms that May came on the banks of the Struma, the sector of the front to which least attention had been given in the previous weeks. These operations of the British XVIth Corps, which was commanded by Lieutenant-

General C. J. Briggs, were primarily intended as a subsidiary feint. If the Bulgarian line broke at any point, then General Briggs was to press forward and occupy the Rupel Pass; but otherwise his task was to engage the Bulgarian Second Army so as to prevent it sending reinforcements westwards while, at the same time, avoiding severe losses to his own men or material. After four days of artillery bombardment the 10th (Irish) Division – the first arrivals in Salonika, more than eighteen months previously – was to advance some three and a half miles on a nine mile front while the 85th Brigade of the 28th Division was to seize two vital Bulgarian outposts on the left bank of the Struma at a point where it turns north-eastwards towards Rupel. This was very different country from Doiran or the Moglena; here the mountains lay several miles back and all the action took place in the open, sometimes on marshy ground but often in fields in which the only cover came from high crops of corn or maize. Almost it might have been Flanders or the Somme, although neither side had the strong defensive works of the Western Front and the countryside had not, as yet, been so deeply seared by battle. Moreover each knew that a determined advance in either direction would lead, inevitably, to the Balkan escarpments. Both the British and the Bulgars suffered considerably in these unhealthy fields and there were frequently sharp encounters between their patrols; yet there are moments when one feels that this was a different war from the one waged on all the other sectors, a contest in which each side boxes shadows; and then unexpectedly finds that the shadow has a mailed fist. It was a strange war, unpredictable and in retrospect almost unreal (although never to the unfortunate sufferer in the trenches).

And so it was on May 15th and May 16th. The Irish captured their villages without meeting any determined resistance. The Bulgars, ludicrously camouflaged beneath sheaves of corn, made ineffectual counter-attacks. The Royal Fusiliers and the Buffs in the 85th Brigade had a tougher task but, under a continuous barrage, they reached the two Bulgarian outposts whose defenders, feeling perhaps that it was futile to offer defiance, resigned themselves to captivity. The XVIth Corps had done all that it was asked to do; and had gained control of a larger area of territory than all the other units. If he were to authorize the continuance of this operation, Milne had to have good news from the Crna or the Moglena.

But by this time it seemed most improbable that any progress at all would be made up in the mountains. There remained, however, one considerable contingent which had not moved at all. This was the Serbian First Army, which comprised three infantry divisions, a cavalry division and the Fourth Russian Brigade. After a week of action on both its flanks in the Moglena, the First Army was still in its trenches between the Crna loop and the Dobropolje.

At first General Bojović, the Serbian Chief of Staff, had informed Sarrail that he was keeping the First Army in reserve in order to exploit any breach in the enemy line. This attitude, although unfashionably optimistic, made sure sense: for the Serbs in the First Army had shown themselves to be magnificent fighters, hardy veterans accustomed to long marches in difficult country, and they were still commanded by General Mišić, who had led them in the assault on the Kajmakcalan eight months previously. But as the enemy line failed to break, Sarrail's demands became more and more insistent. On May 14th, to a brief query asking why the First Army was not assisting the Second Army, he was told that it would attack on the following day. And on May 17th, when there had still been no movement, Sarrail telegraphed to his liaison officer, General Douchy, 'It is absolutely necessary that the Serbs press forward. . . . It is urgent. Drive home the point. I count on you'. Still Mišić would not move: he had not the force to scale the mountain facing him; he would not go forward until the Dobropolje was in the hands of the Serbian Second Army. Yet the Second Army, too, had come to a halt, although not from their own choice: 'The Serbian soldiers and officers are impatient to attack and only await the order', telegraphed Douchy to Sarrail on May 22nd, from Second Army headquarters. It was too late. On the previous day, Bojović, convinced that Sarrail's policy would only expose the Serbs to useless losses without any compensatory gains, formally requested him to call off the whole offensive. That evening Sarrail notified Grossetti and Milne that the operations should cease. The Spring Offensive had lasted twelve days.

The Army of the Orient had captured a few outposts at Doiran, on the Struma and at the foot of the Dobropolje. And for these pitiable acquisitions, 14,000 Allied soldiers – more men than Montgomery was to lose in the twelve victorious days of Alamein – had died, or been incapacitated, or taken prisoner. In any other war Sarrail's offensive would have been written off as a major failure and its author discredited for all time. But by the grim standards of 1917 these casualties were not exceptional. In that same month on the Western Front eleven times as many died in front of Arras alone, with no gain of any strategic significance; and the French losses on the Aisne were even greater. Sarrail's ill-conceived operation looked no more than a minor setback beside the magnitude of this defeat in France. Nivelle, who for a time had convinced the political leaders of both Britain and France that victory awaited him on the Aisne, had failed disastrously. He was despatched to North Africa and Pétain, the saviour of Verdun, took over his head-quarters at Compiègne. The consequences of defeat to any commander on the Western Front seemed automatic. But as yet no such writ ran on the Macedonian Front. Sarrail and his staff remained undisturbed in Salonika. It was a long way from Paris to the Crna.

8 / Conspiracy, Mutiny and Fire

BY THE END of May 1917 the Army of the Orient was stand-ing on the defensive from the Struma to Lake Prespa; and in each of the divisional headquarters, staff officers were holding private inquests on the failure of the spring offensive. There was no denying the fact that the men in Macedonia had just suffered the most severe setback in all their months of Balkan campaign-ing; and it seemed as if almost everyone had a different ex-planation of what had gone wrong. This was as true of the commanding generals as of their subordinates. Sarrail himself was inclined, at first, to blame the weather: the offensive had been postponed because of 'the violent storms of rain and snow' and had been halted by further torrential rain, followed by fog. Later, of course, Sarrail had more sophisticated reasons: the Roumanians had failed to divert Bulgarian troops by attacking in Moldavia; and one of the French divisional commanders, General Lebouc, was hankering after the supreme command at Salonika and had been disloyal to Sarrail. Milne, thinking chiefly of Doiran, was content to explain the failure in military terms – the enemy fire-power had been far greater than had been expected – but he also intimated that there had been con-siderable mistrust between the various national commanders. The Italians, for their part, roundly condemned Sarrail: he took decisions from headquarters far distant from the battle-field; he ignored the advice of men on the spot who knew the topography of their own sectors much better than his staff could ever do; and, above all, he was pre-occupied with the political situation in Greece. The Serbs, too, put the responsibility for failure on Sarrail: they chafed at his system of command and had no faith in his leadership.

Apart from Sarrail's characteristic and unfounded suspicion of Lebouc, each of these explanations has a certain warranty. Spring had been exceptionally late that year throughout Europe – even on the Western Front there had been frequent snow storms in the second week in April – and no troops could scale mountain ridges in such conditions. And the Bulgarian and German artillery had proved well sited and unexpectedly effective. But there is no doubt that Sarrail himself, as commander-in-chief, had made a fundamental strategic error. He should have launched a simultaneous attack on the various sectors of his front while concentrating his forces at the point where he hoped to break through. It was, of course, too much to hope that he would have been able to surprise the Bulgars and Germans; they had been expecting a spring offensive for weeks and they were assisted by an excellent intelligence service. Yet, in preceding each attack by several days of artillery preparation, Sarrail had played straight into their hands. The enemy was given an opportunity to make final defensive preparations along the very positions he intended to assault. An allied force of overwhelming numerical superiority keyed up to a fever-pitch of enthusiasm and inspired by a resolute leader might, even so, have carried the enemy's defences. But not the Salonika Army of 1917.

The truth was that though on the surface these events had been a military reversal, there were far deeper reasons for the failure. The Army of the Orient was in no state to launch the offensive which the politicians in London and, to a lesser extent, in Paris were demanding. A malaise of despair had, in varying degrees of intensity, gripped three of the national contingents – the Serbs, the Russians and the French – in the opening months of 1917. And throughout the summer this lingering discontent was to hamper operations and jeopardize the future of the whole expedition.

The half-hearted behaviour of the Serbs seems to have taken Sarrail by surprise. 'For eight days I have vainly tried by all the means in my power to push them on', he wrote on May 23rd, 'I believe their inexplicable inactivity was the result of desertions in the Serbian Army, gloomy news from Russia, and the hope that our attacks on the Crna and at Doiran would accomplish more than they did'. But was their inactivity so 'inexplicable'? Sarrail himself had had ample warning.

On March 9th Bojović, the Serbian chief-of-staff, had informed Sarrail, 'Serbian troops will only be able to participate in an offensive which is well-planned and capable of gaining decisive results'. And he had gone on to make three demands: no major attack should be launched in Macedonia unless the enemy was heavily engaged on other fronts; all the Allies should participate with all their forces in any Macedonian operation; and the Serbs should receive reinforcements of heavy artillery. Sarrail had given little weight to the Serb's message. He had brusquely reminded Bojović that the Serbian Army 'was under my orders without conditions', and the French Government had sent a stern message to the Serbian prime minister insisting on the 'close collaboration of the Serbian troops with the French troops operating on their flanks in the 1917 campaign'. This was all very well; but Sarrail had been aware for more than two months of bitter internal feuds within the Serbian command. He had let Paris know on January 3rd that the Serbs were taking steps to stamp out a secret political organization in their ranks; but he does not appear to have realized the depth of the wound which the Serbian authorities had inflicted on their contingent. When in March Bojović stated his conditions for Serbian participation in an offensive, he was clearly hoping they would prevent the Allies from undertaking any major operation until the Serbian Army had recovered. For several months the Serbian Army was virtually paralysed.

To understand the Serbs' dilemma it is necessary to go back further still, to the time when the battle of Monastir had ended and the Allies were contemplating withdrawal from the four hundred square mile salient of liberated Serbia in order to rationalize the defensive lines. On December 28th 1916 the commander of the Serbian camp near Salonika, Colonel Dinjić, arrested the chief of military intelligence of the Serbian Third Army at its headquarters at Vostarene near Lake Ostrovo. He was taken to Salonika and charged with complicity in a plot to assassinate Prince Regent Alexander and with attempting to organize a mutiny. If proved, both of these offences carried the death penalty.

The arrested officer, Colonel Dragutin Dimitriević, was no ordinary Serbian soldier. In 1903 as a twenty-six year old captain he had organized the plot which led to the murder of the last Obrenović king and brought the Karadjordević dynasty to the throne of Serbia. Eight years later he had become a founder member of 'Unity or Death' (*Ujedinjenje ili Smrt*), a secret society pledged to add the Serb-populated regions of the Turkish and Austrian Empires to the tiny Serbian kingdom. As the 'Black Hand', prototype of twentieth century terrorist organizations, this sinister society is sure of a place in contemporary history;

and under his code name of Apis, Dimitriević too has won a
fair measure of notoriety. For in 1914 it was Apis who sent
three young students into Bosnia to assassinate the Archduke
Francis Ferdinand; and it was the Black Hand which supplied
their weapons and smuggled them across the frontier. The
Salonika melodrama of 1917 was an epilogue to the Sarajevo
tragedy of three years before.

Between the wars it was widely believed that Apis was brought
to trial in 1917 because the Serbian Government was contemplating a negotiated peace with the Austrians and wished to
remove all who were connected with the Sarajevo crime in
order to obtain better terms. There may be some truth in this;
but it is possible that the Government had a more pressing
problem. For five years Serbian politics had been dominated
by the duel between the military circle around Apis and the
ruling party, the Radicals, under their wily septuagenarian
leader, Nikola Pašić, the prime minister. Although the feud
between the military and civil authorities had died down once
the war had broken out, Apis still had a considerable following
which included a handful of senior officers and a much larger
group of younger men, who had come under his influence when
he was an instructor at the Serbian Military Academy. To them,
Apis was a dedicated patriotic hero, a legendary figure who for
a time had been in their midst and dominated their lives by the
strength of his massive personality. Many of Apis's supporters
were serving with him at Vostarene. Might he, in 1917, have
become a Serbian Venizelos, defying the Government if it sought
to follow a policy unpopular with the patriot officers? It is significant that the original indictment charged Apis with having
conspired with a group of officers 'to subvert the present Government and judicial order under the Karadjordjević dynasty and
to introduce, instead of the parliamentary monarchy, a régime
in which the highest power in the State would be in the hands
of ten to fifteen chosen men who would carry out the will of
this military organization'.

The 'Salonika Trial' (as it is still called in Yugoslavia) did
not open until April 2nd; but the crisis within the army had
come earlier than this, at the moment when Sarrail was seeking
to coax and cajole the Serbs into participating in his projected
offensive. Investigations into Black Hand activities lasted from
the first week of January until the last week of March; they
were entrusted to a commission of officers who were jealous of

Apis's influence and anxious to further their own careers by assisting Pašić to liquidate the Black Hand. But, even allowing for the prejudice of the investigators, the extent of Apis's following was remarkable. As the commission continued with its task, the Serbian High Command became alarmed. It seemed clear to Bojović that nothing short of a complete reorganization of the military administration could cut out this canker. There was a major purge of the dissident elements: one officer in every thirty was suspended, the majority of them (180) being despatched to Bizerta, where they were interned by the French. The proportion in the Serbian Third Army was so high that, on March 30th, Bojović was forced to inform Sarrail that the whole unit had been broken up: three of the infantry divisions and all the cavalry were merged with the First Army, and three other infantry divisions (including the Timok Division in which Apis had served in the Albanian retreat) were attached to the Second Army. So great was the confusion over the Serbian redeployment that, on April 9th, Allied G.H.Q. in Salonika had to despatch two French colonels to search for the headquarters of the First Army; it was just six days before the original date for the opening of the spring offensive. Small wonder that the Serbs proved an uncertain quantity.

The trial itself was a mockery of justice. Apis and his alleged associates faced a specially selected Military Court, all the normal judges having been relieved and replaced. It sat for eighty-one sessions and summoned more than a hundred prosecution witnesses, but the only evidence of the attempt to assassinate Prince-Regent Alexander came from two convicted criminals who were serving sentences for murder and who subsequently admitted, thirty-six years later, that their testimony was perjured. All ten of the accused men were found guilty; but only Apis and two others were executed. They were shot, on the outskirts of Salonika, at dawn on June 26th. There were protests from the champions of the Yugoslav ideal in the allied countries and from the Serbian politicians who opposed Pašić, but the death of Apis did not lead to any overt act of indiscipline in the Serbian armies. Morale, however, remained exceedingly low. Throughout the spring and summer there were numerous instances of men deserting to the Bulgars in the hope that they would be able to return to their native village. When, two months later, Milne visited the Prince Regent on the Serbian Front, he could see for himself the fatigue and depression

of the troops around him. The Kajmakcalan was still in Serbian
hands, and so was Monastir; but it seemed hardly possible
that these weary veterans would ever scale the castellated walls
of the Moglena mountains and eject the Bulgars from Veleš
and Stip and Skopje.

The two Russian brigades were in a far worse state than the
Serbs. By May 1917 they had been active on the Salonika Front
for eight months, with little respite. They had pitted themselves
against the Kenali defences in the grimmest days of the battle
for Monastir, and for five months they had stood on the alert
in the Crna loop, never more than two hundred yards from the
enemy positions. They had fought well, but they were weary
and dispirited. The vain seizure of the village of Orle, on May
9th, by the Second Brigade was the last token gesture of a contingent which had been decimated by sickness and by battle
casualties. Their commander, General Dietrichs, who before
coming to Macedonia had distinguished himself as one of the
ablest of Brussilov's staff officers in Galicia, was a determined
and energetic officer, but on May 18th even he had to ask
Sarrail to allow his brigade a rest period of six weeks in which
to recover from the fatigue of the winter and the constant alarms
of the last few weeks. And the Fourth Brigade, who were serving
with the Serbs, showed even more disturbing signs of unrest,
the men suspecting that they were intended as easily expendable
cannon fodder and resenting the arrogance of both the Serbian
officers and their own commanders. When, a few weeks later,
the Russian language newspaper in Salonika published a plain-
tive appeal for troops to resume the habit of saluting officers,
it was apparently the Fourth Brigade who were the worst
offenders.

Neither the Second Brigade nor the Fourth Brigade were, as
yet, so mutinous as the First and Third Brigades, who had left
Russia at the same time as the Salonika contingent but had
disembarked at Marseilles for service on the Western Front;
for in France the Russians were exposed to insidious propaganda
from Trotsky's group of exiles in Paris and were better informed
about the situation in Petrograd than their comrades in Macedonia. But there is no doubt that the Second and Fourth Brigades
were left confused and uncertain by the political changes in
Russia which culminated in the Tsar's abdication on March
15th and the establishment of a Provisional Government. As

Dietrichs himself wrote on May 18th – curiously enough, the day upon which the moderate socialist, Kerensky, became Minister of War – 'The latest events in Russia, added to the slowness and uncertainty of postal communication and the various rumours and occasional gossip reaching the trenches from the rear and spread around by good-for-nothings, can only strain the men's nerves still further, worrying them and paralysing their will'. Unfortunately, this sorrowful little army, brooding over its hardships and the agony of the homeland, needed far more than six weeks in which to recuperate. Indeed, precisely six weeks after Dietrichs' request had been granted, a Russian detachment which was being re-embarked at the Piraeus to return to Salonika broke into open mutiny and French troops had to be sent in order to quell the disturbance.

Sarrail had not, however, given up hope of using the Russians and even thought that it might be possible to obtain reinforcements from Archangel if Kerensky's Government succeeded in re-vitalizing the Eastern Front. In July, 1917, there were still 18,000 Russian troops in Macedonia and it was decided to re-organize them as an independent division with Dietrichs enjoying a similar status to the Italian commander, General Mombelli. In the last week of July the Russian Division returned to the Front between Lake Ochrid and Lake Prespa, and the Provisional Government even promised to send a full divisional train of artillery to Macedonia in the autumn.

It was no use. Dietrichs was summoned back to Petrograd in August. His successor, General Taranowski, did not reach Salonika until the first week in November, arriving at the very moment when the Bolsheviks overthrew Kerensky's Government and prepared to take Russia out of the war. Marxist agitators had penetrated the artillery brigade and pioneer battalion which landed at Salonika early in October. These reinforcements stimulated the revolutionary unrest. Soviets sprang up in every Russian regiment and the division became a breeding ground of disaffection. Throughout the winter of 1917–18 it remained an embarrassing liability to its allies. In January it was removed from the fighting front and disarmed, some of the men joining the French Foreign Legion and many more continuing under Allied orders as a labour force. There was still one more melancholy episode before the tragedy was played out. On March 12th 1918 over three thousand Russians ran amok at an internment camp near Vertikop, and order had to

5*

be restored by a French cavalry unit with drawn sabres. Ironically, it was eighteen months to the day since the first Russian battalions had fought alongside the French on that very sector of the front.

The French *poilus*, too, were weary of Balkan campaigning in that spring of 1917. Interminable forced marches across the plain and up into the hunched shoulders of the brooding mountains; the boring labour of entrenchment; the sense of desolation as men crouched in their solitary limbo waiting for the shell-fire to reach the predetermined pitch of intensity for them to stumble forward once more across the freezing rock-face; and always the feeling that the enemy knew what to expect, that each side had become caught up in a ritual dance of death, purposeless and repetitious. In France, at that very moment, infantry regiments were erupting in mutiny rather than face renewal of the bloody assault on the German fortifications along the Chemin des Dames. Their compatriots in Macedonia knew nothing of this, but they had drunk too long from the same bitter cup of futility to feel dedicated to any venture of arms. If there was, as yet, no open demand for peace, there was also little confidence in victory. The whole Macedonian war seemed to be one long stalemate.

But, suddenly, two French divisions found themselves on the move – southwards. A solution was at last to be found to the Greek Question. The Ribot Government, which had come to power in Paris at the end of March, was as convinced as Sarrail that King Constantine was still in close touch with the Kaiser. What Briand had shrinked from doing in December, Ribot authorized in May and he got Lloyd George to back him. A former Governor-General of Algeria, Charles Jonnart, was to be sent to Athens as the Allied High Commissioner; he was to inform Constantine that, as Guaranteeing Powers, France and Britain would no longer tolerate his exercise of absolute authority in violation of the Greek Constitution; and, once the King had been given notice to quit, the French were to intervene militarily in Thessaly and the Isthmus of Corinth. The excuse for intervention was, perhaps, of questionable validity and would probably not have been raised had there still been a Tsar of Russia to uphold the dignity of monarchy; but there were, none the less, two pressing reasons for action. Venizelos was alarmed at the growth of radical republicanism among his supporters in Salonika and anxious for a reconciliation with the dynasty, which was clearly impossible so long as Constantine was on the throne; and, above all, there was the tempting bait of the rich harvest of Thessaly, which would not be available to the hungry millions in northern Greece if the artificial division between Venizelist territory and Royalist territory were prolonged. Moreover, the Allied Powers were no longer troubled about the effect which the occupation of Athens would have on neutral opinion; the U.S.A. was now an associate in arms in the war against Germany.

Events moved fast. On June 9th Jonnart arrived off Salamis; on the following evening French troops landed near the Corinth Canal and a mixed division entered Thessaly, encountering some resistance. Late on June 11th Constantine announced his intention of abdicating in favour of his second son, Alexander. On June 14th, with Athens in French hands, Constantine left the country; and on June 27th Venizelos was received by King Alexander and became constitutionally Prime Minister of a united Greece, committed to the Allied cause. It was Sarrail's one victory that summer.

But he was hardly given time to enjoy his success. The grievances of the French Army flickered into acts of defiance in July. Sarrail had always been a vague and remote figure to the men at the front, occasionally descending for a cursory inspection at a moment of pending crisis but normally as distant as Joffre or Nivelle or Pétain, back in Paris. Now he became the target for malicious gossip, much of it salacious and most of it undeserved: it was said that a high-born Russian woman, whom he particularly favoured, had been seen fingering confidential documents on his desk in his absence; it was alleged that he was taking more than a professional interest in the welfare of several nurses (and he had, indeed, married a French nurse that spring). More to the point was the complaint that officers and men attached to Sarrail's Headquarters were able to obtain leave in France, a privilege beyond the reach of the men who had spent those last grim months up in the mountains. It was the leave question that brought matters to a head.

Early in June, after the serious mutinies on the Western Front, it was announced in Paris that the High Command would seek to give every soldier serving in France seven days of leave every four months. It was clearly impossible to apply this scale to troops serving overseas; but the rights of the men

were championed by the radical newspapers and Deputies and
a demand was put forward that any soldier who had not been
home for eighteen months should be entitled to return to France
and visit his family. This posed very difficult problems for Sarrail. In April and in May 1917 more than a quarter of the total
tonnage of mercantile vessels sunk by U-boats all over the
world was lost in the Mediterranean; and in June the German
submarine UC 23, operating from Constantinople, mined the
approaches to Salonika itself. The Allies were short of transports, of escort vessels, and of supply ships. What chance was
there of establishing a regular system of leave so long as the
submarine menace remained so formidable? Moreover, if every
man in Macedonia who was entitled to home leave were to
apply for it, the Army would be seriously disrupted. There
were 195,000 Frenchmen in the Army of the Orient; and 20,000
could now ask for permission to go on leave.

The trouble came in the third week of July when units of the
57th Division, which had been in Macedonia ever since October
1915 and which had spent the last few months under almost
constant bombardment in Monastir, besieged French G.H.Q.
in Salonika with requests for leave. There were no ships available and the men were ordered back to the trenches. A riot
broke out, but order was restored by junior officers. Nothing
however was done to disarm the ring-leaders, and within hours
three regiments were in a state of mutiny and there was a danger
of other units joining in. Generals Sarrail and Grossetti acted
swiftly. They had the advantage of knowing about the mutinies
on the Western Front, which had been kept from the men in
Macedonia by strict censorship, although it is possible that
garbled stories of unrest had reached Salonika by word of mouth.
Grossetti, fortunately, was respected by his troops. He was a
gruff disciplinarian with a Falstaffian figure but a generous
spirit. As a Corps Commander in Champagne he had authorized his wife to find shelter for the poorer soldiers in his units
when they were on leave in Paris. He could understand the
grievances of his troops, even if he could not condone a breach
of discipline. The mutineers listened to him. By personal appeals
and reasoned argument three hundred angry men were re-
assured; but there remained ninety determined mutineers who
had to be disarmed and placed under close arrest. There were
some further acts of indiscipline from a battalion of Zouaves –
but no red flags, no singing of the *Internationale*, and no

bloodshed. It was all over in a few hours. And not a shot had been fired.

By comparison with the revolts at Prouilly or La Coutine on the Western Front, these incidents were of little importance, and when he telegraphed a report of the disturbances to Paris, Sarrail minimized their significance. But they were a warning. Sarrail himself saw that he must lighten the load on the French forces and improve the amenities, such as they were, of Salonika. He was anxious to employ more Greek troops and to bring them to the Macedonian Front as soon as possible. And he gave high priority to opening up a new route of communication with metropolitan France so as to lessen the burden on shipping.

There was one obvious way of avoiding the submarines and minefields in the Aegean and the Mediterranean: make greater use of the Greek mainland. In the previous autumn the last link had been completed in the railway joining Salonika to Athens by way of Larissa and Lamia. So long as Constantine was on the throne, this line was of small value to the Army of the Orient; but with all Greece ranged behind the Allies it was possible to send troops by rail to the small town of Bralo, some 190 miles south of Salonika, beyond Lamia. From Bralo the men were conveyed by trucks over thirty miles of primitive and precipitous roads skirting Mount Parnassus to Itea, a tiny port on the Gulf of Corinth. And from Itea there were transports to carry them across the Ionian Sea, along a route heavily protected by a naval patrol, to the Italian port of Taranto, whence they entrained for Marseilles. By using Itea and Taranto it was possible to cut the time spent in the open sea to little more than twenty-four hours for even the slowest steamer; and the U-boat haunts off the Cyclades and Matapan were avoided.

It is significant that the first convoy came up from Itea to Salonika on July 23rd, only a week after the disturbances in the 57th Division. Leave parties of French troops began to use this route in the following month. By the end of the year the Itea–Bralo road had been considerably improved and more than 30,000 men could be conveyed along it each month. The British, too, used Itea for leave-parties and for sending back to England serious malarial cases. The harbour facilities of Salonika were still essential for the heaviest war material and for contact with the British base in Egypt. But, in time, the Taranto–Itea–Bralo route became the main artery of the whole army in Macedonia; and the problem of shipping troubled G.H.Q.

far less in 1918 than it had done in the first two years of the expedition.

The British troops were in better spirits than the contingents from Serbia or Russia or France. Although disappointed by their failures at Doiran, they remained a well-disciplined force. They had, of course, plenty of vexations – the omnipresent flies; the long delay in replacing stores and spare parts; the exactions of the Greek shopkeepers in Salonika itself and in the towns and villages between the base and the front; and the monotony of the strictly rationed food. Then, too, there were the perverse contradictions of the climate; the bitter Vardar wind that cut through the bones in the icy months of winter; the squelching, slithering mud of spring and autumn; and the parching sun of the summer months, which made all the earth around the trenches as hard-baked as a brick and turned the support roads into dust-bowls in a dun-tanned wilderness. It was a disagreeable existence, with even less opportunity for home leave than the French enjoyed. And it was made even worse by the high incidence of sickness in the British Salonika Force.

The most effective enemy of the British in Macedonia was undoubtedly the malaria-bearing mosquito. During the three years of the campaign ten times as many British soldiers entered hospital with malaria as with wounds caused by enemy action; no less than 34,762 British officers and men – almost the equivalent of two infantry divisions – were invalided home as chronic malarial cases, the majority of them in 1918. Other national contingents were less affected by the disease because the most virulent mosquitoes were in the swamps of the River Struma, a sector of the front manned almost entirely by the British throughout the campaign. At the end of July 1916 the sick rate from malaria in the 10th Division alone was 150 a day, and it was not much lower in the 28th Division. Conditions were no better a year later and the casualty figure continued to rise throughout the summer and autumn of 1917 until it reached a peak on October 16th when there were 21,434 British malarial cases actually in the hospitals, a figure which represented some 20 per cent of the total British force. Although the mortality rate for malaria was not high – only one hospital case in every 207 proved fatal – the large number of chronic invalids meant that at any given moment a high proportion of the British contingent was fit only for light duties. It was a scourge for which there was nothing comparable on any other front during the war. And, of course, the medical services also had to deal with cases of dysentery and the other diseases which have always accompanied an army into action.

Every effort was made to combat malaria. The men were dosed with quinine; pools were filled in or drained; and ninety acres of brushwood were cut to the ground. General Milne himself told the troops that the mosquito-net was 'as important as the rifle'; but there were never enough nets to go round, and in 1916 and again in 1917 the supply did not arrive from England until after the beginning of the most dangerous weeks in the summer. The incidence of malarial cases would have been even worse had it not been for the decision taken at the end of May 1917 to evacuate all troops from the low ground in the Struma and Butkovo valleys. In the second week of June the infantry was pulled back to the right bank of the Struma, a withdrawal in most places of some four miles. The Bulgars had no wish to occupy the malaria-infested villages along the valleys and for some four months there was a no man's land nine miles wide between the opposing armies where only cavalry patrols would venture. This crescent of waste land was a grim admission, by both sides, that as a pest the mosquito now ranked with the locust. It was hard to remember that in peacetime the peasants sought to farm this unhappy valley and that beyond the swamps and scrub were neglected cornfields.

Apart from malaria, the greatest menace to the well-being of the British forces was sheer boredom. There were weeks of inactivity, of passive waiting in the trenches and bivouacs beside Doiran or the Struma looking out at the same line of enemy-held hills. And there were long hours of dismal guard duty at ammunition dumps or transport parks or signal stations, isolated points of habitation well behind the lines in a world of goatherds and grasshoppers. Once the infantry had moved forward from the Entrenched Camp in the spring of 1916, few of the members of the British Salonika Army saw anything of the city from which the force took its name, unless they were attached to G.H.Q. or a transport unit or were sent to recuperate in one of the many hospitals that had sprung up in the suburb of Kalamaria and on the slopes of Mount Hortiach. The men were left to organize their own amusements and entertainments. This was easy enough at Stavros, the delightful little port which the British opened up commanding the mouth of the Struma;

there was swimming and a tennis court and woodcock shooting
and (improbably) a flourishing debating society for the more
earnest souls. And up near the front, where hundreds of men
were concentrated in a small area, it was possible to run football
tournaments; for the Bulgarian artillery obligingly let up when
a match was in progress. In the upper Struma Valley the 28th
Division ran a pack of beagles. The hounds penetrated the
enemy lines on several occasions in their wild enthusiasm; and
the Bulgars always returned them to their owners. It was a
gentlemanly and leisurely war, very different from the bitter
ferocity of France. Even the German airmen seemed a chival-
rous crowd: they were prepared to drop messages over the British
flying-field giving information about the fate of airmen shot
down behind the lines; and once an R.F.C. Major received a
letter from a junior officer who had fallen into German hands
which ran, 'I have just dined with the German Flying Corps.
They have been very kind to me. I am going up to Philopopolis
tomorrow. The Germans have asked me to ask you to throw
them over some coffee on Drama which they want in Mess
here'. Perhaps it was a little difficult for the British to feel heavily
committed to a war in such an outlandish spot of Europe.

While the brass-hats frowned on such sympathetic frater-
nization, they realized to a far greater extent than the staff
officers of any other national contingent that it was essential
to relieve the monotony of the campaign. It is interesting to
find General Sarrail, just ten days after quelling the mutiny in
his own troops, setting out for the headquarters of the British
27th Division, overlooking the Struma valley, to witness the
final events in a three-day horse show. Probably the significance
of the contrast did not escape him, for that autumn the French
belatedly began to attend to amenities for their own hard-pressed
men at the front.

Milne, for his part, had encouraged his army to amuse itself
ever since he assumed command. All available talent was uti-
lized: the 2/4th London Field Ambulance of the Royal Army
Medical Corps, for example, had a band which was trained by
Private R. Vaughan-Williams. Divisional concert-parties were
a roaring success. The most famous of them, 'The Roosters',
presented their first show in a Y.M.C.A. hut at the end of March,
1917, just before their division (the Sixtieth) took part in the
assault on the Doiran defences. Nobody, then, could have foreseen that 'The Roosters' were to live on as a professional company

through two decades of peace and another war. Christmas pantomimes were staged in 1916 and again a year later; and, towards the end of the campaign, the 22nd Division with a nice sense of place and occasion took the measure of the Bulgars by mounting *The Chocolate Soldier*. Inexcusable frivolity? But had there not been a Ball in Brussels on the eve of Waterloo?

The truth was that concert parties, which depended for their success on topical humorous sketches, proved an admirable safety-valve for minor grievances. And there was another outlet, *The Balkan News*. For three years from November 1915 *The Balkan News* was printed each day in Salonika and circulated throughout the British sector despite problems of transport and a shortage of couriers. As its editor said, with justifiable pride, it was 'The first daily newspaper to come into being purely for the needs of an army'. Mingling optimistic news from the major battle areas with gently ironical humour, it lacked the pomposity of an official gazette. Even after half a century, its files show the determination and doggedness underlying the mocking self-pity which was as fashionable in Macedonia as it was in the trenches of Belgium and France.

One grievance of the troops could not be allayed by any amount of sport or entertainment nor brushed aside by a rueful joke in *The Balkan News*: the conviction among the British public, and among soldiers serving elsewhere, that life in Macedonia was pleasantly relaxing, a gentle drift down a backwater of the war. Few people at home knew where Salonika was on the map; even fewer cared. No dramatic incidents from the British lines crept into the headlines of the London newspapers. Letters home described the happier moments – a football tournament or a show put on at one of the divisional theatres or sometimes the sheer beauty of a sunset behind the mountains. It is not surprising that people began to say, 'There's no fighting at Salonika'; and because months would go by with no reports of the British being engaged in battle, it was assumed that Milne's men were basking in idleness. Clemenceau, in his biting way, had described the Army of the Orient as 'the gardeners of Salonika'; the British public credited it with nothing so energetic as gardening. The phantasy went further than casual conversation. Macedonia became the one front in the war to be ridiculed on the music-hall stage: 'If you want a holiday, go to Salonika', the comedians sang in that summer of 1917. Naturally enough, the men who spent hour after hour sweltering in the ravines of Doiran or swatting mosquitoes beside the Struma resented these innuendoes. It was bad enough to be forgotten and neglected, but that had been the fate of other expeditions: to be despised as well was intolerable. A sense of resentment was bred, which lingered on even after the Armistice. Not all the ugliness of war lies in battle.

With the British public questioning the whole Salonika project, the Westerners on the General Staff once again pressed the Government to have done with the wretched thing for all time. The failure of the May offensive had confirmed their pessimistic assessments. The British could not afford to have six divisions and a hundred and fifty merchant ships tied up in such a futile enterprise. It was a luxury beyond the resources of their army and, at that stage in the submarine war, beyond the capacity of the mercantile marine as well. The French had already been told that the British intended to transfer to Egypt the 6oth Division and two cavalry brigades. Now Robertson wanted to extricate the other five divisions, leaving a token force to hold the port of Salonika itself.

This was, of course, the argument of an extremist; but there were other, more moderate, critics who did not hesitate to express their doubts. General Smuts, for example, who on this question was a relatively disinterested member of the War Cabinet, argued that 'The Balkan Front should either be one of our most formidable in men and guns or should be left alone altogether'. Since it made heavy demands on shipping, he considered it 'the least promising . . . of our overseas campaigns'. By implication, Smuts – who, it should be noted, had just visited Haig at his headquarters in France – had moved to the side of the Westerners. And he was not alone.

Yet Lloyd George, who had been so set against Macedonia at St Jean-de-Maurienne, hesitated. He had always disliked the war of attrition in France, and he was beginning to dislike Robertson, Haig and the whole pack of Westerner Generals. Many months ago Lloyd George had claimed that it was possible to gain victory by 'knocking away the props', by isolating Germany from her allies. Now he began to veer back to the position he held at the Rome Conference. He would not, however, go so far as to give his confidence to Sarrail again; and in the first week of June he informed the French that the War Cabinet desired the immediate recall of Sarrail. But when the

French prime minister protested that he could not remove
Sarrail when he was busy engineering the abdication of Constantine, Lloyd George gave way and let the matter drop. He
wanted French support for his other enterprises – the war against
Turkey and a plan to end the stagnation on the Italian Front.
It was better to let the Salonika question rest, for the time
being.

Moreover Lloyd George could see (as, indeed, could Smuts)
that the retention of a British force in the Balkans had political
advantages. In April it had become known that Austria-Hungary
was exhausted by the long campaign on the Eastern Front and
that the new Emperor, Karl, was anxious for a separate peace.
If the Habsburg Monarchy went out of the war, Germany's
hold over Central and Eastern Europe could be broken. The
Bulgars and the Turks would hardly continue the fight in isolation. But what if Germany reacted violently to what was, in
the eyes of the German High Command, no better than treason
on Karl's part? It was always possible that Hindenburg and
Ludendorff, exploiting Pan-German sentiment in the Dual
Monarchy, might attempt a political coup on the Danube (as
the Nazis were to do at Rome in 1943 and at Budapest in 1944
when Germany's allies in the Second World War sought a
separate peace). In such circumstances, the Army of the Orient
might determine the balance of power throughout Eastern and
Central Europe. The quickest route for the Allies to the middle
Danube and to the vital granary of Hungary was still by way of
the Vardar and Morava valleys. And – a point of even more
significance to Lloyd George's reckoning – Milne's men were
the nearest Allied force to Constantinople. Politically it was
most inexpedient to wash one's hands of the Salonika expedition
completely.

Throughout the summer of 1917 the dreary dispute of Easterners and Westerners continued to dominate every discussion
of general strategy. Lloyd George was adamant in refusing to
bring back any of the Salonika force for service in France but
he was becoming more and more attracted to the thought of
a decisive victory in Palestine. When, in June, Allenby was sent
out to command in Palestine, Lloyd George told him that he
wanted 'Jerusalem before Christmas'. If the British people were
to receive this present, Allenby needed reinforcements: and the
obvious place to find these additional troops was the British
Salonika Army. The 60th Division was waiting to embark when

Allenby set out. (So serious was the shipping problem that more than three weeks elapsed between the relief of the 60th Division on the Doiran Front and its actual departure from the port). In July the War Cabinet decided to see if more troops could be brought across the sea to Alexandria. Major-General Webb Gilman, Milne's Chief of Staff, was brought back to London to give evidence before the newly-formed War Policy Committee so that it might attempt a complete re-appraisal of the Balkan theatre of war. And the decisions of the War Policy Committee were laid before an inter-allied conference which met in Paris on July 25th–26th.

At the Paris conference Lloyd George informed his allies that the British had decided to withdraw another division from Salonika and transfer it to Palestine, together with a sizeable proportion of Milne's heavy artillery. He argued that, with the approaching arrival of Greek divisions on the Salonika Front, the Allies had twice as many men in the Balkans as the Bulgars and Germans and Turks. The withdrawal of one British division would weaken the Army of the Orient by only 3 per cent; its arrival in Palestine would increase the strength of Allenby's force by 14 per cent. As more Greek divisions were mobilized, so the British force in Salonika would be reduced even further. He assured the conference, however, that he had no doubt of the value of launching an offensive against Bulgaria as soon as possible; the British had no intention of a complete withdrawal from Macedonia.

The British pronouncement met a violent reception from the French and the Serbs and rather more muted protests from the Italians, Greeks, Russians and Roumanians. No agreement could be reached, and it was decided to thrash out the problem at a further conference in London within ten days. There followed the usual flood of memoranda. Robertson prepared for the coup de grâce:

'The Salonika forces will never materially contribute to the winning of the war, while we may well lose it if we fail to have sufficient shipping to meet all and sundry requirements. As I have always pointed out to the War Cabinet, the Salonika expedition has been from the first strategically unsound. . . . We cannot use the large Army we have there for any offensive, and when we desire to move some of the troops elsewhere for urgent and necessary purposes we are compelled

to consider potential dangers arising from the false position
in which they are placed.'

His memorandum, which was written for the War Cabinet
four days after returning from Paris, advised that Salonika
should be abandoned and a defensive position established in
Greece, which the Serb and Greek forces would hold 'with
the stiffening of three or four French, British or Italian divisions'.

Robertson had, of course, over-stated his case. He knew
nothing of the Balkans and had no concept of the serious political
consequences of the policy he recommended. The Serbian
Government left Lloyd George in no doubt of their view. Victory in Macedonia, they said, was more easily attainable than
in any other theatre of war. With 100,000 more men, success
would be certain; but, conversely, weakening of the Entente
forces would mean that the Serbian Army 'would cease to have
trust in the Allies'. Once again, Lloyd George compromised.
At the London conference, he announced that, while the British
had every intention of transferring the troops as they had said
in Paris, they would not withdraw any additional units without
prior discussion with the Allies, and only then if unexpected
events occurred. Reluctantly, the other delegates accepted the
British decision. They knew that they had at least made it
difficult for the British to pull any more troops out of the Balkans.

The Paris and London conferences widened the gulf between
the Westerners and Easterners and left neither camp satisfied.
The extremes of irritation were voiced by Robertson, on the
one hand, and Sarrail in Salonika on the other. In a private
letter to Haig on August 9th, Robertson showed how badly
he had taken his defeat:

'Our friends the Allies returned to their respective countries
yesterday. The Conference lasted two days. It was of the
usual character and resulted in the usual waste of time. . . .
He (i.e. Lloyd George) is a real bad 'un. The other members
of the War Cabinet seem afraid of him. Milner is a tired,
dyspeptic old man. Curzon a gas-bag. Bonar Law equals
Bonar Law. Smuts has good instinct but lacks knowledge.
On the whole he is best, but they help one very little'.

And at G.H.Q. in Salonika Sarrail treated Milne, the unfortunate agent of the War Cabinet, as though he were a lackey.

His request for French troops to relieve the British Division that was to be moved from the Struma to Palestine was received by the C-in-C with a petulant refusal: 'Who is in command? The General or me?' he growled. Although Sarrail had at his disposal eighteen divisions west of the Vardar, Milne was thus forced to stretch his four divisions over the ninety miles separating the left bank of the Vardar from the mouth of the Struma. It was certainly no 'holiday' for the British in Salonika that autumn; and the two commanders were barely on speaking terms for the rest of the time Sarrail remained in Macedonia.

All this tension in high places was, naturally, hidden from the men. They only knew, in the third week of August, that the 10th Division, the veterans who had been hurried to Salonika from Gallipoli, were on the move to Egypt. These Irish troops (the 'Balkan Harriers') had suffered much undeserved bad luck since that wet arrival nearly two years before – the frustration and hardship of the first winter, the scourge of malaria in the following summer, the enforced withdrawal from their advanced posts beyond the Struma that spring in order to escape from the mosquitoes. And now, as they trundled along the Seres Road for the last time, one final misfortune awaited them: they were to spend their last weeks in Macedonia, not in the comparative comfort of a transit camp, but amid a mass of destitute and panic-stricken refugees. For, in the very weekend they were withdrawn from the line, the whole of the centre of Salonika was reduced, in a matter of hours, to a smouldering ruin.

The Great Fire began in the middle of the afternoon siesta on August 18th up in the oldest quarter, where jutting storeys jostled each other so closely that the narrow street became a wood roofed arcade. After four rainless months, every balcony was tinder dry and with a fierce north-west wind blowing, the city had as little hope of escaping destruction as Chigaco in 1871 or London in 1666. The two oval watering-tanks, which formed the municipal fire-brigade, were hurriedly pulled up the steep alleys by a noisy and confused crowd of men and boys. But this was little more than a pathetic gesture. Soon people were pouring out of their houses, loading possessions on to donkeys or into carts or dragging beds and clothes and household utensils after them in a panic flight towards the waterfront. With virtually no water in the upper town, the walls in street after street began to crash as though they were trees in a flaming forest.

It took some time for the military authorities to realize the seriousness of the fire. As it was a Saturday, many of the soldiers and nurses around the Base were off duty and enjoying themselves. At sunset an Italian band was still playing jaunty marches in Eleftherias Square; and the Royal Engineers' concert party staged *A Little Bit of Fluff* that evening as planned. Dinner was served in the hotels and restaurants, as usual in Greece, at nine o'clock. By that time, however, G.H.Q. had become alarmed and two British fire engines, which had only recently been landed, were in action – the crew of one of them was to continue to fight the blaze, without sleep, for fifty-eight hours. Fire-fighting parties had also been landed from H.M.S. *Latona*, the naval depot-ship. It was becoming clear that the fire was a grievous blow to the poorer people; but still nobody believed that it would cross the Via Egnatia, the old Roman road which formed a social frontier as well as a geographical division through the city. They were mistaken: around ten o'clock that night the fire swept over this barrier. By midnight it stretched in a . mile long arch across the night sky, with the minarets of mosques burning like candles on the altar of destruction.

Troops of all the national contingents around the town were, by now, fighting the flames. As the fire reached the modern part of the city, there were fresh perils. Gas pipes melted, shooting up a fierce blue flame that leapt ahead of the main fire; and an ominous crackle spread down the overhead tram wires. With great haste the pretentious hotels were evacuated, and the waterfront was filled with rich and poor refugees, wondering desperately if only the sea could save them. At one moment they seemed completely trapped, for sparks had set fire to a lighter which, earlier in the day, had been landing tanks of petrol and the burning oil swept over the water; but naval crews succeeded in grappling the lighter and towed it out to sea, where it sank. Army lorries and naval pinnaces managed to convey thousands of refugees to safety on the western fringe of the town.

The British, French and Italians all had military establishments in the city. Although Sarrail s own headquarters had to be evacuated early on the Sunday morning and an Italian supply depot was, for a time, encircled by flames, neither of these buildings was seriously damaged. The British were the worst hit. An ordnance store, filled with hand grenades, had gone up in the course of the night; and when the fire reached the waterfront, British base headquarters were gutted and almost all the stocks of quinine in the depot of Medical Stores were lost, even though the troops fought the fire hour after hour. On the Monday the fire was still burning, but at last the wind changed and by the Tuesday morning it was under control, although the blackened walls continued to smoulder for a fortnight.

Few people perished in the blaze, but eighty thousand were made homeless, and for weeks the military authorities sought to tend them in relief camps, most of which were organized by the British. Rumour, of course, credited enemy agents with having started the fire, allegedly in seven different places at the same time. But there is no reason to suppose that this is the case. It was generally accepted that it had been started by burning oil spilling from a cooking stove. On five occasions in the past century large areas of Salonika had been burnt to the ground. The fire of 1917 was greater than any of its predecessors because Salonika was larger and more densely populated than ever before. Nearly half the city was completely destroyed, including the Byzantine church of St Demetrius.

Although the fire did little damage to the port facilities and therefore failed to reduce the value of Salonika as a base for military operations, it deprived the Army of the Orient of some of the amenities its men most cherished. Salonika had never been a smart town, but in its tawdry way it had been a gay one; and men up in the trenches, who had only passed through the port on their arrival, had always hoped that they might get a few days' leave to go down into Salonika and 'hot it up', seeing if the tales they had heard of the Odeon and the Skating Rink had any basis of truth. Now all these cabarets and music halls were gone. So were the hotels, and Flocca's, the 'fashionable' café where a young officer would take one of the nurses. Only around the White Tower, where the Turks had tortured their prisoners not so long ago could men on leave from the front or recuperating from sickness find a touch of gaiety. Of course, it was still possible to enjoy the natural beauty of the Gulf and to find some peace in the hills behind the town. But there were many high spirits who looked for something noisier; and Montmartre – or was it Babylon? – had gone up in smoke. For the rest of the campaign, Salonika remained a desolate place.

It had been a vexatious summer.

9 / The Fall of Sarrail

In THE AUTUMN of 1917 it seemed to everyone, except the General himself, that Sarrail's days as Commander-in-Chief must be numbered. The Russians and the Italians had asked for him to be relieved of his command even before the battle of Monastir; successive French Governments had been presented with a formidable list of slights and grievances. 'I shall send more troops to Macedonia when there is a General to command them', the Italian C-in-C had bluntly informed his allies. Lord Bertie, the British Ambassador in Paris, who was an abler judge of the public figures in France than most of his compatriots, had also foreseen disaster if the Macedonian campaign were left in the hands of Sarrail. For a time, the victory at Monastir and Sarrail's behaviour and bearing at the Rome Conference, had muted the criticisms. But, after the disastrous confusion of the May offensive, the Italians had renewed their objections to his command and, in the course of the summer, they were supported by Lloyd George and by Pašić, the Serbian prime minister, who came to Paris for the inter-allied conference of July 25th. The reconciliation of Venizelos and King Alexander further weakened Sarrail's position; for the French had consistently maintained that, whatever Sarrail's failings might be as a military commander, he could not be superseded so long as the Greek Question remained unresolved. Now all Greece stood united behind the Allies; and Venizelos, who had spent nine months as Sarrail's neighbour in Salonika and seen for himself the General's interest in Greek affairs, was as anxious to pack him off to France as Joffre had been to despatch him far from Paris in the first place.

Yet Sarrail still had one advantage. When Ribot had succeeded Briand as premier in March 1917, he appointed as War Minister Paul Painlevé, a Radical Socialist Deputy whose faith in Sarrail remained undimmed by the misfortunes of war. And when, early in September, the Ribot Ministry in its turn fell, it was Painlevé who became premier, retaining at the same time ministerial responsibility for the army. Sarrail knew he could rely on Painlevé, who for more than a year had been referred to as 'Sarrail's guardian'. Less than a month before he formed his Ministry, Painlevé wrote to Sarrail:

'I am fully aware of the difficulties of your heavy task and, in particular, of those which have been caused by the pretensions of certain of our allies. As well as looking after the French troops, you have to satisfy, as far as possible, the English, the Serbs, the Italians and the Russians. In that respect, I have every trust in your decisions, for you, being on the spot, are better able to judge the situation than anybody else, and I send you once more my confidence'.

With such backing from the new political leader of France, small wonder if Sarrail appeared undismayed by the coolness of the other Allied commanders. But should Painlevé's Ministry prove as short-lived as its predecessor, the prospect for Sarrail was bleak; unless, of course, he gained a military success.

There was, however, no possibility of launching an autumn offensive that year. The Serbs and the Russians were politically unreliable, the Italians too few. The British had lost two infantry divisions and a high proportion of both cavalry and heavy artillery to Egypt and Palestine; and the Greeks so far had only three divisions in Macedonia, each of them untried units from the Venizelist 'National Revolutionary Army'. On paper the Allies continued to outnumber the enemy forces opposed to them; their military effectiveness, however, was lower than it had been for fifteen months. The French, for example, were so weakened by the decision to allow home leave to veterans that Sarrail had to merge two of his divisions. At any given moment in the last five months of 1917 almost one man in every six in the French Army in Macedonia was absent on leave. Sarrail would, of course, have preferred to hold back the leave parties, but after the mutiny of the 57th Division he dared not take the risk. A resolute Bulgarian attack at that time, with German or Austrian support, would have thrown the Army of the Orient back into the Entrenched Camp, and perhaps even into Thessaly. It was, indeed, fortunate that the attention of the Central Powers was elsewhere.

Yet, curiously enough, Sarrail did gain a victory that autumn. He used his limited forces shrewdly. The Bulgars suspected that he might be contemplating a resumption of the spring offensive. The British 22nd Division made a series of successful night raids on the formidable defences of Pip Ridge at Doiran; the Italians took some German prisoners in a raid on Hill 1050 in the Crna loop; and the Serbs attempted to eject the Bulgars from their outposts on the Dobropolje but had to halt their operations because of heavy casualties. These were all minor actions, but each was staged at a sensitive sector of the front and the enemy was kept on the alert. It was essential to prevent troops from being moved to other theatres of war, to tie down Austrian units that might have been transferred to the north of Italy and Bulgarian regiments that could have helped to end the resistance of the Roumanians. The trouble was that there was no room for manœuvre at any of these points of the Macedonian Front. They could be attacked in force (which was not practicable) or they could be raided; there was no chance of gaining some limited objective, some name which could be added to the list of places taken, a token reassurance in Paris of the value of maintaining a Macedonian Army.

But Sarrail had seen the one area where such a success was possible. West of Monastir, west even of Lake Prespa, lay the political no man's land of the Balkans. Forests of beech and oak and pine rolled over mountains that had none of the bleakness of the Moglena. Geographically this region was regarded as south-eastern Albania but, in character, it was as far removed from the inhospitable Albania of the Serbs' retreat as the Struma valley was from the Peloponnese. There had, as yet, been little fighting in this part of the Balkans. Sarrail had occupied the Albanian town of Koritsa in August, 1916, but had progressed no further into Albania. By road Koritsa was more than 150 miles from Salonika. It was important to hold the town because it was a key position on the route to the Adriatic port of Santi Quaranta, but he had never considered it worthwhile pressing further north. The Italians were extremely sensitive about this area – and, with reason, for the French had encouraged the establishment of an autonomous republic at Koritsa in December, 1916 – but, by September 1917, Sarrail had little regard for Italian susceptibilities. North of Koritsa was an Austrian division. It was based upon the small town of Pogradec which stood on a spur overlooking Lake Ochrid. Pogradec had none of the importance of Monastir or Doiran, but it was at least a place-name and its fall would merit a communiqué.

The capture of Pogradec proved remarkably easy. On September 7th General Jacquemot, with a scratch division of such units of the 156th and 57th Divisions as were not on leave, began his advance through the wooded hills. At three in the afternoon of September 10th the first French units entered Pogradec. By the time he gave orders to halt the advance on September 12th, Jacquemot had taken 414 Austrians and Bulgarians prisoner and had captured a considerable quantity of material and munitions. The French lost 44 men killed and had 131 wounded.

The victory was duly reported to Paris and welcomed by Painlevé. Sarrail, who was adept at handling representatives of the Press, surpassed himself on this occasion. There was no reason for anybody in France to be unaware of Jacquemot's achievement. Pogradec became a legend. When the triumphal Victory Procession moved down the Champs Elysées on Bastille Day 1919, the honours of the French Armies were represented by winged figures along the route, each bearing the name of a battle. 'The Marne' was there; 'Verdun' was there; 'Monastir', oddly, was not. But Sarrail's army was remembered, none the less; the name 'Pogradec' looked down proudly on the marching columns. It was, no doubt, a symbol of something.

Jacquemot was assisted in his advance on Pogradec by the most dubious of all France's allies. For twelve months an unusual flag, a black star on a red background, had flown over a villa on the eastern outskirts of Salonika. It was the standard of His Excellency Essad Bey Pasha. Nobody seemed certain of the origin of the flag; perhaps it was of physiognomic inspiration, for Essad Bey carried magnificent black moustaches which stood out against his permanently choleric complexion. Nobody, for that matter, seemed certain of Essad Bey's origin, either. He was said to be a fifty-two year old former General in the Turkish Army, who owned large estates around Durazzo in central Albania. It was known that he had defended Scutari against the Montenegrins in the Balkan Wars (and it was alleged that he had subsequently sold Scutari to the King of Montenegro for a good price). It was also known that he had hawked the crown of Albania around Europe in 1913, eventually turning against the German princeling who was rash enough to accept it. He had arrived at Salonika in August 1916 in a French warship, having been removed by the Italian military authorities from southern Albania as what might euphemistically be

termed a 'security risk'. He sufficiently impressed the French
for Sarrail to recognize his self-bestowed dignity of 'President
of the Albanian Government'. Several hundred Albanian irregulars trained in Italy and shipped by the Italians to Salonika
were, to the Italians' fury, put by Sarrail at Essad's disposal.
A court, a Government, a Ministry of War, a Ministry of Foreign
Affairs, even a Ministry of Agriculture, were all set up by Essad
in the villa Sarrail had assigned to him. Since Sarrail did not
trust Essad completely, he attached a 'Minister Plenipotentiary'
to his retinue; Venizelos appointed a Greek to keep an eye on
the Frenchman; and Pašić, in his turn, sent a Serb to watch,
impartially, the Greek and the Frenchman and Essad himself.
The Italians, having burned their fingers once over Essad
and a second time over the Albanian irregulars, regarded him
as a sinister antagonist, subsidized by every other power to
thwart Italy's legitimate aspirations in post-war Albania. The
British merely treated Essad as a great joke. In this they were
less than just to him; he deserved admiration as the most plau-
sible profiteer in a city where the business of war was good business.

The 'Albanian President' had, as yet, taken no part in the
military operations, although he had frequently been seen in
Salonika in a General's uniform with an impressive array of
stars and medals jangling on his bovine chest. But in August
Sarrail, short of troops, determined to test the value of the
Albanian contingent. The Presidential villa was evacuated; and
on September 6th Essad, with 500 men, arrived at Jacquemot's
headquarters at Biklishta, south of Lake Prespa. The Albanians
proved a valuable addition to Jacquemot's forces for they could
move rapidly through country which, although not difficult,
was unfamiliar to the French. After the fall of Pogradec Sarrail
authorized Essad to carry out a raid behind the enemy positions
and down the valley of the upper Skoumbi. So successful was
this sortie that the Albanians returned to Pogradec escorting
no less than 156 prisoners. Whatever might be thought of Essad's
political pretensions, there was no doubt that his men were
good fighters.

Sarrail was impressed with the ease of Jacquemot's victory
in Albania. It seemed the one sector where there was comparative freedom of movement; why not press home the advantage
by advancing further along the western shore of Lake Ochrid?
Three columns moved out to the north of Pogradec on October

19th, delayed by a heavy mist which had drifted in from the lake and enveloped the foothills (where the Albanians were, once more, to operate). Nevertheless, some progress was made on that day and the next; the way seemed clear for an advance to Struga and round the top of the lake to Ochrid town, whence pressure might be put on the Bulgaro-German right flank, facing Monastir. It was a sound tactical move. But on October 21st Sarrail received a telegram from the Ministry of War in Paris: a halt was to be called to all operations in Albania. And that night Jacquemot's troops dug themselves in five miles north of Pogradec. Their successors were holding the same line when the final offensive was launched in September 1918.

It is clear from his memoirs that Sarrail was not surprised by the veto on his resumed offensive. Ever since Jacquemot had opened his attack on Pogradec he had suffered from the irritation of the Serbs and Greeks as well as of the Italians. The employment by the French of Essad and his contingent confirmed their worst suspicions: this, they felt, was no legitimate military operation; Essad was to be the political agent through whom the French would win concessions to exploit Albania's untapped mineral resources. On June 3rd 1917 the Italians had jumped the gun by proclaiming the unity and independence of all Albania under the protection of the Government in Rome. There had, at that time, been severe friction with the Greeks, but if the French were determined to exploit Albania, Italians and Greeks were prepared to forget their differences. And so, for that matter, were the Italians and the Serbs. Pašić himself visited Sarrail at G.H.Q. on October 6th and demanded that a Serbian regiment should be moved at once to Pogradec. He was curtly told that such a change in the deployment of the Allied forces was not practicable; and Jacquemot and Essad were authorized by Sarrail to press forward up Lake Ochrid. The Italians fared no better. They requested that the whole of their division should be transferred to Albania where it could be based on Valona, which was already held by Italian detachments. But this would have meant withdrawing eighteen battalions from Sarrail's army and stationing them in the remotest part of the front, where they would have little value in any later operations. Not surprisingly, Sarrail was as unaccommodating as he had been with the Serbs.

By now, the Italians and the Greeks and the Serbs were at one in considering that Sarrail had gone too far. This was no local question; it should be raised in Paris. The vehemence of their allies' representations alarmed Painlevé's Government, and indeed the British; this tiny force on the shores of Lake Ochrid was splitting the alliance. Not even Painlevé could permit Sarrail to defy three of the Allies at the same time: he must be content with holding Pogradec. Thus was the only successful action in the Balkans that year brought to a halt because it had opened up too many political sores. It is possible to feel some sympathy for Sarrail, despite his imperious treatment of the Allied representatives; but the whole episode hardly enhanced his prospects of remaining commander-in-chief.

Little enough happened elsewhere on the Macedonian Front that autumn. In the second week of October Milne ordered the XVI Corps to move forward from the line they had occupied during the malarial season on the Struma. Since it had been deprived of an infantry division and much of its artillery and cavalry, the Corps did not advance so far beyond the river as it had done in the previous winter; but outposts were set up some $2\frac{1}{4}$ miles from the Struma and a series of night raids were made against the Bulgarian positions. Early in November the Argyll and Sutherland Highlanders raided Bulgarian trenches on a hill three miles east of the Vardar after several days of artillery bombardment; but the constant shelling alerted the enemy, and the attackers suffered casualties hardly less heavy than those of the defenders. Doiran remained an unrewarding area in which to mount an attack.

From all the other sectors of the front there was nothing to report, day after day. As the third winter of the campaign set in, the war in the Balkans seemed as frozen as the terrain over which it was – at intervals – being fought. At this moment of enforced inactivity, the most caustic critic of the Salonika Expedition, Georges Clemenceau, came to power in Paris.

It was, in fact, many months since Clemenceau's newspaper, L'Homme Enchaîné, had poured scorn on the 'Gardeners of Salonika'. For all that summer there had been targets for its venomous shafts much closer to hand. In the press and in the Senate Clemenceau mercilessly fulminated against what he considered to be defeatism and treachery. He hounded, in particular, Miguel Almereyda, who had taken German money to run his newspaper, the Bonnet Rouge, and Louis Malvy, Minister of the Interior in all five governments since June 1914, who had subsidized Almereyda for eighteen months and protected him for even longer. Such denunciations could not be ignored. Almereyda was arrested on August 4th; incriminating documents were found in his villa at Saint Cloud; and a fortnight later he was discovered dead in his cell in the Santé Prison. Malvy, a weakling rather than a traitor, was driven from office (and, in due course, put on trial and imprisoned). His disgrace precipitated the break up of the Ribot Ministry on September 7th. Yet Clemenceau persisted in his attacks, feeding his passion for France on his hatred of France's politicians. Malvy may have gone; but there remained his friend, Joseph Caillaux, who had given £1,600 to Almereyda and who was the natural leader of the 'peace' party. So long as Caillaux commanded any support in the country, *L'Homme Enchaîné* still had a task to accomplish.

Painlevé, the sensitive and kindly mathematician who succeeded Ribot, could not last long in this atmosphere. He tried to please too many people. On November 13th he appealed for a week's truce in an acrimonious dispute between two Deputies; his proposal was put to the vote; and Painlevé's Ministry became the only French government during the war to be overthrown by the will of the Chamber. Yet with this fractious disavowal of Painlevé the Deputies played themselves out of the war; for there were virtually only two possible successors, Caillaux or Clemenceau, and both for different reasons had scant regard for the susceptibilities of parliament.

It was, however, for President Poincaré to settle the succession. He distrusted Caillaux but he had no love for Clemenceau, who had opposed Poincaré's nomination for the Presidency in 1913. Yet he had little choice. 'That devil of a fellow (Clemenceau) has all the patriots behind him, and if I do not send for him, his legendary power will kill any other ministry', he wrote in his diary. Disciplining his personal antipathy, Poincaré sent for Clemenceau on November 14th. The third republic had found its Danton – at seventy-six.

Significantly Clemenceau chose to govern France from the War Ministry in the Rue St Dominique. Within weeks his elevation had left a mark on every front on which Frenchmen were serving. Predictably it led directly to the downfall of Sarrail. The General owed his promotion in the first place to Caillaux; and it had been to Malvy he had appealed after his

dismissal from the Third Army in 1915. His contacts with
Clemenceau, on the other hand, had been frigid even before
the Salonika Expedition. There was more than personal ani-
mosity between the two men. Both, technically, were supporters
of the same political party, the Radical Socialists, and there
had been a time when Sarrail sought out Clemenceau with the
same diligence as he waited on those other Radical Socialists,
Caillaux and Malvy. But in 1911 the Party split, with Clemenceau accusing Caillaux of seeking to appease Germany. Thereafter, to Clemenceau, Caillaux was no better than a 'pacifist',
a term which in his vocabulary was hardly distinguishable
from 'traitor'. With the terrifying single-mindedness of a fanatic
Clemenceau indiscriminately attached the same pejorative to
all of Caillaux's associates, whether they were criminal rabble
rousers, like Almereyda, or ambitious servants of the State,
like Sarrail.

Already there had been repercussions of these scandals in
Salonika. When the police searched Almereyda's home on
August 4th they found three confidential military documents,
each of which appeared to have come from the headquarters
of the Army of the Orient. One of them was a report sent by
Sarrail to General Roques, the then Minister of War, after
the Cordonnier Affair, painting the condition of the Army in
the gloomiest possible terms. The other documents were hardly
less damaging: a directive from Joffre on Anglo-French co-
operation; and a report from the French Minister in Athens
on the political situation shortly before the Zappeion tragedy.
It was assumed that Almereyda had communicated the information in his possession to the Germans. There was no suggestion that Sarrail had forwarded the documents to Almereyda,
but Ribot and Painlevé insisted on an inquiry; and a staff
officer in whom Sarrail had shown considerable confidence was
court-martialled and disciplined. Had Clemenceau been in
power three months earlier, there is little doubt that Sarrail
himself would have been accused of negligence.

The future of Sarrail was raised at a meeting of the Supreme
War Council which gathered at Versailles on December 1st.
These had been black weeks for the Allies. With the British
mourning the slaughter of Passchendaele, the Italians in flight
from Caporetto, and the Soviets swept to power in Petrograd,
there was a need for some master authority to co-ordinate
Allied strategy; and it was for this reason that, early in Novem-

ber, the Supreme War Council had been established. The Versailles Conference, although formally the second session of the Council, was the first to be attended by Clemenceau and the first for which there had been careful and detailed planning. Naturally it had far more pressing problems on the agenda than Salonika. But with representatives of Italy and Serbia present and with Venizelos nursing a store of grievances, it was inevitable that the question of Sarrail should be discussed. Lloyd George reiterated the British complaints; Venizelos – with, it must be admitted, scant justice – blamed Sarrail's parsimony for the Greek failure to raise twelve divisions for the Macedonian Front; and the Italian and Serb delegates dutifully spoke from their prepared briefs on Albania and the enormities of Essad Pasha. Clemenceau undertook to examine all these matters; and referred the future of the Balkan Front to an inter-allied committee of military advisers.

It was not, however, the representations of the Allies which settled the fate of Sarrail, although they were hardly displeasing for Clemenceau to hear. He had already made up his mind. Three days before the conference opened, the British Ambassador noted in his diary that the French intended to dismiss Sarrail. Clemenceau was moving swiftly but warily; was he not, after all, 'The Tiger'? In the temper of 1917 it was prudent to retire a General whose name was linked with one's political enemies; if his recall were appreciated as an understanding gesture by one's foreign Allies, it was all to the good; but if the responsibility for summoning him to Paris could be given to another expendable General, what could be better?

Only in this last manœuvre did Clemenceau fail. When the French War Council met on December 6th he declared that Sarrail had proved to be a lax commander of the Army of the Orient and 'had given no account of himself'; he therefore proposed that Sarrail should be put at the disposal of the Commander-in-Chief of the French metropolitan army, General Pétain. But Pétain was too astute to fall into this trap: if he recalled Sarrail, all the Deputies of the Left – who had for long accused him of being a crypto-royalist, contemptuous of parliament – would be clamouring for his own head; and there was no guarantee that this neo-Jacobin, Clemenceau, would help him to keep it. Besides, ever since the fall of Joffre in December 1916, Sarrail had taken his orders from the Ministry of War. Dismissal must come from the Rue St Dominique. Clemenceau saw that it was up to him: 'Don't worry', he assured Pétain, 'If you wish, I alone will assume this responsibility'. On the evening of December 10th he telegraphed a laconic message to Sarrail: 'I have the honour to inform you that, acting in the general interest, the Government has decided to order your return to France'.

It was still essential to move with caution; for Sarrail had powerful friends in the Senate and the Chamber, and he was not the man to accept defeat in silence. There was no point in re-calling a General only to make him a political martyr. Accordingly, an official announcement on December 11th informed the public, with a felicitous choice of words, 'General Sarrail has had to contend with serious difficulties and has rendered great services'. But, on the same day, Clemenceau forwarded to the Chamber a report on the treasonable activities of Sarrail's friend, Caillaux. The Deputies were too concerned with put-ting their own house in order – or saving their own skins – to worry about a displaced General. The Tiger's timing was masterly.

When Sarrail left Salonika on December 22nd it is probable that he planned to let all France know how he had been 'betrayed' by Paris. Already, in 1915, he had refused to be 'Limoged' (sent into provincial retirement); he would refuse again, es-pecially now that the French Army, in a grim hour, was in the hands of priest-ridden reactionaries, like Foch. Certainly he intended to go to Paris. But, in the next fortnight, the case against Caillaux grew blacker and blacker: he was found to have sent hundreds of letters to men who had turned out to be German agents. No accusations of this type could be levelled at Sarrail; but rumour was hard at work. On landing in France, Sarrail was peremptorily ordered to stay away from the capital. More disclosures followed, among them a melodramatic memo-randum in which Caillaux outlined a possible coup d'état which owed much in inspiration to Brumaire, 1799: Sarrail, a saviour fetched back from the East, was to play Bonaparte to Caillaux's Sieyes. There was no evidence that Sarrail knew of Caillaux's phantasy; but should Clemenceau instigate a general witch-hunt, it would be well for Sarrail to keep out of the public eye. After all, even Limoges was preferable to the Santé Prison.

Hence, on January 13th 1918 when a warrant was issued for the arrest of Caillaux on a charge of 'plotting against the interests of the State', Sarrail was already at his home in

Montauban writing his memoirs. By the time they were published in 1920 a radical reaction had set in, and Caillaux had been freed from prison. The General, however, had learned some discretion at Salonika: in all the 415 pages of his book the name Caillaux does not once appear. Yet the final words of the memoirs have some interest: 'You have not been beaten; you do not die without being victors'. It is a quotation from Bonaparte's farewell to the Army of Egypt. A sense of history may, at times, be a spur to disaster.

10 / Guillaumat

CLEMENCEAU HAD LITTLE doubt whom he wanted as
Sarrail's successor. He was convinced that the Army of
the Orient needed Franchet d'Espérey; and President Poincaré agreed with him. It was just three years since d'Espérey's
staff had drawn up for Poincaré the master-plan that would
have carried the war to the Danube. Conditions now were
very different, but if it were possible for any Frenchman to
lead the polyglot army in Macedonia into Serbia and across
to Bulgaria, then General Franchet d'Espérey would accomplish the task. He alone among French generals had maintained
an interest in the southern Balkans and central Europe; and
this was hardly surprising, for he alone among French generals
knew the terrain. The Government was convinced that it would
be a wise appointment; but Foch (the Chief of the General
Staff) and Pétain were reluctant to send one of France's ablest
soldiers to the remotest corner in Europe.

Since December 1916 d'Espérey had been in command of
the Army Group of the North, responsible under Pétain for
the sector of the Western Front from the upper Oise to the
Aisne, with thirty divisions subordinate to him. His reputation
as an energetic and determined commander had grown month
by month, and in October his troops had gained a striking
success on a seven and a half mile section of the Chemin des
Dames at Malmaison. His star was in the ascendant when,
on November 30th, Pétain summoned him to his headquarters
for lunch and told him that Clemenceau was to offer him Salonika. Did he wish to take it?

It was a difficult decision; and Franchet d'Espérey wanted
time to consider it. He motored to Paris and sought the advice
of his friends, including Paul Bénazet, the deputy who had
visited Sarrail in Salonika (and, disastrously, Constantine in
Athens) twelve months previously. If d'Espérey went to Macedonia, he would be giving up a key position covering the defences of Paris for an army which was starved of support and

despised by every figure of eminence in the West. Would this be in his best interests? Would it, for that matter, be in the interests of France? Moreover, d'Espérey was reputedly a political reactionary. If he replaced Sarrail, who was known throughout the Army as an anti-clerical radical, the appointment would provoke howls of protest from the Deputies on the Left. And if he were to remove Sarrail's political camp-followers from Salonika – as, of course, any new commander would have to do – there would be no silencing the Deputies. It would be far better to appoint a General whose political sympathies were unknown. On December 2nd Pétain saw him again: 'If you do not want Salonika, it is time you said so', he declared. D'Espérey made up his mind: this was not the time to go to the east. He sought out Clemenceau's Under-Secretary and informed him that he could not accept the post.

Clemenceau was displeased. At the War Council meeting four days later he still wanted d'Espérey to be ordered to Salonika but he encountered strong opposition from Pétain and Foch. On their insistence it was agreed to entrust the Army of the Orient to General Marie Louis Adolphe Guillaumat, who was in command of the IInd Army at Verdun. A better choice could not then have been made.

General Guillaumat was seven years younger than Sarrail and Franchet d'Espérey. Like Sarrail, he was an infantryman who came from south-western France; and, like Sarrail, he had won praise for his qualities as a divisional commander on the Marne; but there the resemblance ends. While Sarrail waited hopefully in the coulisses of the Chamber of Deputies, seeing no military action until 1914, Guillaumat fought in twelve campaigns before the outbreak of the war. Most of his service was spent in North Africa but he had been with the Foreign Legion in Indo-China and, like Franchet d'Espérey, with the international expedition which helped restore order in China after the Boxer Rising. He could therefore draw on a far more varied experience than any general who had seen battle only from the trenches of the Western Front; and his acquaintance with colonial regiments would be of particular value in Macedonia, for of the eight divisions in the French contingent, three came from the overseas empire. Although never courting press publicity, Gauillaumat was not an obscure unknown among the professional soldiery. He had met all of France's senior commanders in the last decade of preparedness for war and, as an instructor at St Cyr for eight years, he had come across many of the most promising junior officers as well. Yet perhaps his greatest merit, given the circumstances of his appointment to Salonika, was a complete absence of Party affiliation; for a few weeks in 1914 he had been military adviser (*chef de cabinet*) to a Radical Socialist War Minister, Messimy, but contact with the executive failed to kindle political ambition.

The recall of Sarrail implied far more than the displacement of one individual. Guillaumat reached Salonika on December 22nd, only a few hours before Sarrail left. Quietly but firmly, his hand-selected staff-officers were weeded out and sent after their fallen idol as speedily as possible. General Michaud, the chief-of-staff who had shared much of Sarrail's unpopularity when the spring offensive failed, was replaced by Colonel Charpy, who was promoted General at the end of the year. Charpy had served with Guillaumat in the IInd Army and, by the standards of French G.H.Q. in Salonika, was almost terrifyingly efficient. He remained in Macedonia until the final victory, as did most of the other newcomers, the majority of whom arrived soon after Guillaumat. Not all the changes were caused by Sarrail's fall. Illness forced the ablest of Sarrail's subordinates, General Grossetti, to return to France, where he died a few months later. His successor as commander of the French Army in Macedonia was General Henrys, another colonial war specialist, who landed at Salonika early in January. For one reason or another, the French command was fielding a new team.

There was little opportunity for the departing officers to acquaint the new arrivals with the problems of the terrain or with the peculiar difficulties caused by a multi-national army. In many ways this was all to the good, for Guillaumat and his staff could make their own assessments unencumbered by inherited prejudice. Moreover, before Guillaumat left Paris, he received a directive from Foch on the function and future rôle of the Salonika armies; and this directive was counter-signed by Clemenceau. It was amplified by detailed notes from Foch explaining the policy which the Rue St Dominique expected him to pursue. Never before in the campaign had there been such co-ordination between Paris and Salonika.

His instructions were mercifully free from ambiguity. The 'Allied Armies of the Orient' (as the forces in Salonika were now officially termed) were to be based upon the whole of Greece, and not merely upon the port itself. They were to prevent the

enemy from occupying Greece and were to maintain their
existing lines, paying particular attention to preserving contact
with the Italian detachments around Valona in western Albania.
In case there was an overwhelming enemy attack, Guillaumat
should prepare defences in depth; but once the defensive organization had been revised, he was to think in terms of an eventual offensive. He was, also, to arrange for the full participation
of the Greek Army, first in defence and later in the projected
attack upon the Bulgars. Finally he was told to ensure adequate
cooperation with his allies in the defence of the isolated, but
vital, staging post on the island of Corfu.

Guillaumat lost no time in letting the subordinate national
commanders know the details of his instructions. Their immediate task was not dissimilar to the work they had begun
to carry out in the first winter of the campaign. The positions
prepared around the Entranched Camp were strengthened,
and even more was added to the 'Birdcage'. Communications
had to be improved, both in Macedonia and 'Old Greece'.
Much had, in fact, already been done; the surface of the Seres
Road never disintegrated under the strain of the 1918 operations as it had in the previous spring. But there remained vital
construction work to be carried out in regions which had acquired a new significance, the mountainous area between Itea
and Bralo, for example; and there was a need for light railways
and subsidiary roads in both the French and British sectors.
Local labour was used as much as possible and it was found that
some of the Russian detachments were prepared to work as
navvies and pioneers even though Guillaumat had written them
off as a fighting force. Few of the new roads were suitable for
use in bad weather since most of them were converted donkey
tracks; but they would serve as valuable lateral communications
in the spring and summer months, when there was most likely
to be activity at the Front. All this tedious labour ensured that
the Allied Armies would have greater mobility than their opponents in this difficult country when the next offensive came.
The Gardeners may, once more, have been digging; but this
time, to adapt a slogan from a later war, they were 'Digging
for Victory'.

Meanwhile Guillaumat was also improving the system of
command within the French contingent by a series of administrative reforms, the most important of which was the creation
of a common reserve of artillery, which could be despatched

to any sector in which it was needed. At the same time, Henrys's Army became a more self-contained unit, similar in composition and status to the Armies on the Western Front. All this made for greater efficiency; and helped to prevent a recurrence of the misunderstandings which had marred Sarrail's relations with Grossetti's predecessors.

The new Commander-in-Chief was impressed by the potential fighting qualities of Milne's Army and quickly established cordial relations with the British. He was less successful with the Italians. They again pressed the French for permission to move their contingent (the 35th Division) away from the Crna to the extreme left of the Allied line, so that it could be based on Valona. But Guillaumat was no more willing than Sarrail to release eighteen battalions for the Albanian sector. His tact and firmness enabled a compromise to be reached, by which some Italian units were moved to Albania although the bulk of the force remained on the Crna. The Italians, however, were still extremely suspicious of the general policy of the French; they continued to show reluctance to allow the French use of the route from Koritsa to Santi Quaranta. Nevertheless, General Mombelli, the Italian commander, no less than Milne and Bojović, found it possible to work with Guillaumat as he had never been able to do with Sarrail. Gradually the Allied Armies of the Orient began to recover confidence in each other.

Guillaumat's main concern were the perennial problems, shortage of men and shortage of material. He was as eager for reinforcements as Sarrail had been. For the first two months of his command a steady flow of newly-trained recruits was sent from France to fill deficiences in the divisions already serving on the Front. Clemenceau, although an old opponent of the Salonika expedition, was a realist: he would support Guillaumat so far as he could. But the Westerners among the Generals, particularly the British, remained unimpressed by the change in command; they continued to the very end of the war to look upon Salonika as an importunate poor relation. At a military conference in Compiègne on January 24th 1918, Haig even suggested that all the British and French forces in Macedonia should be brought back to France. None of the soldiers raised Haig's proposal at the subsequent meeting of the Supreme War Council, and he may never have meant it to be taken seriously: was it worth handing the Germans the key to the eastern Mediter-

6*

ranean and abandoning the Serbs and the Greeks in order to
fetch twelve weary and malaria-plagued divisions to fill the
insatiable trenches of France and Flanders? It was far too late
to back out of the Balkans, as Clemenceau and Foch realized.
Yet it must be admitted that there were moments in the months
of crisis which hit London and Paris that spring, when Haig's
proposal looked tempting and twelve British divisions were, in
fact, sent to France. Had the British and French contingents
been fit front-line troops, several divisions might well have been
ordered to the Western Front. It was all very well for Guillaumat to commend their spirit and bearing; the wiseacres in
London preferred the sobering evidence of the hospital returns.

Yet unexpectedly Milne received a slight strengthening of
his fire-power in the early months of 1918. Allenby had taken
Jerusalem early in December and there were siege guns to
spare in Palestine. A battery of 8 inch howitzers, capable of
making some impression on the concrete emplacements of the
Grand Couronné, was transferred to Macedonia in January.
Four batteries of six inch howitzers, withdrawn from Macedonia in August, were returned in February and early March.
At the same time, one of Milne's chief opponents faded into the
background. On February 18th the indomitable 'Wully' Robertson, a soldier great in heart but limited in vision, handed over as
Chief of the Imperial General Staff to Sir Henry Wilson. The
new C.I.G.S. – who is not, of course, to be confused with his
namesake, Sir Henry Maitland Wilson, the commander of
XII Corps at Yanesh – was a Western Fronter by experience
and conviction, and within five months Lloyd George was
complaining in exasperation that he was 'Wully *redivivus*'. But
he was also ambitious – as a brother officer cuttingly remarked,
'He got into a state of sexual excitement whenever he saw a
politician' – and he was at first anxious to show independence
of judgment. Hence, although Wilson would not spare a man
or a gun from the B.E.F., he was at least prepared to look at
requests from Salonika with no greater repugnance than he
showed towards Palestine and Mesopotamia. And this, no
doubt, was the best that Milne could expect.

It was clear, however, that if Guillaumat wanted new blood
for his armies, he had to seek it elsewhere than in London or
Paris. He found it primarily in the parts of Greece which had
refused to participate in the National Revolution, and also in
an unlikely addition to the Serbian Army.

Among the officers who came out to Greece at the same time
as Guillaumat was General Bordeaux, who had served in the
French military mission in Athens from 1911 to 1914 and was
now appointed Inspector General of the Greek Army. Sarrail
had put French officers at the disposal of Venizelos as soon as
Constantine went into exile, but they had made little progress.
It was the responsibility of Bordeaux to reorganize, train and,
as far as possible, re-equip the Greek Royalist Army so that it
could take its place at the Front in Macedonia. The 'Corps of
National Defence' (the old 'National' Army under General
Zymbrakakis) had been serving in Macedonia since the end
of 1916, principally in the British sector; and by January 1918
it was some 30,000 strong. But there were another 22,000 men
mobilized in Athens, Larissa, Lamia and Patras. General Bordeaux had to move these reserves to Macedonia and replace
them by newly-trained (and trustworthy) conscripts, many of
whom would come from the districts in Greece which felt least
committed to the cause with which Venizelos had identified
their country.

It was a difficult task. Even among the Greek divisions sent
to Macedonia there were units of questionable loyalty: two
detachments at Lamia and Larissa mutinied while on their
way to Salonika, early in February. But the General could
rely on the support of King Alexander. He would not tolerate
acts of indiscipline. He sought a soldierly obedience as resolute
as his father, Constantine, had received in the halycon days of
the Balkan Wars. It was, of course, as much in his interest as
in the interests of the Allies that the Greek Army should cease
playing politics. Courageously he visited the dissident troops
in Lamia, refusing clemency to their ringleaders and making
it clear to the others that Venizelos's Government enjoyed
his full confidence. When a group of conscripts defied their
officers and pillaged a village, he gave orders that two of the
trouble-makers were to be shot. He would brook no nonsense.

Gradually, the persistence of General Bordeaux and the determination of Alexander enabled the Greek Army to be re-
constituted. The King made his sympathy with the Allies mani-
fest to all his subjects, visiting Salonika and conferring with
Guillaumat, Milne and Prince-Regent Alexander of Serbia.
But there remained two unresolved questions. Were the townsfolk of Athens and the other cities behind their King, or did
they still feel loyal to the exiled Constantine? And how would

the Greek Army fare in an attack upon the Bulgars? Guillaumat himself was optimistic over the answers to both these
questions; and before he returned to France in June, events
had shown he was right.

There was, of course, no possibility that the Serbs could
augment their forces by levies from within the old Kingdom,
as the Greeks had done. The occupying authorities, whether
Bulgarian or Austro-Hungarian, administered the Serb lands
with an iron hand. Resistance to the invader was kept alive in
southern Serbia and the Sumadija by guerrilla bands which,
from time to time, raided isolated enemy posts and destroyed
bridges (although never on the scale of the Partisan War a
quarter of a century later). Some local inhabitants were con-
scripted into Bulgarian regiments in regions which the Sofia
Government had long claimed. Occasionally, a deserter would
slip into the Allied lines maintaining that he was a Serb by
race and wished to fight for the liberation of his country rather
than serve the invader who had denied his nationality. But such
rare additions to the Serbian Army were more than offset by
Serb deserters who responded to the enticement of Bulgarian
propaganda and the promise that, once they contracted out
of the war, they could return to their native village. Apart from
moments when morale was exceptionally low – in the summer
of 1917, for example – the number of such desertions was small,
but the problem remained potentially serious, posed as it was,
not by cowardice, but by the sheer homesickness of a simple,
peasant people. Another year spent in frustrating inactivity
among the border mountains of the homeland might prove
disastrous.

This pull of nostalgic patriotism had, however, beneficial
effects in the wider world, away from the Balkans. It attracted
back to Europe thousands of South Slavs whose families had
emigrated to the United States. Others came from South America
and from Australia. Many enlisted in the Serbian Army at the
first opportunity but some were uncertain for what cause they
were fighting. If Prince-Regent Alexander needed men to make
the 'Greater Serbia' of which Pašić spoke, then this could have
little appeal to the Catholic South Slavs of Dalmatia and Croatia, who formed at this time the largest section of Yugoslav
emigrants in the United States. If, on the other hand, there
were a guarantee that the Serb Government would support
the creation of a united South Slav State, a 'Yugoslavia', then

it might expect the backing of many Croat and Slovene and Montenegrin emigrants as well as of the Serbs. On July 20th 1917 the leading spokesmen for the Yugoslavs in exile, Ante Trumbić, a Croat from Dalmatia, signed an agreement with Pašić at Corfu affirming the unity of the Serbs, Croats and Slovenes and declaring that a Yugoslav Kingdom (under the Serbian dynasty of Karadjordjević) should be established after the war. Although most Yugoslav politicians distrusted Pašić – and not without reason – the 'Corfu Pact' appeared to broaden the basis of Serbian war aims. It removed many of the hesitations which had held back Yugoslav patriots from joining a narrowly Serbian army.

The largest source of new recruits for the Serbian Army in 1918 was the crumbling Eastern Front. A Serbian Military Mission had gone to Petrograd in 1916 in order to organize Serbian detachments from among the prisoners-of-war captured by the Russians in their early offensives again the Austro-Hungarian Army. In time, Croats from Bosnia and Dalmatia (and, in fewer numbers, Croats from Slavonia and Slovenes) wished to join the 'Serb Volunteer Division', seeking to constitute a genuinely Yugoslav Corps. These volunteers fought valiantly on the Roumanian Front for over a year, suffering heavy casualties and receiving short shrift from their former commanders if they were so unfortunate as to be recaptured. But once the Russians ceased to offer effective resistance in the summer of 1917, they wished to transfer to the Macedonian Front. The Allies, naturally, were anxious to have these experienced troops in Salonika; but how were they to get there?

The first division, some 10,000 strong, was able to leave Russia while Kerensky was in power. Although it took them weeks to secure transport to Archangel, the rest of the journey was comparatively straightforward. Travelling round the North Cape to Cherbourg, they were conveyed to Taranto along the normal route and reached Salonika at the end of the year. But their compatriots in the second division were, by then, still in Russia. The Bolsheviks had seized power and put every obstacle in the way of their journey. This was a smaller force of no more than 6,000 men, but Soviet Commissars insisted on interviewing each man to assure themselves that they really wished to travel to Salonika. Denied the west, they turned eastwards and moved slowly along the Trans-Siberian Railway and the Chinese

Eastern Railway to Port Arthur, which was then in the hands
of the Japanese. Thence they were carried, in such ships as
were available, to Hong Kong and eventually across the Indian
Ocean to Port Said, and so to Salonika. The first company of
this second division, which mostly comprised men from Bosnia
and Herzegovina, arrived at the Serbian camp at Mikra, outside Salonika, on March 29th; it had travelled nearly 14,000
miles in eleven weeks. By the middle of April, all these tough
and determined veterans were in Macedonia, eager to resume
their circumambient journey to their homes in Sarajevo and
Mostar.

The 'Serb Volunteers', as they were generally called, were
the wonder of Salonika that spring, just as the Russians had
been in the summer of 1916. They were welcomed, not only
by the Serbian Command (who viewed their political pro-
clivities with some suspicion), but by Guillaumat, by Milne,
even by the Italians. What counted was not so much their numerical strength as their spirit. Here were men who still believed
that victory would be won in Macedonia, who had travelled
through a revolution and around Asia in order to reach this
gloomy, despised and forgotten theatre of war. Many of the
new arrivals were attached to the existing six divisions, which
were hopelessly under strength, but the Vardar Division was
transformed into a composite South Slav force, with one brigade
entirely Serb and the other comprising these volunteers from the
rest of the Yugoslav lands. Appropriately, they were to be
among the first troops to break the Bulgarian positions in September and to enter Belgrade six weeks later.

With the arrival of 18,000 'Serb' reinforcements and with the
Greeks taking over sectors on the Struma and on the right bank
of the Vardar, Guillaumat began to examine the possibility
of a limited offensive. He informed Foch on March 1st that,
although he could not as yet undertake the reconquest of southern Serbia or penetrate into Bulgaria he thought that it would
be possible to ensure that the enemy retained his forces in Macedonia by a series of probing attacks to test the defences. He had
reached agreement with the Italians, and he therefore planned
joint operations with them in May in Albania, south-west of
Lake Ochrid, primarily to engage the Austrians and prevent
their units moving to other battle areas. The British XVI Corps,
with Greek support, would occupy a number of villages beyond

the Struma; and there would be a Franco-Greek assault on a Bulgarian salient west of the Vardar in May.

General Briggs was able to mount the Struma action earlier than the other two enterprises. But things went badly for the XVI Corps that April. The Bulgars almost cut off a battalion of the Cheshire Regiment in fields which gave them little cover; and the Cheshires suffered heavily. A battalion of the Rifle Brigade which had entered the village of Pros nik received the full force of an artillery bombardment. In attempting to pull back to the British lines, it was caught, as the Cheshires had been, in open country and suffered as grievously. The Greeks at the same time occupied five villages and held their line against Bulgarian counter-attacks, but here, too, there was a disappointment. Half the Greek casualties were caused by the premature explosion of their own hand-grenades. There had been a serious weakness in Greek training.

Far more success attended the French and Italians in Albania. The Allied columns occupied 120 square miles of what was, technically, enemy-held territory to the north of the Santi Quaranta route. This advance, spectacular so far as mileage goes, was, however, of little significance. There were few Austrian detachments in this part of Albania and grim ranges of stark mountains continued to separate the allies from any worthwhile objectives. Even so, just as the Greek misadventure with hand grenades had a negative importance in planning any future offensive, so close liaison between aeroplanes and fast-moving columns on the Albanian Front suggested a method of preventing the enemy from digging himself into fresh positions once a breach had been made in his main defences. Guillaumat's new team was learning its task.

There seemed now to be a purpose about all these operations. And so it was, too, with the best-known combat of the Guillaumat period, the attack by the Greeks, with French support, on the Bulgarian salient at Skra di Legen on May 30th.

The Skra di Legen is an irregular-shaped rocky summit some ten miles west of the Vardar, just on the Greek side of the frontier with Yugoslavia (or, as it then was, Serbia). Inaccessible even today, it was fifty years ago far more remote than the Kajmakcalan or the Dobropolje, although in miles it was so much nearer to the main routes of communication. The Allied positions were served by a winding track which twisted over two mountain ridges down to a railhead beside the Vardar at Gumendye, more than twelve miles to the south-east. Until the French engineers gave this track the appearance of a road, it was impossible to bring up supplies, let alone heavy guns. And even when the road had been given its face-lift, there was no certainty that it would stand up to the tasks imposed upon it by even a limited offensive. Apart from a half-hearted attack by the French in May 1917, there had been little activity in this region. But the Skra di Legen was far more than a geographical obstacle. Heavily fortified, with shelters under protective slabs of rock and a cluster of machine-gun emplacements rising like steps on the face of a cliff, it was in many ways a complementary position to the Grand Couronné, which lay a similar distance from the Vardar on the opposite bank. Just as Pip Ridge and the 'Devil's Eye' dominated the Doiran sector, so the defences of the Skra di Legen, which ran for nearly two miles along a spur projecting from the main Bulgarian line, determined the fate of any attack launched along eight miles of bleak rock-face on the right-bank of the Vardar. If ever a general assault were to be made on the Bulgarian front, the Skra di Legen (and its support lines) had to be captured. And this mission, Guillaumat entrusted to the Crete Division and the Archipelago Division of Zymbrakakis's 'National Defence' Army.

Throughout the last fortnight of May, French and British guns were smuggled up through the valleys and sited around the village of Ljumnica, whence they commanded the flank of the Skra and the Bulgarian support lines. Among the artillery was the 8 inch howitzer battery which had been sent to Milne from Palestine in January. Other French artillery was further to the west, where the opposing trenches were more than two miles apart. The Bulgarian observers noted increased artillery activity and air reconnaissance as early as May 22nd; but they were puzzled by Guillaumat's intentions. And he, for his part, did his best to keep them guessing. The whole front, on both sides of the Vardar, erupted into activity on May 28th. Patrols were out around Doiran and in the French positions beside the Vardar. The shells crunched down, alike on Pip Ridge and on the Skra. But still the Bulgars were uncertain: where would the attack come? Which was the feint? Surely the British did not intend to go forward again up Jumeaux Ravine and Pip Ridge?

At five minutes to five on the morning of May 30th, with the sun coming up behind them, the Greek troops scaled the Skra. The Bulgars were taken by surprise. Half the machine-gun

Salonika from the air, January 1917

Venizelos inspecting Greek Nationalist troops, November 1916

British mule sleigh in the Struma mud

Newsvendor, Salonika 1916

The Black Watch lead the 77th Brigade up into the hills

Doiran: Pip Ridge from the British lines

emplacements seemed unmanned; and the Greeks reached the Bulgarian lines almost as soon as the creeping artillery barrage. Within little more than an hour the Greeks had captured, not only the Skra, but the Bulgarian positions to the west as well. Only in the east was there a hard fight and even that was settled by the end of the morning. The Bulgars counter-attacked in the afternoon and in the following night but nothing could dislodge the attackers. If the Skra were to be regained, it would be neces- sary to bring up reinforcements and mount a carefully-planned operation. So great was the hatred of Bulgar and Greek, that it would never satisfy the Bulgars to accept the loss of a position to their traditional enemy.

Guillaumat expected the Bulgars to respond aggressively. He withdrew the Greeks, replacing them by more experienced French troops. But the Bulgarian attack never materialized. The Greeks had been so successful that a whole Bulgarian Regiment, the 49th, had, according to their own account, been eliminated. And the only reserves they could muster were of poor quality and verging on mutiny. It was the worst rebuff the Bulgars had suffered for over a year.

The Skra di Legen, an unknown mock-Italian place-name, became famous overnight in Athens and all the other cities of Greece. A defeat of the Bulgars by Greek troops, a resumption of the cavalcade of victory in the Second Balkan War – this was the news all Greece wished to hear. The personal prestige of Venizelos reached a new height, not least in the towns where he had been far from popular. There had been difficulties in mobilization in the Morea: the victory at the Skra removed hesitations. Suddenly the war became fashionable, even popular. Sophisticated Athenians had evolved a gloomy formula to prove that the Bulgars would win the war. In 1913, they argued, the Greeks had beaten the Bulgars but the leading Greek officers had been trained in Germany. With the departure of Con- stantine, the Allies had removed these Potsdam-minded officers and the army had been reorganized by the French. But the Germans now occupied more than one-fifth of France and had despatched staff-officers and specialists to bolster up the Bulgars. Therefore Germany was militarily superior to France and the Bulgarian Army, being German trained, was superior to the Greek. News of the victory of the Skra destroyed this false logic. The Greeks had captured more than 1,600 Bulgars and even 200 Germans (mostly signallers); and less than 500 of the attackers had been killed. Therefore the Greeks were better soldiers than the Bulgars and the Germans. How fortunate were the Allies that they should receive, in that same summer, not only the American Expeditionary Force but the new Greek divisions as well! Victory was now assured. As an Italian officer wryly observed, 'In the cafés of Athens there was little to choose between the Marne, Gorizia, the Somme, Brussilov's offensive and the Skra di Legen'. Pogradec in the autumn and the Skra di Legen in the spring – the battle honours were, indeed, mounting.

Guillaumat was well pleased with the action. The Greeks had moved forward fearlessly and had held on tenaciously to the positions captured in the morning. Even if patriotic pride understandably inflated a local success, the courage of the Greeks showed that they were a force worthy of respect. By the autumn he hoped there would be seven Greek divisions on the Macedonian Front, with three more in reserve. In March he had told Foch that he could undertake a modest operation along the Vardar and the Struma; now he cast off much of his caution. His staff began to prepare for a powerful offensive on both banks of the Vardar, with Greek attacks on the Struma and a Serbian diversion further to the West. But ten days after the capture of the Skra, Guillaumat was suddenly summoned to Paris. He was needed on the Western Front. By the time he left Salonika on June 9th his new plan had not even been committed to paper. But he left with one firm conviction in his mind: the Allied Armies of the Orient must go over to the offensive that autumn. As it happened, his greatest service to the troops he was leaving lay still in the future.

11 / 'Desperate Frankie'

THREE MILES NORTH-EAST of Salonika the Seres Road
begins to climb over the first low hills that separate the
city from Lake Langaza. At one point the road sweeps around
a hillock overlooking a water-course, dried up for most of the
year. In the spring of 1918 the British converted these slopes
into a terraced ampitheatre and there, on March 23rd, 16,000
men gathered to watch the final of the British Salonika Army's
Boxing Championship. General Milne was present and as his
guest, General Guillaumat, came down the steps towards him,
the band played the *Marseillaise* and all the British troops
stood 'rigidly at attention'. No doubt it was, in part, a gesture
to France; but it was also in honour of a commander who had
won general respect. As an eye-witness wrote a year later, 'It
was a magnificently impressive moment'.

But what, one wonders, were Guillaumat's thoughts that
Saturday afternoon? The news had just been released that in
France the Germans had launched their long-awaited offensive
two days previously. Forty-three divisions, backed up by a
superiority in heavy guns of nearly three to one, were moving
relentlessly towards Amiens. The *Kaiserschlacht* – the decisive
battle which Ludendorff was convinced would win the war
for Germany – had begun. It would be hardly surprising if
Guillaumat, who had spent over three years on the Western
Front, was thinking of more testing combats than anything
afforded by his ally's improvised boxing ring.

That very morning a German shell fell in the Tuileries Gardens; and for the next four months Paris was to be under intermittent bombardment from a German gun seventy-five miles
from the capital. The news from France remained grim for
many weeks. On five occasions Ludendorff threw the German
Army against the joint British, French, American, Belgian and
Portuguese forces; and each time it seemed that the front might
break irretrievably. Had the Germans reached the mouth of
the Somme or had Paris fallen, there was little purpose in

retaining the Army of the Orient at Salonika, or indeed any-
where else. Against this sombre background, Guillaumat's advance in Albania and the Franco-Greek victory at Skra di
Legen seemed puny achievements, and the old rivalry of Westerner and Easterner as petty and irrelevant as a disputation of
medieval schoolmen.

It was not until May 27th that Ludendorff began the most
menacing of all his offensives. Seventeen German divisions
attacked a weak point held by the French Sixth Army on the
Chemin des Dames. The line cracked and the whole of the
Army Group of the North was flung into retreat. Within nine
days the Germans had advanced thirty miles and reached the
Marne, east of Chateau-Thierry. Hurriedly Foch, who had
been made Generalissimo of the Allied Armies at the end of
March, summoned up reserve divisions from the British, French
and American armies. The offensive was checked; perhaps the
Germans had even run into danger by creating an indefensible
salient; but there was still alarm in Paris.

Failure in the High Command in the west could never be
tolerated. Clemenceau considered removing Pétain, who had
remained responsible for all the French forces on the Western
Front. Yet, if Pétain went who was to replace him? Supposing
a successor were needed for Foch? Clemenceau had to find someone who was calm and energetic and able to inspire confidence
among troops of many nations. There seemed one obvious can-
didate among France's senior commanders. Guillaumat was too
capable a general to remain in Salonika at such a time. His
place was in France; and on June 6th he was duly summoned
there in all haste. It was Clemenceau's intention that he should
serve, in the first place, as Military Governor of the capital;
but if the Allies suffered a reverse he would be at hand, to replace
Pétain or even Foch. For the moment, both retained their appointments, although five corps commanders were relieved of
their posts.

But the Chamber demanded a scapegoat of some eminence
and if Foch and Pétain were spared, it was not easy to find one,
for the Allies had been overwhelmed by sheer weight of men
and munitions rather than through weakness in any individual
general. Clemenceau, however, was too much a Jacobin to
deny the parliamentarians their victim. His bloodless guillotine
fell on the commander of the Army Group of the North, Franchet
d'Espérey. On the afternoon of June 6th a message reached his

headquarters at Provins ordering him to relinquish his command and set out for Salonika as successor to Guillaumat. Like Sarrail three years before, he was held to have failed on the Western Front and was promoted to a distant theatre of war; and, again like Sarrail, he was determined to redeem his reputation (whereas Guillaumat had been content merely to make his).

At 10.30 on the morning after his dismissal, d'Espérey called on Clemenceau at the War Ministry. The Tiger had not forgotten his refusal of the Salonika command when it was offered to him six months previously, and there was little warmth about his reception.

'Well, General,' Clemenceau began unpromisingly. 'You are, then, going to Salonika at last?'

'Yes, prime minister, but the conditions are no longer the same as they were last December.'

'Quite so. You are going there now as someone sent to Limoges.'

'Limoges? How is that?' d'Espérey replied with spirit. 'I was a subordinate: I become commander-in-chief.'

'Ah, yes,' responded Clemenceau, with more amiability, 'you understand the situation. Like you, I know the guilty one; but I have had too much difficulty in setting up the unique system of inter-allied command to destroy it without the gravest reason. Your Group of Armies suffered a severe set-back; I must calm down parliament. The post I am giving you is proof that I bear you no ill-will. . . . Set out as soon as you can. . . . All will go well.'

It was a curious exchange of words, characteristic of both men. Neither liked nor trusted the other, but each respected the very qualities in the other which he found antipathetic. D'Espérey was at heart smarting under his treatment. He was too proud a man to serve as a whipping-boy. Yet in private he consoled himself by maintaining that Macedonia would give greater scope for his talents than warfare in the trenches of France. A few hours before he left Paris, he scribbled a hasty note to his friend, Le Chatelier: 'I am not angry at being sent there, as I don't approve of the Foch-Pétain way of doing things. It will certainly defeat the Boche, but at the cost of men, of time and of money. These fine fellows have no imagination.' And in a postscript he added: 'I was not consulted. Clemenceau needs Guillaumat. My name was on his desk. He assigned me the post. I could only obey.'

Franchet d'Espérey left the capital on the evening of June 11th. He had not called on Foch. He had, as his biographer says, received 'no more military instructions than a colonel taking over the command of a regiment.' He did not even await the return of his predecessor. That night, somewhere between Paris and Rome, d'Espérey's train passed the express carrying Guillaumat back from Salonika: the two commanders-in-chief were not to meet until after the Allied Armies of the Orient had achieved their triumph.

For the remainder of the campaign Franchet d'Espérey was to hold the stage in the Balkan theatre of operations, and it is as well, at this point, to interrupt the narrative of events and consider what sort of a man it was who had been whisked so swiftly from the upper Seine to the Vardar.

A casual glance at a formal portrait of Franchet d'Espérey provokes a casual reaction: here, one feels, is a typical French general. Just as Seeckt with his monocle or Ludendorff and Hoffmann with their stubble hair suggest the ruthless rigidity of the Prussian military tradition, so d'Espérey's massive head and short, square frame seem characteristic of provincial France. One dismisses him as of little interest and passes along the gallery to the more striking figures, the ascetic Galliéni perhaps, or the genially obese Joffre. But closer inspection of d'Espérey reveals a more enigmatic personality. The body may be that of a peasant, but the aquiline profile with arched nose and wilful chin has about it an air of Roman nobility. The jet-black moustache trimmed closely over the firm lips looks menacingly uncompromising. The cap sits jauntily on the left eyebrow as though he were a Gallic Beatty. Dark eyes, which seemed empty at first, challenge startlingly from the flushed furnace of a face. With head leaning a little forward and tunic tightly constricting the waist, there is a touch of aggressive arrogance in the way he holds his body; but the overriding impression is of energy and vigour and resolution. It is the picture of a man who will not tolerate slackness or brook opposition to his plans. It radiates authority.

Franchet d'Espérey never completed his memoirs, but even without his own account, we know plenty about him. Like all great commanders, he inspired devotion and faithful hagiographers on his staff have recorded his virtues with the diligence of monastic chroniclers. He never smoked; he ate substantial

meals, but hurriedly so as to waste as little time as possible;
he had a phenomenal memory for detail; he would sweep through
the routine desk-work at his headquarters as though he feared
that an In-tray filled with documents would of itself make him
a sedentary bureaucrat. He wished always to be on the move.
He would be up in the saddle for a canter at five in the morning.
And (like Milne) he was not a commander who could stay
isolated from the front-line. Bumping along the broken roads
in his staff car, he would descend unexpectedly on distant units
and command posts, a terrifyingly propellent general. Everywhere
he jotted notes on what he saw, building up a private intelligence service which he could use with devastating effect to get
his own way in conference. By nature, he was blunt and straightforward, hating intrigue and never practising it. Throughout
his life he retained the unsophisticated sense of humour of a
young lieutenant in an African colonial regiment, heartily –
and at times embarrassingly – jovial, a bear dancing. But he
was also unpredictable and impulsive; an irritating incident
or a rebuff would make him brusque and unapproachable, a
bear growling.

He had already impressed the British on the Western Front.
After meeting him for the first time, Haig wrote: 'He seemed
an active, determined little man and gave me a feeling of greater
confidence than the majority of French officers with whom I
have had dealings had done.' And Brigadier-General Spears,
less patronizingly, described the 'galvanic shock' he had given
to the staff officers in France when he took over the Fifth Army:

'He moved quickly, almost fiercely, bent arms keeping time
like those of a runner with the movement of his legs. His
dark eyes were piercing, his voice sharp, his diction precise.
Olympian, the whole weight of responsibility rested on his
shoulders alone. He kept all in their place by his manner.
Never did he solicit or permit advice or suggestions, which
indeed no one would have dared to offer. He was a genuine
commander. . . .'

Now, three and a half years later, the Olympian was coming
to the foot of Olympus. He had learnt much, although he did
not always remember his lessons. Nowadays he would even
listen to others, provided that their advice did not run counter
to his own intentions. At heart he remained a fighting general

in a hurry. The British, with typical linguistic indolence, soon gave up all pretence of twisting their tongues round the pentasyllabic French of his name. Irreverently, they dubbed him, 'Desperate Frankie'; as a nickname, it was not so wide of the mark.

Travelling by way of Brindisi and Athens, Franchet d'Espérey arrived at Salonika in the evening of June 17th. He was met by the acting commander-in-chief, General Henrys, and a group of senior officers. Bluntly he told the group assembled on the quay, '*J'attends de vous une energie farouche*' ('I expect from you savage vigour'). Immediately on landing, he paid a courtesy call on the allied commanders and on Prince Alexander of Serbia, who impressed him considerably. But no time was to be wasted on social pleasantries. Abortive projects of Sarrail's staff must be considered anew. Guillaumat's preparatory work on an offensive had to be reassessed. Temporarily disciplining his impulsiveness, the new commander-in-chief settled down to paperwork.

Yet d'Espérey liked none of the proposals placed before him. The official plan of operations, agreed three months previously, was too traditional and too cautious. It concentrated on the Vardar, and that was what the enemy would expect. Dryly he noted in his diary: 'It did not at all correspond with my intentions.' Nor was he encouraged by a telegram from Paris, despatched five days after he landed at Salonika, informing him that a detailed directive was on its way by special messenger and that, pending its arrival, he was to continue the preparations for a limited offensive begun by Guillaumat. He was convinced that somewhere along the mountain front there must be a point where it was possible to break through the enemy's line and throw him into confusion. If Paris could only propose an advance of a few kilometres, as though Macedonia were a sector of the Western Front, then he would go up into the mountains himself and determine the character of the offensive before the directive reached him. The man who had talked best sense to him in Salonika was Prince-Regent Alexander, and on June 28th (Serbia's National Day and the fourth anniversary of the Sarajevo assassination) Franchet d'Espérey set out for the Serbian front in the special headquarters' train which had been fitted out by Sarrail two years previously and hardly used. With d'Espérey travelled the Voivode Mišić, the general whose men

had stormed the Kajmakcalan and who was now to replace
Bojović as Serbian Chief of Staff.

The advanced headquarters of the Serbs were at Yelak, a
clearing in a forest of fir-trees some 5,500 feet up in the Moglena mountains eighty-five miles north-west of Salonika. On
three sides of Yelak towered bare and jagged summits. No
general schooled in the military academies of western Europe
would ask his army to attack over terrain such as this unless
he were out of his mind. But Mišić, who had established the
command post at Yelak before he became Chief of Staff, thought
otherwise. If the crests of the mountains could be seized and the
enemy line broken, the valleys and ridges beyond ran towards
the upper Vardar, along the natural line of advance and not,
as further to the east or to the west, across it. It is true that
for many miles these routes were little more than goat-tracks
and bridle-paths; but the Serbian soldiery, although primitive
by western standards, were tough and self-sufficient, the best
infantry in Europe for a task such as this. Mišić had already
converted Prince-Regent Alexander to his plan; but could he
win over a newcomer, a graduate of Saint-Cyr? Sarrail had
studied this region more than once and it had figured in his
plan of February 1917, but, in the end, he had decided against
it because of the impossibility of moving guns across the formidable mountain-chain. Guillaumat had shown that it was possible
to site artillery for a limited offensive in difficult mountain
country at the Skra di Legen; but Mišić was, like d'Espérey,
asking for something more than a local success. It seemed as
if Mišić would have a hard task to sell his plan of operations
to the new commander-in-chief. He had brought a believer in
a war of movement to inspect a region in which even the mules
could stumble forward only after heart-breaking delays.

Mišić, Alexander and d'Espérey lunched at Yelak on June
29th. In the afternoon they mounted horses and climbed, with
painful slowness, another 2,000 feet up to the crest of a mountain called the Floka, where the Serbs had hewn an eyrie in the
bare rock. From the Floka, d'Espérey could study the whole
Bulgarian defensive system. He could look down on a pyrami-
dical mountain known as the Sokol, less than four miles to the
north-west, which formed a key position in the defences. Six
miles to its west he could see a twin peak, the Vetrenik. Between
the two ran the broken and formless ridge, the Dobropolje,
the southern spurs of which had been vainly assailed by the

Serbs in the spring of 1917. All three names – the Sokol, the Vetrenik and the Dobropolje – were to figure again and again in the operational orders of the next few months. And so too was the Kozyak, a slightly higher mountain which stood out clearly three miles further northwards and which formed the Bulgarian second line. The scenery was awe-inspiring; scrub over the limestones on the lower slopes, belts of conifers straggling over the valleys, the long line of bare summits sharply defined in the crisp mountain air.

Every field commander in the Balkans had looked out over country such as this, but to d'Espérey it was a new experience. His position was unenviable. He was being asked by the enthusiastic commanders of a foreign force, which he had only recently encountered for the first time, to authorize an offensive far more ambitious than his instructions would permit over a region which his two predecessors had written off as unassailable. Common sense dictated the rejection of the Serbian design out of hand. Pétain and his staff had often complained, back in France, that d'Espérey was impulsive. Now he hesitated. There was much in the project that appealed to him. A major attack on the Dobropolje would certainly take the enemy by surprise. Moreover, the Serbs were clearly filled with that 'savage vigour' for which he had asked from his own officers; a rebuff would have an adverse effect on their naturally volatile spirits. It was no easy decision.

D'Espérey rode down to Yelak and spent the night there. By the following morning he had made up his mind. He telephoned General Charpy, his chief of staff back at Salonika: light machine-guns were to be found for the Serbian soldiery; Italian labourers were to be drafted to work on the access routes to the Moglenitsa; carrier-pigeons were to be despatched immediately to Yelak in case the overburdened line of communication broke down. Mišić, Alexander and d'Espérey met once more in conference. The whole Serbian Army, reinforced by two French divisions, would go over to the offensive with the immediate object of breaking through the Bulgarian defences. Mišić, no doubt remembering the difficulties he had encountered with Sarrail, asked that the French units should be placed under his command. When d'Espérey gave his consent, Prince Alexander stood up and silently shook his hand. Less dramatically, d'Espérey recorded the meeting in his diary: 'A long serious conversation with the Prince. After having seen the terrain I laid down the basis of our operations. In place of a local operation, it will be a decisive attack in which the whole Serbian Army strengthened by two French divisions will participate and which will break through the crust. Agreement is complete.'

Thereupon d'Espérey returned to Salonika, and by July 6th his staff were able to hand Mišić a memorandum headed 'Summary Study of a joint Offensive Action on the Macedonian Front, with the principal operation on the Dobropolje'. It was precisely one calendar month since, back at Provins, Franchet d'Espérey had received his appointment to the Salonika command. Whatever other criticisms might be levelled at him, nobody could accuse the new commander-in-chief of dilatoriness.

It was an achievement to have reached 'complete agreement' with his Serbian allies, but d'Espérey and his staff were still acting on their own. There was a wide divergence between his intentions and the instructions which had been prepared for him in the Ministry of War in Paris. And London, as usual, was several months behind even Paris in its assessment of the situation in the Balkans.

The directive from the Ministry of War, which Clemenceau had signed on June 23rd, reached d'Espérey on July 2nd. With the first paragraphs he fully concurred: it was, said Clemenceau, essential to relieve the Western Front by going over to the offensive in the outer theatres of war, and the Allies should, accordingly, seek to crack the Bulgarian defences by 'a general and concerted action'. So far so good; but with the rest of the instructions d'Espérey had little sympathy. He was ordered to continue the series of local combats which had begun at the Skra di Legen in the hope that it would be possible to dislocate the enemy front and mount a major offensive in the autumn. This whole concept ran counter to d'Espérey's convictions. He considered that limited actions of this type must waste lives and material. He wanted to retain such strength as he had for a knock-out blow at a decisive moment on a vital sector of the front. Yet, rather than find himself in conflict with Paris, d'Espérey chose to delay a reply to the directive. Clemenceau had, after all, specifically mentioned the need to 'exalt the morale' of the Serbs and Greeks by assigning them objectives to attack. And this instruction d'Espérey's staff were prepared to carry out to the letter.

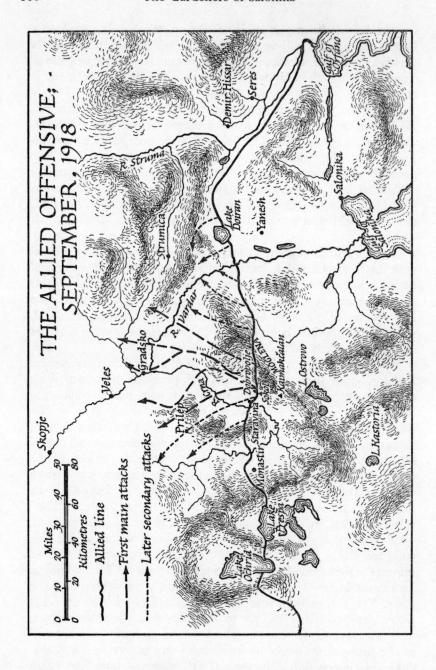

THE ALLIED OFFENSIVE;
SEPTEMBER, 1918

Ironically, while d'Espérey was fuming indignantly over his orders from Paris, Clemenceau was defending him from Lloyd George. The British had not been consulted over d'Espérey's appointment, and they complained that the French were keeping them in the dark over their intentions for the Salonika campaign. The storm burst at the session of the Supreme War Council which opened at Versailles on July 2nd. Lloyd George blamed Clemenceau for placing a general who had suffered a reversal on the Western Front in command of the inter-allied force in Macedonia without prior agreement and 'for issuing orders for an offensive there without consulting the Supreme War Council' which, at its last session, had agreed on a defensive policy in that theatre of operations. Clemenceau was unusually disarming. He accepted the need for a joint appointment to the command in future and he assured Lloyd George that he was not proposing any attack that would weaken the strength of the Allies on any other front. 'He himself, from the commencement had been wholly against any Balkan expedition. He had never believed that an offensive would give satisfactory results. Could he then be accused of wishing to start a grand offensive in the Balkans? So utterly opposed was he to any such proposals that, at one time, he had suggested withdrawing the whole of the troops from Salonika.' The British were mollified by this somewhat evasive reply and the Council formally agreed that their military representatives should meet and 'report as to the desirability of undertaking an offensive in the Balkans', and that, 'pending the result of their inquiry, no general offensive shall take place'.

The military representatives, with diplomatic advisers, duly gathered in the Trianon Palace a week later. The War Office delegated Major-General Sackville-West to look after its interests; only two months previously he had expressed himself in favour of the evacuation of the whole British force from Salonika. But the pace was set by the chief French delegate, none other than Guillaumat himself. The late commander-in-chief had found that, with the stemming of the German tide in France, there was little enough for him to do as Military Governor of Paris and he was therefore ready and anxious to devote all his time and energy to championing the army he had left in Macedonia. He had, he assured the conference, complete faith in the eventual success of any offensive in Macedonia; the Allies had men of sufficient quality and numbers to defeat

the Bulgars. His enthusiasm swept away the objections of the
British. It was agreed that the military representatives should
look more fully at the possibility of a general offensive. Curiously
enough the British insisted on a caveat which would assist
Franchet d'Espérey in his resolution to go beyond his terms of
reference; for it was formally recorded, 'That it is not desirable
to carry out this offensive unless it leads to a victory of more
than local importance'.

Sackville-West soon realized that he had made a greater concession to the Easterners than he had intended. A couple of days
after the conference he asked Guillaumat for detailed information on eleven points concerning the nature of the advance
and the reasons for believing that the Bulgars would suffer a
major defeat. Guillaumat hedged: only the present commander-
in-chief could give the general plan and answer such questions
fully, but he assumed that the main attack would fall between
Doiran and the Crna. It would succeed because, while the
Allied force was better suited to mountain warfare than it had
ever been before, the Bulgars were short of reserves and unlikely to receive reinforcements from the Austrians, Turks or
Germans owing to the pressure on other fronts. It was difficult
to find flaws in the French logic, but the War Office remained
unhappy.

The French received support from an unexpected quarter.
The American representative at the conference, General Tasker
H. Bliss, was given permission by the British to ask Milne for
his views. Technically, this was an unorthodox proceeding:
the United States was not at war with Bulgaria; and Milne,
strictly speaking, was a subordinate commander whose duty
in the first instance was to reconcile the narrow interests of
Britain with the general strategy laid down by Franchet d'Espérey. But it had the merit of providing the Council with views
which were entirely independent of the French, for, as yet,
Milne had no inkling of d'Espérey's intentions. Milne's reply
to General Bliss was as confident as ever: he was sure that an
attack in Macedonia would have consequences far beyond the
narrow battle-area. He did not, however, like the proposal by
Guillaumat in March for the main attack to be launched between the Vardar and Doiran, as he considered that, in that
particular sector, the advantage in numbers and fire-power lay
with the enemy; but he favoured an advance up the Struma
to the Rupel Pass, and he commented particularly on the oppor-

tunities which would be opened by a successful assault on the
Serbian sector. While tactfully admitting that the Supreme
War Council was alone qualified to judge whether or not the
time was ripe for an offensive in Macedonia, he concluded:
'In my opinion an offensive here at the psychological moment
may have more than local effect and should be prepared for'.

The die-hard Westerners in the War Office were being out-
manœuvred, but they were prepared to go down fighting. In
June no less than twelve British battalions were withdrawn from
the line on orders from the War Office for transfer to the Western
Front; and three days after Milne telegraphed his reply to
General Bliss, the C.I.G.S. was recommending the War Cabinet
to replace all the British units in Macedonia by Indians and
abandon any intention of going over to the offensive in that
theatre of operations. By mid-July Clemenceau knew that d'Espérey was contemplating a more ambitious project than his
original instructions had authorized, and the War Office learnt
of his intentions from Milne on July 25th. It was bad enough
that an offensive was in the offing; it was even worse that Milne
should have asked for his troops to be brought up to 'fighting
pitch by sending the necessary ammuntion and reinforcements'
by the second half of September. An irate message was despatched to Clemenceau seeking clarification of the instructions
sent to Franchet d'Espérey. Clemenceau replied that preparations
were being made in accordance with the decisions taken by the
military representatives at the Trianon, and that d'Espérey
had been forbidden to launch an attack until he had received
formal permission (which would depend upon the consent of
the allied governments).

The whole matter was threshed out at a further conference
of the military representatives of Britain, France, Italy and the
United States at Versailles on August 3rd. For the last time
Sackville-West brought out all the old arguments against an
offensive. With authoritative certainty the French countered
each objection: it was made clear to Sackville-West that Foch
himself desired the attack to take place in order to worry the
Germans on yet another front; and it was claimed that only by
allowing the Balkan allies to liberate their occupied territories
could the morale of the Greek and Serb Armies be sustained.
One concession of importance was made to the Westerner's
viewpoint: on the insistence of the American, General Bliss,
it was agreed that the preparations in Macedonia must not be

allowed to divert men or material or shipping from the Western theatre of war. But the final resolution of the conference afforded Franchet d'Espérey far more support than he might have expected a month previously: preparations for the offensive were to be 'pushed on with all speed'; and d'Espérey was to be left 'free to launch this offensive at the moment he considers most favourable, unless new and unforeseen circumstances arise'. The British had not yet given their final approval to the attack – which, indeed, they still regarded with great repugnance – but it would be extremely difficult to refuse consent once d'Espérey had completed his preparations.

By August 3rd all the preliminaries for the offensive were, in fact, well advanced. Hundreds of labourers – some of them Russians, some Bulgarian and Turkish prisoners of war and some local civilians – were engaged in opening up the approach routes to the Moglenitsa. It was clearly impossible entirely to prevent the enemy knowing what was going on, but it was hoped that he might, at least, be kept unaware of the scale of the preparations. In the later stages secrecy was vital and the polyglot force of navvies was replaced by regular units of French pioneers and engineers. There was a need for cunning, patience and restraint. Each night saw a fever of activity, but at dawn the camouflage nets went up and throughout the daylight hours a deceptive quiet settled over the valleys. The most remarkable achievement of all was the placing of the heavy artillery. Twelve 155 mm. and 105 mm. guns were slowly hoisted up by means of tractors and tackle on the Floka, more than 7,700 feet above sea-level. And two more batteries of heavy guns were carried up to the summit of another peak almost as high. Each gun needed two tractors to shift it, and the work made slow progress. But after a fortnight of toil the batteries were in position, dominating not only the Dobropolje and the Vetrenik, but even the second line of defences on the Kozyak. And the Bulgars had no suspicion of the fire-power which was being massed against them.

Each of the main national contingents – French, Serbian and British – was responsible for working out the detailed plan of operations within the general framework of d'Espérey's proposals. The Greeks and Italians were in a different situation. Most of the Greek force (five divisions with one in reserve) had been placed under the command of General Milne, but another two Greek divisions were attached to the Army Group of the French General d'Anselme and a ninth Greek division formed part of the main French Army of the Orient, under General Henrys. It was intended that, at a later stage in the operations, the Greek commander-in-chief, General Danglis, would assume command on the Struma front. The main Italian force was completely independent of d'Espérey's army and had problems of its own in Albania, but the Italian 35th Division was included in Henrys' Group and posted on the loop of the Crna, where it had valiantly held the trenches facing Hill 1050 for nearly two years. One contingent was ignored by Head-quarters: neither Franchet d'Espérey nor the Italian com-mander, General Ferrero, had any use for the Albanian levies of Essad Pasha. When a signal from Paris demanded to be informed what had happened to the army of the man whom Sarrail had welcomed to Salonika as President of the Albanian Government, d'Espérey curtly telegraphed in reply that it now numbered 13 men.

There were far more urgent problems than a wayward Al-banian adventurer, and throughout the torrid days of July and August the staff officers were hard at work in each of the command headquarters. The vital breakthrough was to be achieved by the Serbs under Mišić on the six mile sector between the Sokol and the Vetrenik. He was to be supported on his left flank by the Army Group of General Henrys and on his right by the three divisions of General d'Anselme. An impor-tant subsidiary attack was to be launched by the British XII Corps in front of Doiran with the XVI Corps thrusting towards the Blaga Planina and the Belasica Planina from the eastern shore of Lake Doiran, and a further advance was to be made across the Struma. General Henrys had completed the plan for his Army Group as early as July 23rd, but General d'Anselme had to reorganize his sector and the operations order was not ready until August 24th. Mišić handed over the orders he pro-posed to issue for the Serbian Army to d'Espérey's staff on July 27th, but the commander-in-chief insisted that they should be amended. He was determined on the acceptance by all the national units of an important principle: there was to be no delay in following up the initial assault; support troops were to be brought into the attack before the enemy could deploy his reserves, and the second line of enemy positions overrun and carried with the greatest possible speed. This was a signifi-

7

cant innovation in Macedonia: failure to develop early tactical
successes had been one of the bitter lessons of the actions of
the autumn of 1916 and the spring of 1917.

It took Milne far longer to perfect his plans. He needed men
and he needed shells and, although he was far from sanguine
that he would get his way, he was determined to try and squeeze
all he could from a reluctant War Office before making his
final dispositions. He met with little response. On four occasions he telegraphed urgent requests for ammunition and particularly for supplies of gas shells. He even sent his Deputy
Quartermaster-General back to London to plead for one more
8-inch howitzer battery. There was nothing doing. So monu-
mental were the Westerners in their parsimony that Franchet
d'Espérey himself was at last, early in August, moved to telegraph to Clemenceau asking him to intercede with the War
Office so as to ensure that Milne received some ammunition in
time for the offensive, which was by then only six weeks away.
At last the rounds of ammunition were promised, and eventually
one-fifth of the shells requested by Milne reached the Doiran
front, less than twenty-four hours before the bombardment was
due to begin. Apart from the arrival of some Indian drivers
for the ammunition train and of a small supply of Lewis guns,
Milne received no reinforcements. He was forced to undertake
the final offensive short of mules and horses, short of spare
parts for his lorries, and with his ammunition supplies peri-
lously low. And, although he could not foresee it when he prepared his operational orders, his men were to be hit by a new
scourge. Already debilitated by malaria, they were, from the
start of September, seriously weakened by an epidemic of 'Spanish' influenza, which was so virulent that one whole brigade
had to be withdrawn from the front. Not since the Crimea had
any British commander asked for so much from an army of
sick men.

But by August 17th Milne had completed his provisional
plans. There was to be a preliminary assault by units of the
27th Division on what was known as the 'Roche Noire Salient'
to the west of the Vardar so as to deceive the enemy into believing that the main thrust was to come up the valley itself.
But, as the commander-in-chief had requested, the principal
blows were to be aimed at that grim bastion above Doiran,
with a secondary thrust east of the lake. The precise timing of
the British attack was left undecided. All that Franchet d'Es-

pérey asked was that it should be launched when the offensive on the other sectors of the front had 'made a certain progress'. This vague formula had the merit of giving Milne far greater independence of judgment than Sarrail permitted him to exercise in the earlier actions; but it could be argued that the British commander, as a partial executant of a comprehensive plan proposed elsewhere, was in no position to determine what progress had been made in the Moglena; and that, in consequence, there was a danger of the attack at Doiran being launched too soon. Milne has, in fact, been criticized on this very count (most recently by a veteran of the campaign, Mr Charles Packer, in his book, *Return to Salonika*). Yet, clearly, one of the prime tasks of the British operation was to prevent the Bulgars from moving troops to the other battle areas. Not for the first time in Macedonia, they had to engage the enemy in strength in a region to which, for the sake of prestige, he attached great significance and where he had placed crack troops of high morale. It was no less likely that the attack might come too late. The British were cast for as exacting and bloody a rôle as their allies further to the west, but it would hardly be so dramatic.

While the final preparations were being made, Franchet d'Espérey noted in his diary: 'The cardinal difficulty of the soldier's craft is neither to neglect details nor be swamped by them'. His general instructions showed a concern with the minutiae of battle that is rare in the twentieth century. He was insistent that each unit realize it must continue the attack towards more distant objectives once the forward positions were seized. The metaphor which he used in his directive likened the operation to the taking-off of a squadron of aircraft: the initial assault was intended merely to get the attack 'airborne'. Each unit was to push forward with boldness. 'March in several columns to outflank the enemy directly one column meets with resistance', he wrote. 'Each column should be covered by an advance guard and should keep touch with the neighbouring columns. Watch your flanks and your rear'. The enemy was to be given no chance of preparing new positions. After more than two years of trenches and barbed wire, the Salonika armies were to wage open warfare. 'Desperate Frankie' conveyed his own aggressive spirit to the troops.

Yet he had still not received the go ahead from Clemenceau, and time was running out. On September 4th Lloyd George summoned a conference at 10 Downing Street. Milner, the

War Minister, and Wilson, the C.I.G.S., were present and Guillaumat was sent over from Paris to put the case for an immediate offensive in Macedonia. He was at his most persuasive: the Allied Army was 'good and well found'; 'provided that the mountain artillery which had been promised was sent, there was good prospect of success; the attack could be begun in a week or two by the Serbs who were practically ready'. The British withdrew to another room to deliberate. Wilson still disliked the project, but it evidently kindled a dying flame in Lloyd George. His old enthusiasm for a thrust into Central Europe returned; and he swept aside Wilson's objections. 'The British Government', Guillaumat was informed, 'give their consent to the proposal so far as it concerns them and the British troops'. It was all he wanted.

There were still the Italians to consult. As soon as Guillaumat returned to Paris, he was off again, this time on the Rome Express. Franchet d'Espérey was becoming anxious. All was ready and further delay might prove disastrous: the enemy could discover what was afoot; and there was the risk of the weather breaking. To make his position clear, d'Espérey even sent a staff officer by plane to Rome to ensure that Guillaumat understood the situation. He need not have worried. Guillaumat took the Italians by storm as he had taken 10 Downing Street; they gave their consent.

Triumphantly Franchet d'Espérey made a laconic entry in his diary: 'Tuesday, September 10th. I receive from Clemenceau authority to commence operations when I judge it suitable. Artillery fire to open September 14th. D. Day ('*Jour J*'): 15th September.'

He had won the battle against the Westerners: now there remained only the enemy.

12 / 'The Enemy is in Retreat'

O N THE EVENING of September 13th the Voivode Mišić
rode once more up to the observation post on the Floka
where he had explained his project to Franchet d'Espérey
eleven weeks previously. It was for him to decide whether or
not operations should begin. He would spend the night in the
cramped dugout near the summit. If thick mist veiled the mountains at dawn or if grey rain-clouds swept towards him from the
Vetrenik, then the batteries around and below him would
remain silent, hidden by camouflage-nets for another day, perhaps even longer. For Franchet d'Espérey could not afford a
false start. He was willing to wait until the weather was good;
once the guns began to thunder out, then he would have no
second chance. And the old Serbian general up in the mountains,
with his peasant's nose for bad weather and his veteran's eyes
for a battle, would be far better placed to foretell the prospects
of the day than any meteorological expert back at G.H.Q.

At five in the morning the eastern peak of the Vetrenik shone
pink against the rising sun. A strong wind blew across the valleys
from the Vardar, swiftly dispersing the few puffs of mist that
had lingered after dawn. There were no ominous clouds, not
a scent of rain in the air. It did not take the Voivode long to
make up his mind. A code signal was despatched to every unit
between the Vardar and Monastir, '*Mettez en route quatorze
officiers et huit soldats*'; and each battery commander knew that
on September 14th at 8 a.m. he was to open fire. There were
barely two hours to wait.

The machinery of the great offensive was put in motion.
Over five hundred guns poured their shells into the enemy
defences along eighty miles of front. By the standards of Verdun
it was nothing; but it was without precedent in the Balkans.
And as the gunners had their day, thirty-six thousand French
and Serbian and Italian infantrymen waited with their rifles
ready. Behind them were eighteen squadrons of cavalry. The
Bulgars and the Germans caught unprepared in this sector

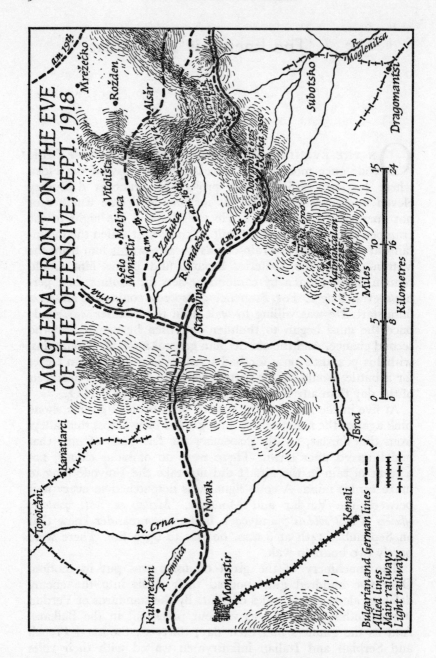

MOGLENA FRONT ON THE EVE
OF THE OFFENSIVE, SEPT. 1918

were outnumbered three to one. Just one more dawn and all
the seventy-five Allied battalions would be moving forward.
Just forty-eight more dawns and the Serbs would re-enter their
capital city.

The bombardment continued throughout the morning of
September 14th, with the greatest concentration of fire falling
on the six miles which separated the western crest of the Vetrenik from the Sokol. A German writer describes how the 'iron
storm', as he calls it, reached 'hurricane force' by ten in the
morning. For more than six hours without intermission the
shells continued to fall on the mountainside, throwing up grey
cascades of rock as they exploded. By the afternoon the air was
thick with smoke and the waiting men battered by the constant
roar, horribly amplified by the ravines and valleys. Although
the wind lay in the opposite direction, the rumble of the bombardment could be heard by the British troops moving up to
the Doiran positions forty miles to the east of the Vetrenik,
sinister thunder on the left. Suddenly in mid-afternoon it seemed
as if the gunners took a siesta. All was quiet, apart from the
high drone of French reconnaissance aircraft seeking to take
photographs of the damage. For half an hour the hot guns
cooled; and then the bombardment began once more, and
continued until darkness swept down on the battlefield.

Now and again, like some distant summer storm which might
blow itself out, the guns could be faintly heard at the headquarters of the 'Army Group von Scholtz' in Skopje, more than
sixty miles to the north, over four distinct ranges of mountain.
General von Scholtz, who had made a name for himself at
Tannenberg, was responsible for the so-called German Eleventh
Army, which was commanded by General von Steuben (with
headquarters at Prilep). It consisted of seven Bulgarian divisions
with the staffs of two German army corps, and the Bulgarian
First Army (three divisions under General Nerezov, with headquarters at Dedeli, eight miles north-west of Doiran). Von
Scholtz's Army Group thus covered more than 130 miles, from
Lake Doiran to the mountains west of the Albanian frontier.
He was not surprised that the Macedonian Front had suddenly
erupted. At the start of the month reports from intelligence
agents in Switzerland had let him know that Franchet d'Espérey
was seeking permission for an offensive; and he was well aware
of the intensive use that had been made in the preceding fortnight of the railways from Salonika to the various sectors of the

Allied line. But he had assumed that the main attack would be made some ten miles west of the Vetrenik–Dobropolje–Sokol sector, with the Kajmakcalan serving as an observation post in much the same way as Mišić did, in fact, use the Floka. Von Scholtz also thought that there would be a secondary attack up the Vardar, a belief strengthened by the costly feint launched by the British 27th Division on the Roche Noire Salient on September 1st. The opening of the Allied bombardment merely confirmed both of his assumptions. The shells were falling on his positions from the Vardar to Monastir, and it was not until after the brief lull in the afternoon that he became aware of the particular attention which was being given to the region of the Dobropolje. So confident was von Scholtz he had correctly read d'Espérey's intentions that, while the bombardment was at its height in the morning, he gave orders for a Bulgarian regiment and a Saxon Jäger battalion to be hurriedly moved south-westwards from Prilep to cover the approaches to Monastir, which was more than twenty miles from the sector threatened by the Allied concentration. In the late evening reports of Serbian patrol activity in front of the Sokol reached German headquarters and, somewhat belatedly, the German and Bulgarian artillery began to attend to the Allied batteries in that area. When, at 10.30, the Bulgarian 30th Regiment intercepted a French battalion patrolling no man's land on the Dobropolje, von Scholtz's staff began to see that they had been deceived. But by then it was too late to take any effective counter-action; the Serbian infantry were due to go forward at 5.30 in the morning and throughout the night the artillery duel hampered the movement of troops.

Franchet d'Espérey had thus succeeded in one of his main intentions. He had ensured that the main assault along the Dobropolje would catch the enemy High Command off its guard, even though Salonika had a notorious record as a repository of confidential information. But it soon became clear, on the morning of September 15th that, in another respect, d'Espérey's plan was working less happily. The artillery barrage had, indeed, made gaps in the wire and obliterated many of the advanced trenches. But it had left little impression on the enemy batteries, or – a more immediate obstacle – on the nests of machine-guns, cunningly sited in the rock and often protected by concrete emplacements so that nothing but a direct hit would put them out of action. Moreover, as yet, the Bulgarian

front-line troops showed none of the war-weariness which was
creeping rapidly over their country. And if the Serbs were
adept at fighting over this unrewarding terrain, then the same
was true of their Balkan rivals, the Bulgars.

The Serbian Sumadija Division stormed up the south-western
slope of the Vetrenik by tracks which twisted around the steep
slopes like paths on the face of a cliff. The eastern Vetrenik
was an even tougher obstacle, with a heavy fire coming down
on the attackers as they hauled themselves forward, scrambling
for footholds in the rock. The Vetrenik was not in Serbian
hands until the early afternoon. Between the Vetrenik and the
Dobropolje the 17th French Colonial Division (which contained four battalions of Senegalese) spent two gruelling hours
holding off five Bulgarian counter-attacks on the heights known
as the Kravički Kamen. There the enemy held positions on a
plateau pocketed with ridges which, in the course of the morning, were stormed and lost and stormed again by both sides
in confused fighting so that, by noon, French and Bulgars alike
were exhausted. Not until four o'clock in the afternoon did
the indefatigable Sumadija Division, advancing from the Vetrenik, go forward with the bayonet alongside the French and
Senegalese and carry the defences. The Dobropolje pyramid
was known to be well-fortified and it proved a difficult obstacle.
The French had to use flame-throwers for the first time in
Macedonia, to overcome fanatically brave resistance by Bulgarian machine-gun units; but in less than two hours fighting
the pyramid was seized, and the Allies were thus provided with
a forward observation post from which artillery bombardments
could be directed on to the second and third lines of defence.
The Sokol, on the other hand, held out all day; only after dusk
were the Serbs and the French together able to carry the summit in a frenzied rush forward. On their flank the Yugoslav
Division, the volunteers who had travelled so many thousands
of miles to fight for their cause, crossed the old frontier between
Greece and Serbia early in the evening in a moment of high
emotional enthusiasm, many of them singing national songs and
(disconcertingly) breaking rank to embrace French comrades-
in-arms fighting beside them. Their objective, the Kozyak, lay
three miles to the north but they moved forward in high spirits,
their fervent patriotism a drug rendering them impervious to
all danger.

Now, as the gun flashes lit the night sky, came the critical

7*

moment upon which Franchet d'Espérey had laid particular emphasis. There could be no pause for congratulation. Mišić ordered his men on; they must press forward through the night. They did so; and by dawn on September 16th the Yugoslav Division was ready to assault the Kozyak, while the Timok Division faced a ridge to the north-east of the main Bulgarian defences, having thrust six miles forward in twelve hours of hard night marching. And to the west the Serbian First Army had joined in the attack, fording a stream two miles beyond the frontier. The offensive was, indeed, 'airborne'. It had taken longer than d'Espérey had expected for the assault troops to seize the advanced defences, but he had never insisted on a rigid timetable and already his commanders in the field were looking towards further prizes.

But the fighting on September 16th was no less grim than on the previous day. On the Kozyak the defenders threw back attack after attack, until the strain became unbearable and shortly before dusk, the Bulgarian defence cracked. Even so the Kozyak was not yet completely in Serbian hands, for a German reserve battalion was rushed up from the neighbourhood of Prilep and dug in on a ridge north of the Kozyak. Yet the sudden giving way of the Bulgars was symptomatic. They had tended to mass their men in a single line and, in consequence, their losses had been heavy. More seriously still, they had as reserves only troops of low calibre. Von Scholtz was alarmed. He had hoped that the Allied assault would peter out once the attackers encountered sustained resistance – this, after all, had been the experience of May 1917. But now it was the Bulgars who were dissipating themselves. He took drastic steps to prevent what he feared would become a rout: he ordered General von Reuter, who had been in command of his reserve, to go with his staff officers to the new position north of the Kozyak and, with revolver in hand, to stem the flight of the Bulgars; and, at the same time, he telegraphed to Hindenburg at the headquarters of the Supreme Command Staff requesting the immediate despatch of a German division to hold the advancing French and Serbs.

At Spa, where Hindenburg and Ludendorff were anxiously analysing reports of Allied concentrations on the Western Front, von Scholtz's message received scant attention. If anyone was to bolster up the Bulgars, it must be Austria-Hungary. Hindenburg forwarded von Scholtz's request to the Chief of the Imperial and Royal General Staff, Arz von Straussenburg. But General Arz could give no positive assurance of help, for Austria-Hungary, hardly less than Bulgaria, was weary of war; and, on the very day that Mišić had set the guns firing along the mountain ranges, the Habsburg Emperor issued a vain appeal for peace, without consulting his German ally. Within a fortnight both Hindenburg and Arz were regretting that they had not given greater priority to von Scholtz's plea for reinforcements, but for the moment it seemed a minor matter. Von Scholtz would have to make do with a German composite brigade, which could be brought by sea from the Crimea to Varna on the Bulgarian coast and thence to the front: it was unlikely that the movement of the brigade would take more than a fortnight, and there was always the prospect of a division of the Imperial and Royal Army arriving – sometime. There was no sense of urgency.

While awaiting a reply from Hindenburg, von Scholtz had taken some precautions with the limited troops at his disposal. He authorized von Reuter to organize the broken and confused units into a composite division and, if the Allied attacks persisted, to retire in good order to the third line of defence. But before von Reuter could even begin to carry out his task, Major-General Rušev, in command of the Bulgarian 2nd Division, had ordered a withdrawal to the third line as soon as the Kozyak was lost. It seemed almost as if the 2nd Division had panicked, for it had fallen back without warning either of its neighbours. During the second night of the battle they had to extricate themselves hurriedly from the risk of flank attacks; the French and the Serbs harried them relentlessly.

Franchet d'Espérey had every reason to be pleased when he assessed the reports from the battle area on the morning of September 17th. A salient twenty miles wide and six miles deep had been driven into the enemy Front. There could be no doubt that 'the offensive had made a certain progress'. It was now essential to prevent von Scholtz from plugging the gap with troops moved from other sectors. The time had come to press forward east of the Vardar. The British and the Greeks were to complete their preparations to attack the positions around Lake Doiran on the following morning.

Meanwhile, Mišić's army continued throughout the day to exploit its success. Hardly a shot was fired as it moved forward during the morning towards the enemy third line; and General

Henrys's army, to its left, also met little resistance. But the
German battalion which had fought so stubbornly on the Kozyak, the 13th Saxon Jägers, once again held off all the attacks
of the Yugoslav Division on the right flank of the advance, even
though the German unit was under strength, short of ammunition and without much of its equipment. If von Scholtz had
been able to concentrate all the German battalions in the Balkans on this one sector, he might well have halted the Allied
advance, but the policy of the High Command had been to use
the German troops as a leavening for each of the Bulgarian
armies, and while the situation north of the Dobropolje was
becoming desperate, there was the equivalent of a German
division inactive to the east of the Struma.

Yet General von Reuter assured von Scholtz that he could
hold the third line of defence. And so, no doubt, he might have
done had it not been for Major-General Rušev. For as the
Serbs moved cautiously forward to the main Bulgarian lines
at three in the afternoon, Rušev repeated the manœuvre that
had so nearly brought disaster on the previous day; he ordered
the Bulgarian Second Division to fall back behind the Crna
rather than wait to be attacked. Once again there was some sound
sense behind Rušev's decision, for the Crna is a swift-flowing
stream which cuts its way through the mountains in narrow
defiles, difficult to cross. But Rušev had given the order without
consulting either of the divisions on his flank. For the second
day running the Serbs had the good fortune to find a gap nearly
five miles wide facing them and, by dusk, their vanguard was
able to reach the Crna more than six miles north of the point
on the river from which the offensive had started. German
troops were still strongly entrenched to the west of the Crna;
but the ultimate Allied line of advance was to be north-eastwards up the river towards its junction with another mountain
stream, the Belasnica, and in due course to the Vardar; and it
was this very region that had been left denuded of defenders
by Rušev's abrupt withdrawal.

Nor were Rušev's troops the only Bulgars to avoid battle.
Eleven miles to the east some of the regiments in the Third
Division were in a state of mutiny. Von Scholtz had no alternative but to order a retirement behind the Belasnica during the
night of September 17th–18th. But now the battle of the Dobropolje, as French military historians have called the first stage
of the offensive, was won. An arrowhead, which at its apex

was fifteen miles north of the old Allied lines, had been thrust into the enemy defences. And, as von Scholtz looked at his map on the morning of September 18th, he could see clearly enough that the arrow was pointing directly up the Crna. If it continued at its present rate of progress, it would reach the Vardar and the supply depots at Gradsko within three days. Once Gradsko fell, his whole Army Group would be split in two. This prospect was bad enough: but he had, on that morning, a more immediate concern; the offensive was spreading eastwards to his left flank around Lake Doiran, and he now had to guard against an advance across the Bulgarian frontier itself.

In the small hours of September 18th a deceptively inconsequential code message was telephoned to each divisional headquarters in the British command, '508 bottles of beer will be sent to you'. It was a signal that the attack was to be launched at eight minutes past five that morning, one hour and three-quarters before sunrise. There had been weeks of heartbreaking training, much of it on what claimed to be replicas of the eventual objectives. Everyone knew full well what was coming; the only question was when, and now that doubt had been finally resolved.

While the French and Serbian troops had pressed forward over ground which was new to them, the XII Corps were once again to fight their way across ravines and up hills that were full of bitter memories. So much seemed unchanged after sixteen months of watching and waiting: General Wilson still had his headquarters down at Yanesh; the ghost town of Doiran itself remained near and inaccessible, suggesting at times a mirage, with its one minaret shimmering in the heat haze; and over the ramshackle houses, the trenches and the lake loomed the triple humps of hills – the Petit Couronné, the Grand Couronné and Pip Ridge, with the Devil's Eye observing day after day every movement for miles around. Many veterans of the earlier battle were still in the line, for no less than fourteen of the twenty-two infantry battalions which had taken part in the two assaults of 1917 remained on that same three miles of front. Of course, sickness and the arrival of fresh drafts had changed the composition of the individual units, but each contained a core of hardened warriors who knew what hell awaited them now that the order for battle had been given.

There were, none the less, significant **differences** between the situation in the spring of 1917 and the autumn of 1918. Most ominous of all the changes was the greater strength of the Bulgarian defences: the batteries were by now shielded with casemates of reinforced concrete; and concrete dugouts and concrete machine-gun nests had been sited in the hills. Conversely, the most heartening development on the Allied side was the arrival of the 'Seres Division', under General Zymbrakakis, which comprised three regiments of Greek infantry and one of French Zouaves, and which was to hold the three-quarters of a mile of trenches down by the lakeside and lend support two miles further inland, west of Jumeaux Ravine. Yet, despite this addition to Milne's army, the Allies were outnumbered in this sector by the defenders, partly because so many of the British battalions were ravaged by malaria and influenza. The Bulgars here were not merely stronger on paper; they had far more spirit than their compatriots along the Crna, and their divisional commander on Pip Ridge, General Vazov, was an able soldier, idolized by his men. It was a grim prospect for the waiting infantry.

There were changes, too, in the plan of operations. Ever since the near disaster of the previous year, a night attack had been ruled out. This time the first troops were to go forward in the murk before dawn. And there was to be no lengthy period of preliminary bombardment. Gas-shells were directed at the enemy's batteries during the night in the vain hope that the gun-crews would be put out of action before morning, but there were not enough shells for a long and sustained barrage. The greatest attention was given to the tactical innovation, the assault by the XVI Corps on the defences of the Blaga Planina, seven miles north of Doiran. It was by means of an out-flanking movement of this character that the Greeks had forced the Bulgars to evacuate Doiran in the Second Balkan War, and it was hoped that a similar manoeuvre, provided it were not detected by the enemy, might considerably ease the task of the XII Corps, attacking from the south. To deceive the Bulgarians, the artillery of the 28th Division, which was to cover the XVI Corps, remained silent in the night before the battle.

The XII Corps opened the attack. The Greeks on the lakeside swept forward as they had done at Skra di Legen. Within three-quarters of an hour they had emerged from the scrub and low hills and entered the town of Doiran, establishing themselves more than a mile from their original lines. Another

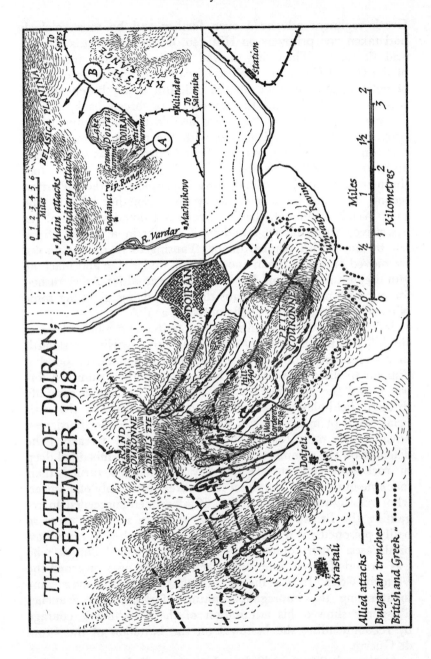

THE BATTLE OF DOIRAN,
SEPTEMBER, 1918

Allied attacks ⟶
Bulgarian trenches ▬ ▬
British and Greek " ⋯⋯⋯

Greek regiment advanced even further and by seven o'clock had taken 700 prisoners on Hill 340, between Jumeaux Ravine and the town. Then they moved forward up the steep slope of the Grand Couronné itself towards the Bulgarian second line of defence, another mile up the hill. But there the enemy fire was so formidable that the Greeks were forced back, and in the course of the day they were unable to make any further progress. All went well at first with the attack of 22nd Division, on the Greek left, and the Petit Couronné was surrounded and firmly in Allied hands within half-an-hour; but here, too, the men were unable to make any impression on the Bulgarian second line, and there were heavy losses. Further left still, the 11th Welch Regiment, 'having been well dosed with rum' (as a survivor wrote later), found itself caught in a pocket of gas left by the British bombardment. 'Pausing to fit on gas masks, we moved on again. Then another stop, under rifle and machine gun fire, to take them off. We had several casualties. As we rushed for our first mark, stick bombs dropped among us lifting some of us off our feet, but some fell not to rise again'.

It was a similar story from other units. The whole slope of the hill was under a pall of smoke and dust, swirling westwards in a breeze from off the lake. Battalion commanders found it difficult to discover what was happening as they stumbled forward, and the landmarks which had been studied so carefully through field-glasses were obliterated. Yet beneath the artificial cloud of battle the 7th Battalion, South Wales Borderers, advanced for more than a mile and a half until it reached the defences on the summit of the Grand Couronné, embedded deep in rock and concrete. Desperately the Bulgars turned their machine-guns on the battalion from three sides; only one officer, who was slightly wounded, and fifty-five men succeeded in regaining the British lines and thirty of these survivors were so badly poisoned by the British gas cloud that they became hospital cases. Their commander, Lieutenant-Colonel Burges, who was wounded three times and taken prisoner, was awarded the Victoria Cross. It was the nearest that the British ever came to storming the impregnable natural fortress, and Franchet d'Espérey showed his admiration of the Welshmen's courage by recommending the bestowal on the battalion of the Croix de Guerre.

At times it seems as if there hung over Doiran on that first day of battle much of the glory and vain heroism of Balaclava.

Sick men and weak battalions spent their lives like bullets on the open slopes. The heaviest casualties of all fell on the 66th Brigade (the 12th Cheshires, 9th South Lancashires and 8th King's Shropshire Light Infantry) which was called upon to advance up Pip Ridge and which was mown down by machine-gun fire from in front and from both flanks. The enemy position remained unshaken and only one in three of the attackers suc-ceeded in regaining the comparative safety of the ravine from which they had scrambled a few hours earlier.

By ten in the morning it was clear that the attack had already failed. General Wilson had followed the course of the battle from his advanced headquarters on the Piton Rocheux, three miles behind the British line. Wearily he telephoned General Milne, who had come up to Yanesh; they agreed that there could be no resumption of the assault that day. But, if they could muster the men, they would go forward again tomorrow; Franchet d'Espérey was determined that not a single Bulgarian unit should be allowed to slip away to the other side of the Vardar.

Much now depended upon the XVI Corps attack on the Blaga Planina, for if real progress were made in that region there was a chance of cutting the communications of the de-fenders of Pip Ridge and the Grand Couronné. But this was a very different type of operation. Four and a half miles of flat and wooded plain separated the outposts of the two armies north of the lake. It was necessary for the attackers to descend the steep slopes of the Krusha Range by donkey-tracks and mop up the advanced Bulgarian posts in a series of small woods before contact could be made with the main Bulgarian defences.

Half an hour after the start of the battle at Doiran, signal rockets sending down a cascade of silver and gold stars burst over the north-eastern shore of the lake. So far so good; the Greek Crete Division had captured the outposts in the woods. But thereafter all was confusion. The Greeks had never even met the officers of the British troops who were supporting them, and there was a complete failure of the two allies to understand each other's needs. No British guns supported the first Greek attack, for there was virtually no communication between the infantry and the artillery. By noon the situation had improved, but there was still no breach in the defences. A second attack was ordered for the middle of the afternoon. Through some quirk in the fortunes of war – perhaps deliberate, perhaps accidental – the long grass, parched and dry in the summer heat, burst into flame as the foremost troops of the Crete Division were creeping forward through the open fields. That same high wind, which had scattered the gas clouds on the other side of the lake, fanned the flames until the Greeks were sent scurrying back to the shelter of the foothills pursued by a tide of fire. The whole enterprise was a sorry failure.

That afternoon, at five o'clock, General Wilson ordered preparations to begin for a further assault on the hills above Doiran next morning. Two of the Greek regiments (the Seres Division) were still able to raise enough troops for an attack, but otherwise Wilson had to turn elsewhere. He brought the 77th Brigade up from reserve and summoned back the 65th Brigade, which only twelve days before had been withdrawn from the line because of the high incidence of sickness. Franchet d'Espérey authorized the transference of the Zouave Regiment, which had been attached to the Greeks, to the XII Corps.

The attack of September 19th was no more successful. It was the turn of the Scottish regiments (the 12th Argyll and Sutherland Highlanders, the 8th Royal Scots Fusiliers, the 11th Scottish Rifles) to match the valour and determination which the Welsh and English infantry had already shown. Yet, tragically, the parallel with the Crimean campaign was even more marked than on the previous day. Blunders and misunderstandings proliferated: orders not to attack which reached the men too late; messengers lost in the murk of battle; an advance by British troops through their own barrage; and a complete failure on the part of the Zouaves to reach the point from which they were to launch their attack. Not a single trench or outpost was taken and retained that day. Within six hours Wilson and Milne had seen that they were asking the impossible: they agreed that nothing could justify the losses which would follow fresh attacks up the slopes of the hills.

Thus, after two days fighting, the Allies were left with the gains they had made early on the first morning – Doiran town and the Petit Couronné and its approaches. The casualties were staggeringly high. More than one British battalion was reduced to a quarter of its effective strength; and the British losses alone were twice as great as those suffered by the French and the Serbs in the initial attacks on the Dobropolje. Yet, while their allies had the consolation of a victory, the British had moved towards a stalemate of exhaustion. They had, none the less, fulfilled one of their tasks: not a single Bulgarian unit which was in the line when the first attack was made fought on any other sector of the front. It was, unfortunately, a negative achievement; and the men whose courage had made it possible passed unnoticed by a public dazzled with spectacular triumphs elsewhere.

General Nerezov, the commander of the Bulgarian First Army, had tried for many years to look and think like a Prussian staff officer; and by 1918 he was able to carry a Hindenburg moustache and have the hair on his shell-shaped head shaved in a style of which Ludendorff would have approved. These affectations were not unjustified. He was probably the ablest officer in Bulgaria and certainly the most audacious. The repulse of the British attack on the morning of September 18th delighted him. He visited the front line troops, took note of the prisoners; and decided on a plan fully in character. These opponents of his were clearly sick and weary and under-strength. If he could persuade the Bulgarian Second Army on the Struma to move forward from Seres, he was prepared to counter-attack at Doiran. Together the two Bulgarian armies would converge on Salonika itself while Franchet d'Espérey's best troops were deep in the mountains around the Crna.

Wasting no time, Nerezov telephoned Bulgarian G.H.Q. at Kyustendil, seventy miles to the north, that very morning. The commander-in-chief had, on the eve of the Allied offensive, gone to Vienna to visit an ear specialist and his responsibilities had devolved upon his deputy, General Todorov, a wily old goat-beard who was expert at every manœuvre round the conference table. Nerezov's message came at a fortuitous moment, for Todorov was about to set out for Prilep where the Germans wished to confer with him. It promised to be a tiresome meeting: there would be recriminations over the behaviour of the Second Division on the Crna and reproaches at the mutinous state of the Third Division, to their left; and it was unfortunate that, on the previous day, Todorov had telegraphed to Hindenburg desperately pleading for at least six German divisions to be sent to Macedonia. But now Nerezov had given Todorov new heart. Here was clear evidence of the vigorous aggressive spirit of the Bulgarian Army. The German commanders would speak of falling back; but a Bulgarian was proposing to advance on

Salonika. Nerezov's proposal would silence the German critics; perhaps Todorov almost believed in it himself.

The conference assembled at the headquarters of General von Steuben in Prilep. No disturbing news had come in that morning and, for the last time, the Germans and Bulgars had freedom to decide on their course of action. Todorov put forward Nerezov's proposal. But where, asked the Germans incredulously, were the material and transport to be found for a sudden advance? The whole idea was far too risky. Then, argued Todorov, they must fall back to a natural mountain defence line through southern Serbia and the ranges south of Sofia. He spoke as one who knew his Balkans, but it was far too drastic for his German ally. Von Steuben wanted to entice the French and the Serbs deeper into the mountain valleys so that, at the right moment, the Eleventh Army and the Bulgarian Third Division, with the backing of German reserves, could fall upon their flanks. The best way to deal with the dangerous arrowhead was to snap it off. Everyone around the conference table was convinced that with each mile he penetrated into the mountains Franchet d'Espérey's supply problem would become worse and worse. Todorov accepted the German plan and the Prilep meeting broke up. There would be a gradual, and orderly, withdrawal.

Todorov, it is interesting to note, had no experience of the Doiran Front. Before being recalled to Kyustendil he had commanded the Second Army, with his headquarters at Sveti Vrach on the upper Struma, twenty miles north of the Rupel Pass. Nerezov, on the other hand, had spent two years building up the defences of Doiran; he was so identified with the region that the Bulgars had re-named one of the hills in his honour. Todorov did not understand the significance of Doiran for its defenders. When he returned from Prilep, as a matter of course he issued instructions for the First Army to fall back as part of the general retreat. The order struck Nerezov as more devastating than any British barrage. He had hoped to receive the command to go forward; sadly he realized that the line his men had held so stubbornly was to be evacuated without a shot being fired.

A Bulgarian writer describes how the First Army, in the clear moonlight, was preparing to meet renewed British attacks and even, perhaps, to go over to the offensive. Now, before dawn on September 20th, the operational order for a retreat went out from Nerezov's headquarters at Dedeli: the First Army must fall back to cover the withdrawal of the Third Division on its right. In a stunned silence the divisional commanders returned to their advanced positions. It had been a bitter blow for them, but they felt there was one small crumb of consolation: they, at any rate, were not retreating under pressure from their adversaries.

It was the airmen who first let Milne know what was happening. Two De Havilland 9s of 47 Squadron, R.A.F. reconnoitred the Vardar and Strumica valleys on the morning of September 21st. At 10.40 one of their observers noted: 'The defile west of Rabrovo on the Strumica–Rabrovo road was packed with transport, and round Rabrovo were anything up to 500 lorries and H(orse) T(ransport) waggons waiting to go up the road'. The significance of the report could not be missed: Rabrovo was two miles north of Nerezov's headquarters at Dedeli. And it was the same on every road leading back into Old Bulgaria. The enemy was in full flight.

That night British patrols found the outposts facing them empty and deserted. An uncanny silence had descended on Pip Ridge. A few hours later the Seres Division moved up the Grand Couronné. The dead still lay unburied on the slopes where they had fallen four days previously. But now the Greeks met no resistance. The Devil's Eye and all the other concrete emplacements had been abandoned. As an officer wrote at the time, the Bulgars had 'packed up and cleared off'. There was nothing for the British to do but admire the complexity of the defences which had defied them for so long. It was a moment for relief rather than for exaltation.

Yet there was little time for sad heart-searching. The long columns of lorries and horse-drawn vehicles moving slowly along the impossible roads were mercilessly bombed and machine-gunned by the R.A.F. Not a German plane was to be seen and the Bulgars themselves offered little resistance. It was the first occasion upon which air power had been brought to bear on Balkan troops. Burnt and twisted lorries, dead animals and dead men blocked the route of escape. Regiments which, less than a week before, had been in a state of high elation were unnerved. They had grown accustomed to the never-ending thunder of enemy guns and they had met the challenge of poison gas with resolution; but, as the steep sides of the ravines closed in to

left and right of them and the road ahead seemed impenetrable, there was no escape from the swooping planes unless
each man could fend for himself. Panic-stricken, the retreating
troops fled over the mountain paths, leaving guns and stores
and supplies abandoned by the side of the road. Todorov and
his German allies had envisaged an 'orderly retreat'. They had
no notion of the havoc created by air attacks on a slow moving
column caught in the confines of a rocky valley. An army ceased
to exist.

   Meanwhile, Milne was hastily mustering troops to pursue
the enemy. The XII and XVI Corps must move forward with
all possible speed, despite the sweltering heat and their weariness. Not all could understand what was happening. The brilliant young painter, Stanley Spencer, was serving as a Private
in the 7th battalion of the Royal Berkshire Regiment. He recorded his experiences with the sensitive eye of an artist: 'We
went by a special track which had been much camouflaged.
As the track turned among the hills the camouflage screens
reached across it over our heads like a grim reminder of triumphant bunting. They consisted of chicken wire and bits of rag.
It was very mysterious to see the rags passing over our heads
in the increasing darkness, like bird heralds coming from what
I was walking into'. But next day, as the Berkshires advanced,
they found no sign of the Bulgars. Spencer's forebodings seemed
unmerited. Instead of charging the enemy with fixed bayonet,
he found himself bathing in the river under a blistering sun.
'All felt something extraordinary had occurred. Was the war
coming to an end?' It was a question posed by thousands of
men in this strange and unpredictable campaign.

Franchet d'Espérey and Mišić were fully alive to the danger
of being trapped in a narrow pocket, and there was never any
serious likelihood that the Germans would be able to carry
out the plan which had looked so promising around the conference table in Prilep. The Serbian First Army had been seeking to establish a bridgehead west of the lower Crna ever since
the morning of September 18th, and on the following day,
General d'Anselme's troops had, with Greek support, begun
to enlarge the breach on the western flank by storming the slopes
of a 7,000 foot mountain known as the Dzena, an operation
which lasted almost forty-eight hours. By now the Bulgarian
Third Division was beginning to dissolve completely, although

Prince Boris (who was to become ruler of a defeated Bulgaria within a fortnight) fearlessly drove from one threatened unit to another, desperately seeking to put new heart into his men.

By noon on September 22nd there was little doubt that all was going well for the Allies. The Serbs had, on the right, reached the Vardar twenty miles north of the old battle-line; and, on the left, they had established themselves west of the Crna. The Italian 35th Division had taken Hill 1050, which was to them what the Grand Couronné had been to the British. With the good news of the Bulgarian retreat confirmed by air reconnaissance, Franchet d'Espérey issued a general order to each of the Allied Armies of the Orient:

'The enemy is in retreat on the whole Front between Monastir and Lake Doiran. We have now to rout him, to take prisoners from his ranks, and to capture his material by an unceasing and resolute pursuit. Outflank resistance and push forward light detachments, which should establish themselves on his line of retreat. The cavalry, whose hour is come, should precede the infantry columns and open the way for them.'

The hour of the cavalry had, indeed, come. So far there had been little enough for the horsemen to do in Macedonia, apart from patrols along the Struma. But now the campaign was becoming fluid. Much would depend on the cavalry division attached to the Serbian Second Army. But, above all, Franchet d'Espérey relied upon the 'Brigade Jouinot-Gambetta', the cavalry group in General Henrys's army.

This French colonial brigade consisted of the 1st and 4th Chasseurs d'Afrique, a section of armoured cars and six squadrons of Spahis from Morocco, natural horsemen with proud traditions of their own. Mounted on Barb stallions as sure-footed as any mountain goat and with long hair streaming out from beneath light blue turbans, the Spahis made a terrifyingly impressive mobile column. Their commander, General Jouinot-Gambetta, was hardly less impulsive than Franchet d'Espérey. He was the nephew of the great radical statesman of the early years of the Third Republic, Léon Gambetta, who in 1870 had flown out of beleaguered Paris in a balloon so as to organize the resistance of provincial France; and the nephew had much of the uncle's initiative and enterprise.

For six days Jouinot-Gambetta had waited impatiently on

the outskirts of Florina. He was convinced that the offensive would, in time, give him the opportunity of leading his brigade, not merely into Serbia and to the Danube, but into Germany itself. But only on September 22nd did he receive his orders from General Henrys. His Brigade was to seize Prilep and wheel westwards to destroy the retreating enemy columns. The Brigade rode out to Novak and the next morning moved through burning villages down the Crna valley, with the sound of munition dumps exploding as the Bulgars fled north-eastwards. What was probably the last great cavalry march in the continent of Europe had begun.

The Brigade rested its horses at Dobrusevo that morning; and, at that moment, it was overtaken by Franchet d'Espérey himself, who as usual was visiting by motor-car the various units along the Front. D'Espérey verbally countermanded Henrys's orders and instructed Jouinot-Gambetta that once he had taken Prilep he was to move on to Skopje itself. This was a far more ambitious undertaking, for Skopje was nearly sixty miles by road from Prilep and the most important town in Macedonia after Salonika.

The advance-guard reached Prilep at 1 p.m. on September 23rd and found that the town had been evacuated by the Germans and the Bulgarians. The Serb inhabitants were so exhilarated that they mobbed the young officer who commanded the first patrol and carried him on their shoulders to what had been the German headquarters. It was just five days since Todorov had arrived there with Nerezov's proposal of a counter-offensive. Apart from the burning remains of the stores, there was no sign now of the enemy. When Jouinot-Gambetta himself arrived a couple of hours later he found that the picturesque little town, with its white minarets, low wooden houses, and rows of black cypresses, plane-trees and almonds had 'an enchantingly oriental atmosphere'. (It still does today, although the minarets and most of the wooden houses have long since vanished.)

Next morning the brigade resumed the march into the hills towards the Babuna Pass. More than twenty miles to the north-east, the 17th Colonial Division of General Pruneau and the Yugoslav Division were also moving towards Skopje up the Vardar river; and that same day (September 25th) they succeeded in entering the vital town of Gradsko. Around Gradsko the Bulgars and Germans had erected a sprawling village of huts and had filled them with stores and supplies to

carry to any point on the Macedonian Front. Hindenburg himself described Gradsko as 'the most important centre of all
communications in the Macedonian theatre of war'. The town
was stoutly defended by both German and Bulgarian detachments, but faced by an outflanking movement the German
commander pulled his men back, and all the stores went up
in vast spirals of black smoke. There was no longer any talk
from the German side of catching the Allied force on its flanks.
All that the Germans could hope was that the invaders would
outpace their supply columns. A year later Hindenburg wrote
in his memoirs, 'It seemed impossible that without rest the
enemy would be able to bring his strong formations forward
to Uskub (Skopje) and the frontier of Old Bulgaria. How would
he overcome the difficulty of supplies, for we had utterly destroyed the railway and the roads?' When, in due course, Franchet
d'Espérey read Hindenburg's words, with justifiable pride he
scribbled in the margin of the book, 'He did not know me!'

Yet it was, indeed, no ordinary or conventional army that
Franchet d'Espérey was ruthlessly pressing forward towards
Skopje (against the advice of even his own subordinate commanders). The Serbs were the hardiest troops in Europe: they were
tough and they were frugal, travelling for days without regular
rations, living off the countryside. The Spahis, too, gave few
problems on this score. But the swift advance began to tell on
the colonial infantry. On the day after his men had entered
Gradsko, General Pruneau wrote in a letter: 'My *poilus* have
their clothes in rags and most of them are bare-footed. We
have moved at such a pace that all replenishment was out of
the question. On some days we have covered forty kilometres
(twenty-five miles). . . . But it is this rapidity that has made
our victory great and complete'. So, no doubt, it was – but it
would be another four days before the bare-footed *poilus* had a
chance to recuperate.

The Brigade Jouinot-Gambetta had the best chance of reach-
Skopje first; but it would never be strong enough to fight its
way through determined opposition by any heavy concentration of troops. In the early hours of September 25th Jouinot-
Gambetta reached the foot of the Babuna Pass. The Serbs had
made a stand there during their retreat in 1915, and the Spahis
began to climb up the winding track with caution, half expecting the clear moonlight to glint on the muzzles of defending
machine-guns. All remained silent, however; until suddenly

the French saw a body of men coming towards them. But it was not the enemy: Italian prisoners of war were taking advantage of the chaos in the retreating army to make their way back to the 35th Division.

By ten o'clock in the morning the Brigade had reached the summit of the pass, and, now, at last it met the enemy. The Bulgarian Fourth Division, which had pulled back before it could be engaged by the main frontal assault in the mountains, was desperately defending Veleš, and the Serbian First Army could make little progress. Jouinot-Gambetta was faced with a difficult decision: should he assist the Serb infantry to break through to Veleš and the Vardar route to Skopje, or should he leave it to engage the main enemy force and strike out northwards on his own? The land to his left looked uninviting – wild peaks nearly 6,000 feet high, sprawling woodland. There was no road for his armoured cars, merely tracks barely shown on the map. Yet if he remained on the recognized route it was clear that he would be able to advance only at the pace of the Serb infantry and the enemy would dispute each mile, summoning up all his reserves to defend Skopje. Franchet d'Espérey wanted Skopje in Allied hands as speedily as possible. Jouinot-Gambetta had no real choice: leaving the armoured cars to assist the Serbs and giving the Spahis orders to fight a holding operation against possible pursuers and then follow him as soon as they could safely disengage, he took to the mountains at Starigrad. From then on, the Brigade was on its own: French hadquarters had no idea of its whereabouts; and Jouinot-Gambetta lost all contact with the rest of the advancing army.

The Brigade trudged on across the ranges of the Golesnica Planina throughout September 26th. The men soon abandoned all attempts to ride their horses; they had to lead them painfully along the winding, narrow paths. On the first day they covered eleven miles. Jouinot-Gambetta allowed them a rest of four hours and then they moved on through the night, climbing higher and higher for another ten miles. At dawn on September 27th they were 5,000 feet up in a wooded gorge and both men and horses were near exhaustion. Throughout that day they rested, hoping that the Spahis would catch them up. Early on the third morning the Brigade was re-united and the whole force began the descent to the Vardar valley which was reached late that afternoon, seven miles south of Skopje. The men were surprised to find the railway, the vital artery for all the enemy armies, unguarded by patrols. They spent that night, still un-observed, in open country west of the main road and railway route into the town. The lights of Skopje burned brightly ahead of them until a heavy autumn mist swept down from the moun-tains and enveloped both the attackers and their objective.

Jouinot-Gambetta could easily have been courting disaster. He had with him only three weary cavalry regiments, with no artillery beyond the light 37 millimetre guns which pack-horses had carried across the mountains. He had no idea of the strength of the defenders. Perhaps it was as well that he did not know: for the city had a garrison of seven battalions, the majority of them Bulgarian, but commanded by a German colonel with a sizeable German contingent. To support the defenders there were four batteries of guns and an armoured railway-train, which had already caused havoc at Gradsko and Veleš. But there was a marked contrast in the morale of the opposing forces; although tired, the Moroccans were in high spirits while the Bulgars were despondent and on bad terms with their German ally. The whole town was full of rumours of imminent disaster. In panic, the Bulgars had already set fire to ammunition dumps which threw up red and black flames and 'made the cypresses burn like giant torches'.

The mist lifted soon after eight in the morning of September 29th, and, as the sun came up, the Bulgars south of the town were startled to see squadrons of Spahis riding down on them. It seemed as if the wild stories circulating on the previous even-ing were true. The High Command might believe the main enemy force to be twenty miles away, but here was the advance guard already at the approaches to the town. The Bulgars broke off the fight and ran.

It was a different matter with the German detachments. As the Chasseurs approached the burning railway station, they came under heavy fire from the armoured train and a German counter-attack forced the French patrols to fall back. But the Spahis had crossed the river and were now wheeling round so as to move into the town from the north. All that the Ger-mans could do was to save themselves and get the armoured train away. Belching out black smoke as the stoker tried to raise full pressure, the train pulled out to the north with the machine-gun bullets making no more impression on its steel waggons than peas thrown into a cullender. Yet although the train escaped, the main prize was in the hands of the French

by nine o'clock. Five heavy German guns were captured with
their ammunition and there were 139 German prisoners taken,
as well as more than 200 Bulgars. As in Prilep, the Serb population was deliriously happy. 'The women kept kissing our
hands while crying with joy', wrote Jouinot-Gambetta later,
looking back on it all.

At 10 a.m. a French aeroplane flew over and the Brigade
arranged panels on the grass to inform the pilot that they were
in control of the city. It seems as if Franchet d'Espérey's headquarters could hardly credit the news of Skopje's fall, for four
hours later two more aircraft came to verify the report. The
doubt was understandable. Since leaving Prilep, Jouinot-
Gambetta's Moroccans had covered 57 miles in six days, over
some of the most difficult country in the Balkans. When his
patrols entered the city the main Serbian Army was still, by
road, thirty miles to the south.

It was true enough: the second largest town in Serbia had
been liberated. And that evening Franchet d'Espérey was able
to pass on his information to Bulgarian delegates who had come
to sue for peace. The war was, indeed, coming to an end for
Bulgaria. The cavalry had seized their hour when it came.

13 / Orient Express

THE DRIVE ON Skopje was not alone responsible for bringing the Bulgars to the point of surrender, and in many ways it represented a more ominous portent for the Germans than their ally. Unquestionably the most serious menace to the Bulgars came from the British and the Greeks. Once the R.A.F. had confirmed that the enemy was pulling back, the 27th and 28th Divisions had pressed forward rapidly from the Grand Couronné up into the Belasica Planina, and the Greek Crete Division had advanced into the hills north-east of Lake Doiran. At the same time Milne moved the XVI Corps over to his left flank, intending that it should drive the enemy out of the Strumica valley and penetrate into Bulgaria itself. General Briggs, the XVI Corps commander, established his headquarters at Stojakov on September 24th, with Doiran eight miles to the north-east and with Djevdjeli and the Vardar valley two miles below him to the west. His forward troops had made contact with the retreating Bulgars on the previous day in the mountain pass five miles further north, and although the advance was delayed by constant shelling, the Derbyshire Yeomanry rode across the Bulgarian frontier near the village of Kosturino early on September 25th, closely followed by the infantry of the 79th Brigade.

As yet there was no serious threat to Sofia or any other town of importance in Bulgaria. The capital was one hundred and thirty miles from Kosturino, over five ranges of mountains running across the natural line of advance. A people devoted to a genuine national cause could have checked the invader and left him to the mercy of a grim winter. But the Bulgars had long since lost all enthusiasm for the war. Ever since the formation of the Balkan League in 1912 successive governments had followed ambitious policies well beyond the country's resources of manpower and material. The total population before the Balkan Wars was under $4\frac{1}{2}$ million: 55,000 trained soldiers had perished in the Balkan Wars alone and another 100,000 had already died in the campaigns of the Great War. There had thus been a higher proportion of the active population in Bulgaria killed by war over the preceding six years than in Germany or France. All this was grim enough: but the effects of the war went far beyond the stark record of lives lost. Such industry as the country possessed was geared to the German military machine. Agriculture was particularly badly hit, for the land was starved, not only of fertilizers and mechanical means of cultivation, but also of the able-bodied peasants who could gather in the crops. With the western countries ranged against Bulgaria, there was no market for the vital export, tobacco. A small group of businessmen made high profits from German contracts, but for thousands of workers there was nothing but increasing burdens and the menace of near-starvation.

By 1918 the war had, in fact, failed to give the Bulgarian people one tangible reward for their sacrifices, and conditions were ripe for a revolution. With the experience of Mother Russia in their minds, the ruling class feared for its very existence. King Ferdinand, sensing the danger, made a gesture to appease public opinion in June when he dismissed his pro-German Ministry and invited Alexander Malinov, a moderate democrat with Western sympathies, to form a government. Malinov was able to organize a more equitable distribution of food supplies but the High Command prevented him from carrying out his original intention of opening negotiations for peace. Yet commonsense was making it clear to some of the senior officers that the best course for Bulgaria was to get out of the war. On September 16th, from Second Army headquarters at Sveti Vrach, General Lukov sought permission from Ferdinand to put out feelers to the Allies. But Ferdinand knew by now that once he broke with the Germans he would probably forfeit his throne. His reply to Lukov was a peremptory, 'Go out and get killed in your present lines'. It was an order Lukov had no intention of obeying.

As the armies wavered in the face of the Allied offensive, and the onslaught from the air turned the retreat into a rout, the latent unrest in the country broke into open acts of defiance. On September 23rd and September 24th left-wing socialists organized Soviets in Pechaev, Berovo and Tsarevo Selo. A day later, while the first British units were crossing the frontier, mutinous bands of deserters tried to take over Bulgarian General Headquarters at Kyustendil and commandeered railway trains

to take them back to their homes and families. The most re-
bellious spirits made for Radomir, a small manufacturing town
halfway between Kyustendil and Sofia, where there was already
a powerful republican movement. With the whole structure of
society challenged, Ferdinand gave way to the joint pleading
of Malinov and Lukov and authorized General Todorov to send
emissaries to British Headquarters to seek a cessation of hostilities.

The British troops had no idea of the situation within the
country they were invading. After spending a night in Kosturino the Derbyshire Yeomanry rode off along the road towards
Strumica early on September 26th. They had covered only a
short distance when a huge German-made staff car approached
them with a white flag mounted on a pole beside the driver's
window. Inside the car were two Bulgarian officers with a
letter from Todorov to Milne asking him to intercede with
Franchet d'Espérey so that Bulgaria could obtain a two-day
respite from battle while negotiations took place for an armistice. The car was sent on to Milne at Yanesh and eventually
to Franchet d'Espérey himself. But he had no intention of giving
the retreating Bulgars a breathing space: the officers were sent
back to Strumica while he telegraphed Clemenceau for approval
of the conditions which he wished to impose on Bulgaria. Meanwhile the Allied advance was to continue.

Once the rumour spread that Ferdinand was seeking peace,
the disorders in Bulgaria worsened. A republic was formally
proclaimed in Radomir on September 27th and several thousand insurgents began to march on Sofia. The only Bulgarian
troops in the capital loyal to the king were his personal body-
guard and a detachment of young military cadets; but the
German 217th Division, which Hindenburg had ordered to
be transferred from the Crimea to the Balkan Front, had arrived at Varna and it was hurriedly concentrated in Sofia where,
without much difficulty, it broke up the rebel troops. By now
all the responsible authorities in the capital had come to see
the urgent need for an armistice, and the acting American
chargé d'affaires, as the representative of the only western
power not at war with Bulgaria, sought to mediate, sending
pressing telegrams to Washington in the hope that diplomatic
intervention might stave off a communist revolution, and trying
to contact Franchet d'Espérey.

Again peace delegates set out by car for Salonika. Again it

was the Derbyshire Yeomanry who conducted them through
the British lines. But now the delegates included General Lukov
and a member of Malinov's cabinet. When, at 4 p.m. on September 28th, they reached Salonika Franchet d'Espérey received them with studied coolness. They had hoped that Bulgaria might revert to the status of a neutral power: Franchet
d'Espérey would have none of it. He presented them with his
terms: all Greek and Serbian territory must be evacuated;
all arms and weapons of war were to be surrendered; German
and Austrian troops should evacuate the country; the Allies
were to occupy strategic points in Bulgaria and use Bulgarian
railways to prosecute the war against their other enemies; and
the Bulgarian Army should demobilize, apart from three divisions and two cavalry regiments. They were far harsher terms
than Lukov had expected and he sought time to consider them.
The delegates spent the following day vainly striving to modify
the proposals, but Franchet d'Espérey was adamant. That
evening he received confirmation that Skopje had fallen. Immediately, he insisted on an additional clause providing for the
surrender of the Eleventh Army (technically a German unit)
which was, for the most part, west of Skopje.

Lukov knew that he was beaten. Every one of Franchet
d'Espérey's conditions was accepted. At 10.10 that night the
Armistice was signed: hostilities between Bulgaria and the
Allies were to cease at noon on the following day (September
30th). It was sixteen days since Mišić had given the order for
the guns to open up; with less than one per cent of the country
occupied by the invaders, Bulgaria had surrendered.

The news of the Bulgarian collapse was received with surprised
jubilation in London and Paris and with alarm at German
Headquarters in Spa. Lloyd George had long ago insisted that
the best way of bringing Germany to her knees was to 'knock
away the props'; now, as Hankey wrote, 'The first of the props
had fallen'. For the first time it began to look as if the whole
edifice of German power might soon tumble down. Heavy
blows were already being aimed at a second prop, Turkey,
and the Italians were preparing to move against Austria-Hungary.
On the Western Front Foch had opened his great converging
battle against the German positions on September 26th. With
Franchet d'Espérey's army free to advance into Central Europe
it seemed that the Germans might be caught in an even greater

pincer movement, extending over the whole continent. 'It was recognized at once that the end had come', writes Churchill, who was on a mission to Paris at the time.

Hindenburg and Ludendorff, for their part, did not minimize the significance of the Bulgarian Armistice. The link between Berlin and Constantinople was sundered. That, in itself, was serious; but what was even worse, German and Austrian troops had to be found from somewhere to stem the imminent advance to the Danube. When the first reports reached Spa that the Bulgars were seeking peace, the Supreme Command, which had played down the earlier requests for troops, hurriedly ordered three more divisions from the Russian Front to the Balkans and also sent the Alpine Corps, a division specializing in mountain warfare, from France. The 217th Division was moving west from Sofia at the time of the Armistice, with an Austrian Division from the Ukraine behind it. Another Austrian division from the Italian Front and the German Alpine Corps were moving down through Serbia, but it would be several days before any of these reinforcements could be in action. To hold the French and Serbian advance, the Germans had only the scattered units in the Eleventh Army – the rump that was left once the Bulgarian contingents had passed into prisoner of war cages – and the newly arrived Austrian 9th Division, which was fifty miles up the railway from Skopje at the time the Jouinot-Gambetta Brigade captured the city.

The German commanders had little confidence in the ability of these reinforcements to keep Franchet d'Espérey's men tied up in southern Serbia and away from the approaches to the Hungarian plain. 'A new army was being formed in Serbia, but how weak those troops were!' wrote Hindenburg, a year later, looking back on the great crisis of his life, 'Our Alpine Corps had scarcely any effective units, and one of the Austro-Hungarian divisions which was on its way was said to be completely useless as it consisted of Czechs, who would presumably not fight'. Since Germany's resources throughout Europe were 'manifestly diminishing' Hindenburg felt compelled to seek 'an honourable end' to the war. Ludendorff, too, thought that the time had come for peace: 'Out situation could never get better, only worse', he later wrote.

Late in the afternoon of September 28th – about the same time that Lukov and his peace delegates arrived at Salonika – Hindenburg and Ludendorff held their famous conversation at

8

Spa in which they admitted to each other that the war was lost. The following day they formally requested that a peace offer should 'be issued at once'. The civilians in the German Government could not believe that the situation was so desperate. They played for time, but Hindenburg was insistent. On October 3rd 1918, he wrote: 'As a result of the collapse of the Macedonian Front and the weakening of our western reserves which this has brought about, and now that it is impossible to make good the very considerable losses which have been incurred in the battles of the last few days, there is, so far as can be foreseen, no longer a prospect of forcing peace on the enemy'. It was a decisive message; the first German note seeking the mediation of President Wilson was despatched within forty-eight hours. Hindenburg's words were a tribute to the importance which the Germans attached to the events in Macedonia – although a cynic might feel that they were, in part, a means of exculpating armies over which the Field-Marshal had more direct responsibility. The Hindenburg legend tended to beget other myths: but this was in the future.

The war was, however, far from over. Between the despatch of the first peace note and the signing of the German Armistice at Compiègne there were thirty-six days of diplomatic negotiation and political conference. Throughout these five weeks the fighting continued between the main combatants; for, although the Germans and their allies knew that they were defeated, the shape of the future map of Europe would depend on the movements of the rival armies in the last spasm of the war. An armistice line in a disputed area could – and did – prove difficult to expunge at a peace conference.

Franchet d'Espérey was well aware of these considerations. Ever since his arrival at Salonika he had acted as Allied proconsul for all south-east Europe. He knew what he wanted and he was determined to get it. He had ridden roughshod over Clemenceau's instructions; he had determined of his own accord the form of the victorious offensive; he had hustled his government in order to secure allied consent for his plans; and he had drawn up the conditions imposed upon Bulgaria. It was an effective way of exercising authority, but it was hardly calculated to win him friends. In Paris there were plenty of soldiers and politicians ready to snipe at him – some smarting under alleged affronts, some jealous of his success, many genuinely alarmed by his independent spirit. Clemenceau lent a not unsympathetic ear to all complaints, and added some more himself. On the very day that the Bulgars made their first overture to Franchet d'Espérey, Clemenceau was planning to recall him and to send out Guillaumat again. The Bulgarian surrender put an end to this manœuvre, but in the weeks ahead d'Espérey was well aware of the enmity shown towards him in Paris; perhaps he even exaggerated it. He had his own immediate war aims: they did not coincide with those of Clemenceau; they were completely at variance with Lloyd George's. There were endless telegrams between his headquarters and Paris, and much bitterness was engendered. In the end nobody had his way: an unsatisfactory compromise gave rise to lasting recrimination.

The General's views had changed very little in the four years since he had first propounded them to Poincaré. The idea of entering Germany across central Europe continued to obsess him. On October 2nd 1918 he wrote to Le Chatelier:

'I can with 200,000 men cross Hungary and Austria, mass in Bohemia covered by the Czechs and march immediately on Dresden. If the Boches dig themselves in along the Rhine, that will be the way to prise them out which is most economical of human life and especially of Frenchmen. There is no doubt that my sudden appearance in Bohemia would send them crashing down. But at Supreme Headquarters they have such rigid views that it will be there as it was with Macedonia, where they believed everything was impossible.'

A month later, only nine days before the Armistice, he told a British general that after taking Budapest he would march on Dresden. He did not believe that the battle against France's principal enemy would, or should, end so soon. Inwardly convinced that he was the preordained instrument of Nemesis, he sought to carry the lessons of war into a region of Germany hitherto remote from the conflict. For the sake of Europe's future, the horrors of invasion and occupation should be brought home to all the German people. For the rest of his life he was convinced that the myopic preoccupation of Clemenceau and Foch with the Western Front robbed France of her opportunity. In this belief he was less than just to both of them.

Clemenceau was no more magnanimous towards the Germans than Franchet d'Espérey; but he was, perhaps, more conscious of what was politically possible. He understood, as Franchet d'Espérey could not, the will of the French people. To him, as to them, it was essential to end the war as speedily as possible. For every minute that it lasted a French soldier was killed or maimed for life. Retributive justice might find its way into a peace treaty, but it could have no place in determining strategy. Moreover Clemenceau knew that even had he shared Franchet d'Espérey's views to the full he could never have imposed them on his allies. Lloyd George had no interest in central Europe: the capture of Prague or Dresden left him unmoved; only the occupation of Constantinople fired his imagination. The Italians looked on every military advance through the South Slav lands with disfavour; they already regarded themselves as the residual legatees of the Habsburgs and had no wish for the inheritance to be squandered on an enterprise for which they had so little sympathy. But, above all, it was the Americans who would not have supported any prolongation of the war. The truth was that with more than four million casualties before the final battles began, the European allies had not the power, singly or together, to determine the continent's destiny. Everything depended upon the willingness of the United States to remain an 'Associate' in the struggle against Germany and Austria-Hungary. The arguments put forward by Franchet d'Espérey were completely antipathetic to the noble idealism which President Wilson believed could alone salve the collective conscience of the belligerents and ensure a lasting peace.

These complexities remained hidden from G.H.Q. at Salonika. Franchet d'Espérey's immediate concern was to reach the Danube. He made this clear to Milne at a conference four days after the Bulgarian Armistice came into force. The British Army would advance through Bulgaria to the Danube southeast of the Iron Gates and enter Roumania. The main French Army, with Greek and Italian support, would move forward on the British left, reaching the river west of the Iron Gates; and the Serbs would thrust on through Niš and up the Morava valley. A French division, with Serb and Greek detachments, would expel the Austrians from eastern Albania. As for operations against Turkey, this could well be left to General d'Anselme with a composite corps containing a French division, a British division and a few Greeks. Milne did not like this plan. It seemed to him that he should be despatching his troops to the Bosphorus, not

the Iron Gates. Dutifully, he ordered the first dispositions to
be made in accordance with Franchet d'Espérey's instructions;
but he telegraphed his objections to London at the same
time.

The British had already made up their minds on the future
use of Milne's army. They had always regarded Turkey as
second only to Germany among their enemies. Even before the
trauma of Gallipoli obsessed their minds, the sanctuary afforded
to the *Goeben* and the *Breslau* had affronted them: there were
few incidents in the whole war that had evoked such universal
satisfaction in Britain as the attack by the submarine E 11 on
shipping berthed at Constantinople in May, 1915. It was essential for Britain to humble the Turk in his capital city. The elimination of Bulgaria meant, for the British, the opening of a new
route to the Straits, not to the Danube. As Lloyd George wrote,
'It was clear to us that our success in Bulgaria would now enable
us to exert considerable additional pressure on Turkey from the
north, with a view to helping her surrender'. Lloyd George had
only been restrained by Balfour and Milner from peremptorily
ordering the British Salonika Army to be taken away from
Franchet d'Espérey's command and put under Allenby for an
advance on Constantinople. On October 4th – the day on
which d'Espérey was unfolding his future plans to Milne – Lloyd
George left for a conference with Clemenceau determined to
secure French backing for his scheme to switch the British
force to the frontier of Turkey, preferably with Allenby as
commander-in-chief.

Hankey's diary gives a vivid impression of the conference.
Clemenceau was 'much put out' by the British proposal. He
was particularly indignant at the suggestion of placing Milne
under Allenby: any march on Constantinople from the north
should be the responsibility of Franchet d'Espérey as it 'was
part of the fruits of his victory'. But Foch was, from the British
point of view, more reasonable; he conceded that there was
much to be said for an advance to the Turkish capital; and the
statesmen went on to discuss the more agreeable topic of the
Armistice terms to be offered to the Sultan's representatives.
At this point, Milne's telegram arrived with details of his conversation with Franchet d'Espérey: 'The Prime Minister was
absolutely furious', Hankey noted. But Clemenceau, too, was
displeased with d'Espérey for having created political problems
over the future of both Turkey and Albania by the division of

his armies. He dictated 'a very sharp telegram, rapping Franchet d'Espérey on the knuckles for dividing the armies'. Lloyd George, for his part, agreed to allow the British Salonika Army to remain 'under Franchet d'Espérey, provided Milne commanded the section ordered to march on Constantinople'. A directive was telegraphed to Franchet d'Espérey that afternoon (October 7th): he was to liberate Serbia, renew contact with Roumania and with any forces that were well-disposed to the Entente in southern Russia, and isolate Turkey. A second telegram made it clear that the British were to be mainly responsible for an advance on Constantinople although detachments representing the French, Italian, Serbian and Greek armies were to be included in the force; a token British contingent was similarly to be attached to the section of the Allied Armies of the Orient which would move towards the Danube.

The British had not gained all their points, but they had forced a decision which was to be of momentous importance for the future of eastern Europe. The despatch of an over-whelmingly British force to the centre of Ottoman power committed Britain for more than a decade to a positive policy in the eastern Mediterranean and beyond: it ensured that she would play a predominant part in the crises which marked the emergence of Kemalist Turkey and in the creation of a satellite system in the Near East. No doubt with Allenby's victories in Palestine it would have been difficult for her to play any other rôle in this part of the world and, in a sense, the eastward movement of Milne's army merely confirmed a tendency that underlay other international agreements in the preceding years. More significantly, the conference showed that Britain was prepared to withdraw from active participation in the reshaping of central Europe. France was to keep watch on the Danube. The true parent of the 'Little Entente' – that embryonic regional grouping of Roumania, Yugoslavia and Czechoslovakia under the patronage of the Quai d'Orsay – was Franchet d'Espérey.

One immediate, and unforeseen, consequence of the conference's decision was the end of all fighting for the British Salonika Army. The last shots had been exchanged on the morning of September 30th. Although there were still many days of battle ahead of the French and Serbian armies in the Morava valley and beyond, the Bulgars remained inactive as the British flooded into their country and the Turks concluded an Armistice before

Milne's men reached the frontier. Only one British battalion (10th Devonshire Regiment) crossed the Danube into Roumania and when the Armistice with Germany was signed it was still south of the river, in Bulgaria. It reached Bucharest in time for the victory celebrations.

There was, however, plenty of exhausting marching ahead of the British at the start of October. Every gun limber and ammunition waggon was fully loaded and, as it advanced, each battalion had to send out reconnaissance parties ready for instant action. The route to the Turkish frontier lay across mountains, cold and bleak in the autumn rain. 'Here', writes a former member of the Royal Field Artillery, 'the track was literally the bed of a stream, rough and boulder strewn, with deviations through bushes and scrub where the river bed became impossible. The wear and tear on men, animals and waggons was severe; horses would jib, poles or traces or axles would break, and vehicles would turn over; long traffic jams resulted, and everyone was tired or angry or both'. On October 30th the advance units reached Dedeagatch, with the Turkish frontier less than ten miles away and the long pencil of the Gallipoli peninsula projecting westward out across the sea; but that day the Turks signed an armistice in Mudros. Most of the troops who marched to Dedeagatch never saw Constantinople. Only one brigade was moved to the heart of Turkey, taking over the forts at the Dardanelles and Bosphorus under the command of General Wilson and mounting guard in the city itself. The remainder found themselves, in due course, marching back again along the same awful roads into Macedonia. Frustration and disappointment remained the lot of the British force to the very end of the campaign.

Meanwhile fierce battles were being fought in Serbia. The German and Austro-Hungarian occupying forces were exactly equal in number to the invaders; they were better equipped and more easily able to get their supplies up to the front. The Serbs, however, came as liberators: they were in rags and the soles had been worn out of their boots, while fallen bridges and deep pot-holes in the roads denied them sustenance or replenishment from their depots far to the south; but somehow they managed to cover ten miles a day, moving forward among their own people, who not only brought them food but even fought alongside them with weapons that had been long hidden or were stolen from Bulgarian dumps. The Serbian High Command frowned at the insurgent detachments, for many of them were inspired by a simple egalitarianism which ran counter to the prevailing mood of Serb politics; but the men in the field knew that without the popular insurrection they would never have been able to maintain the advance. North of Skopje a German battalion offered such stubborn resistance that it seemed as if the Serbs would never get through. Up the steep sides of the valley was a goat-track leading to a flat promontory which commanded the German defences. If mountain guns and ammunition could be carried up the hillside, the Germans would be at their mercy. With great difficulty the soldiers brought the guns up over the rocks; behind them came a long file of women from a liberated village, each nursing a shell under either arm: the Germans were forced to withdraw. As they were to find once again a quarter of a century later, there was no way of keeping down a people in arms.

The Austrian 9th Division, recruited from Bohemia and Moravia, offered little resistance. The Czech soldiery made common cause with their fellow Slavs at the first opportunity. By the end of the first week in October the Morava Valley lay open as far as Niš where the Germans of the Eleventh Army, with Austrian reinforcements, were still fighting stubbornly. General von Scholtz had by now been removed from Serbia to the Roumanian Front, and all the defenders were under the command of Field-Marshal von Kövess. He knew the Serbs and he knew the forests and valleys of their homeland; for, in 1915, he had commanded the Austro-Hungarian forces which had crossed the Danube and forced the Serbs to set out on their long retreat. But von Kövess could not work miracles. Nothing but bad news reached his headquarters in Belgrade on October 11th: the Italian XVI Corps was driving the Austrians back through Albania; a German Corps was lost in the mountains around Prizren; the French were astride the railway from Niš to Sofia; and Niš itself was about to fall to Serbian troops. His only course was to pull his troops back in as good order as possible to the very frontiers of the Dual Monarchy. He must abandon Serbia and put the broad trench of the rivers Danube and Sava between his men and the invaders: surely by now they must have outrun their supplies? A weary army would receive no help in the plains along the river.

With the fall of Niš, the Serbs had, indeed, come to a halt. They had advanced over a hundred and seventy miles in three

weeks of continuous battle. Now they waited for four days for
French support to reach them. Had the Serbs been able to push
on, then the Eleventh Army could well have been routed. As
it was, the Germans were able to fight a stubborn rearguard
action at Paracin on October 22nd; but it could not affect the
eventual outcome of the campaign. By now the Serbian First
Army was fighting in the wooded hills of the Sumadija, the
region where, more than a century before, 'Black George' (the
grandfather of their king) had first raised the standard of Serbian independence. On the last day of October patrols of the
First Army reached the heights of Topcider, above Belgrade
itself. Before them lay their capital, clustered around the limestone crag of the Kalemegdan; and below it, dull grey under
the autumn sky, the great sweep of the Danube was broken
by scores of boats ferrying the enemy back to the Hungarian
shore. On November 1st 1918 as on August 1st 1914, Serbian
batteries on Topcider exchanged shots with the monitors of
the Danube flotilla. The wheel of war had come full circle.

Franchet d'Espérey's last directive from Clemenceau had instructed him to complete the liberation of Serbia: this had now
been achieved, for the Yugoslav Division had reached the
Drina, the river which marks the boundary of Serbia and Bosnia, on the same day that the First Army entered the capital.
It was no secret that the goal now was southern Germany:
preparations began for an invasion of the Hungarian plain.

The Dual Monarchy was, however, in its last days. The
Italians launched their offensive at Vittorio-Veneto on October
24th and, as the Austro-Hungarian Army crumbled, the subject
nationalities proclaimed their independence. A National Council
in Prague took over the administration of Bohemia and Moravia
on October 28th in the name of the Czecho-Slovak Republic.
In Zagreb on the following day, the Croat Diet declared that
Croatia-Slavonia, Dalmatia and Rijeka were henceforth part
of 'the national and sovereign state of the Slovenes, Croats and
Serbs'. A similar proclamation was issued from Ljubljana on
October 31st and from Sarajevo a day later. The Habsburg
armies concluded an armistice with the Italians at Padua on
November 3rd.

All these developments favoured d'Espérey's plans. The
French Army of the Orient and the Serbs were on the Danube.
After learning of the Padua Armistice, d'Espérey despatched a

8*

telegram to Clemenceau proposing that he should carry 'the front to the southern boundary of Germany in collaboration with the Italians'. It was not to be. The Supreme War Council had already decided that operations against Germany should be subordinated to Foch. And Foch, for his part, had assigned the chief responsibility for an advance through Austria and into southern Germany to the victorious Italians. The Allied Armies of the Orient were virtually ignored: it was a rebuff that rankled in their commander's mind.

At this stage events in Hungary played into Franchet d'Espérey's hands. In the last days of October the legal responsibility for government in Hungary was entrusted to Count Mihaly Karolyi, an idealistic aristocrat who had for years led a party sympathetically inclined towards the Entente. Anxious to assert Hungary's independence in the eyes of a disbelieving world, Karolyi refused to consider himself bound by any Armistice concluded in the name of the Dual Monarchy. If he could convince the leaders of the Allied countries that he was establishing a democratic republic in due accord with the principles of Wilsonian liberalism, he hoped that he would be permitted to retain the ethnically Slav and Roumanian areas of 'Historic Hungary'. Fondly clinging to this illusion, he set out for Belgrade on November 5th at the head of a delegation of well-meaning lovers of liberty. They would meet the representative of republican France; and he would surely understand their point of view. They little knew Franchet d'Espérey.

The commander-in-chief was still in Salonika when Karolyi set out for Belgrade, but he took the road northward that afternoon. It was a victor's progress: a night in occupied Sofia, with defeated Bulgars obsequiously attentive; floral reception, speeches and military band in liberated Niš; dinner at Serb G.H.Q., with Prince-Regent Alexander radiating waves of Pan-Serb enthusiasm; and at 5.30 on the third afternoon, entry at last into Belgrade where triumphant arches spanned the streets. Small wonder if all this adulation fanned Franchet d'Espérey's self-esteem. His divisions were on the Danube. It seemed of little importance, just then, that Clemenceau and Foch had ignored his grand strategy. He was master of central Europe. 'For the first time since 1809, a French army is marching on Vienna!', he declared in pardonable anticipation. The Bonaparte complex – that supreme occupational neurosis of French commanders – was claiming another victim. In such a mood of elation, only

ninety minutes after his arrival, he summoned the wretched
Hungarian delegation to his presence.

Franchet d'Espérey possessed a strong sense of theatre and
he was determined that the Hungarian act of abnegation should
be played out in a manner worthy of the occasion. There was
no electricity in Belgrade that night, for the retreating Germans
had wrecked the installation. Karolyi and his party were ushered
into an elegant salon incongruously lit by two huge oil lamps
placed on a mantelshelf before a gold-rimmed mirror. The
General made an appropriately dignified entrance, assuming
a magisterial attitude with his back to the mirror. Karolyi read
a long prepared statement, explaining how the Hungarian
people had been forced into war by a feudal and reactionary
Government, backed by Prussian militarism. From time to time
d'Espérey allowed the journalists to see him make a gesture as
Karolyi read on and on: a nod of approval when he said that
he would carry out agrarian reforms; a disdainful dismissal
with the right hand of Wilsonian sentiments of international
solidarity; an imperious rejection of a proposal that Hungary
should be occupied only by the French, the British, the Italians
and the Americans, not by the Czechs, Serbs, Roumanians or
'colonial troops'. And when at last Karolyi had finished, d'Espérey made a brief and frigid reply: Hungary could not be
regarded as a neutral power for she was a vanquished state. He
handed Karolyi the printed conditions of armistice and left to
dine with French and Serb staff officers: he appears to have made
a good exit.

It is impossible not to feel sorry for Karolyi. His country
was in anarchy: everywhere there was a shortage of food and
fuel and his authority was challenged by opportunists among
his own followers. His only hope of winning the confidence of
the Hungarian people and of establishing the democratic society
in which he genuinely believed lay in constructive cooperation
with Hungary's former enemies. Yet here in Belgrade he had
encountered a victorious General who was enjoying power which
he knew would soon be curbed by the government which had
appointed him. D'Espérey, for his part, hated the Magyars
only slightly less than he hated the Germans. Although he
respected Karolyi personally as a man of honour, he despised
the rest of his delegation as ideologues. Hence he turned on
Karolyi all the venom which he would have used on an intransigent Magyar nationalist and on a man of the extreme

Left. There was little that the Hungarian could do except send a telegram of protest to Clemenceau – which d'Espérey refused at first to transmit – and return to Budapest to persuade his colleagues of the need to accept the General's conditions. More than half of the old Hungarian Kingdom was to be occupied by the French, the Serbs and the former 'subject peoples'. If Karolyi could achieve nothing better than this, his days as saviour of Hungary were numbered. A man of peace became the last victim of the Salonika armies.

Franchet d'Espérey did not wait for the formal acceptance of his terms. The Serbian and French armies moved rapidly into all the lands that the South Slavs sought to include in their new kingdom. Roumania, which had made a separate peace with Germany six months previously, re-entered the war on November 9th, with the backing of a French military mission and the certainty of doubling her size at Hungary's expense in the eventual treaty. Italian troops staked their claim to the Adriatic coast and Albania. An American battalion was brought from Italy to Kotor in order to keep the peace between the rival contestants – the only United States troops to serve in this theatre of operations. D'Espérey himself returned to his headquarters at Salonika still hoping that he would receive orders from Foch to advance into Germany. But the final decisions were taken on the Western Front. On November 11th d'Espérey made a characteristic entry in his diary: 'A telegram from Paris announces the general armistice. Germany has capitulated. I hope the conditions are severe. I have not been consulted nor even notified of the conversations, notwithstanding that my troops were in Hungary, and that – unique action in this war – I have occupied two enemy capitals, Sofia and Constantinople'. He had done all that was expected of him; and much that was not.

14 / 'Without the Laurel'

ONCE THE ARMISTICES had been signed the Allied command wasted little time in clearing out of Salonika. On December 14th Milne transferred his headquarters to Constantinople, where Franchet d'Espérey and his staff followed him a few weeks later. Each of the combatant nations considered that its men had a different task to perform in the uncertain years of readjustment, and units which had spent many months in close proximity were soon thousands of miles apart. Thus, by the spring of 1919, the headquarters of the British 27th Division were at Tiflis in Georgia, eleven hundred miles east of its old camp above the Struma; and the advanced Serbian divisions were in Klagenfurt, giving substance to a dubious Yugoslav claim to Austrian Carinthia, more than six hundred miles north-west of their former lines in the Moglena Mountains. Jouinot-Gambetta's Spahis were in Hungary, and the Italians divided between Albania and Adalia (in Asia Minor). The main Greek Army had occupied Smyrna at the start of what was to prove a disastrous attempt to achieve the 'Greater Greece' of which Venizelos had dreamt for so many decades. Around Salonika itself there were no more than a few battalions left.

Technically the 'Allied Armies of the Orient' remained in being for two years after the fighting had come to an end, and Franchet d'Espérey could still style himself commander-in-chief. It was, however, an empty title which permitted him little authority. He was able to lend support to Yugoslav ambitions at the Peace Conference and to pay ceremonial visits to Bucharest and Belgrade. When it seemed as if the Hungarian communists of Bela Kun would impose their will on central Europe, d'Espérey was allowed to intervene decisively. But gradually his men were sent home and demobilized; for the most part, he remained in Constantinople, querulously questioning each diminution of his forces, chafing at his powerlessness to shape events. When at last, in November 1920, the inter-allied command was formally abolished, he was thankful to return to North Africa where he believed a worthy mission might yet await him.

On July 14th 1922 Franchet d'Espérey was created a Marshal of France, receiving his baton at a moving ceremony on the most historic date in the republican calendar. It was a belated recognition of a triumph which had been virtually ignored in the Victory Procession through Paris three years previously, and it afforded d'Espérey and his devoted staff some satisfaction. But scant notice was taken of the men who had fought their way through the Balkan mountains. No streets in Paris were re-named in honour of their victory. No campaign medal was issued. Already they had become a 'forgotten army': perhaps they expected it.

Certainly the British contingent had long known of its low rating in the public esteem. A fortnight after the Bulgarian surrender, the Bishop of London (Dr A. F. Winnington-Ingram) arrived in Salonika and, in the next week, visited every British fighting unit in Macedonia and Bulgaria (no mean achievement for a sixty year old ecclesiastic). The Bishop swiftly became aware that the men whom he met were 'sore and disappointed' at their neglect by the British public. From Sofia he decided to despatch a 3,000 word letter to *The Times* in London in order, as he said, 'to plead for full justice to be done at home to the work of the Salonika Army'. The letter is an impressive record of a unique episcopal visitation: the Bishop wrote of the men's resentment at music-hall jokes made at their expense; he described how he had found on arrival that the doctors and nurses were caring for 31,000 men sickened by malaria and influenza; he gave a vivid description of the Grand Couronné and Pip Ridge positions (which he inspected only a month after the Doiran battle); and he praised the help which the troops had given to the people of Salonika after the great fire. It was a highly effective vindication; and *The Times* commented editorially, 'These men in our Eastern Armies have had the dust and toil, without the laurel, of the race to victory'. But the letter was printed too soon to achieve its purpose. It appeared in *The Times* on Tuesday, 8th November: on the following Friday the German Armistice was signed and, in the exhalation of triumph in the West, the Bishop's plea passed virtually unnoticed. There was to be no hero's return for the veteran from Salonika.

Yet, if the soldiers were forgotten, old controversies were not. Now from the armchair sanctuary of retirement the Westerners in Britain and France could write their memoirs, and the whole Salonika policy was roughly handled. It had been a waste of men and material. So far from contributing to the final victory, it had postponed a decision by dissipating the limited resources of the Allied Powers in a remote and unimportant theatre of war. It was, in short, 'an ulcer', as the Peninsular War had been to Napoleon.

Apart from Sarrail's highly personal apologia, the former commanders in Macedonia said little. Now and again Franchet d'Espérey gave a growl of disapproval, but he was fully occupied in Morocco. Milne, with a Scotsman's economy of words and a serving officer's natural reticence, did not break his silence until ten years after the final victory. But at last he contributed a special article to *The Times* calmly and precisely recapitulating what had been achieved by the Salonika Army. Only once did he allow himself a phrase of recrimination: he complained of 'the mass of uninformed criticism, almost vindictive in its cruelty, which has saddened the last days of many who gave their sons only too willingly to the service of their country'. Yet he did not minimize the significance of what had been done. 'It is certain', he wrote, 'that but for this expedition the gallant army of Serbia must have succumbed, and in all probability the great nation of the Yugoslavs would never have been born'. Citing Hindenburg's message to the German Government appealing for peace on October 3rd, he claimed that it was the defeat of Bulgaria which precipitated the whole collapse of the enemy forces. His opponents remained unconvinced.

The men who determined the military thought of the interwar period in Britain and in France were not prepared to concede that the Macedonian campaign had any lessons for the future. It seemed a curiously irrelevant anachronism, remote from the real centres of power politics. No one contributed any study of the Balkan operations to the *Army Quarterly*: and the standard histories of the war dismissed the Macedonian sideshow in a few cursory pages. Salonika was always good for a jibe: but where on earth was it, anyhow?

This myopic neglect of south-eastern Europe had its effect on the early strategy of the Second World War. Despite – or, perhaps, because of – limited British and French pledges to Greece, Roumania and Turkey, the Allied leaders preferred to ignore the Balkans. Only General Weygand, Foch's right hand man of 1918 and twenty-one years later the commander of the French Army in the Levant, thought otherwise. In the opening week of the war he argued that in order to avoid the stalemate imposed by the fortified lines across western Europe, the Allies must seek the cooperation of the Balkan nations, land in Salonika and use it as a base for operations against Greater Germany. But nobody took Weygand's proposal seriously. When it became clear in 1941 that Hitler was about to invade Greece, General Wilson – a nephew of the former commander of the XII Corps – was hastily sent from Libya to Athens to co-ordinate Allied defence plans. He had no more information about the situation he would find than Sarrail and Mahon a quarter of a century before him. Hitler had feared the striking power of a British air-base at Salonika: he need not have worried. German armoured columns advanced along the Vardar and Struma valleys with such speed that it was impossible to defend Salonika. The Greek frontier was crossed at dawn on April 6th 1941: at 8 a.m. on April 9th the first German tanks rumbled into Salonika. Within three weeks the swastika flag flew from the Acropolis in Athens and the Allies were out of south-east Europe. Another three years were to elapse before they returned.

Most of the leading personalities in the Salonika campaign were dead before the débâcle of 1941. Mišić had lived for only three years after his triumphant entry into Belgrade. Sarrail, reinstated as a military pro-consul in mandated Syria for a few disastrous months in 1925, died in 1929, his obituary hardly noticed in the widespread mourning for Marshal Foch. Guillaumat became the last commander of the French army of occupation in the Rhineland; his funeral almost coincided with the entry of German troops into Paris. Venizelos headed four governments in post-war Greece but died in France in 1936, where he had fled a year before, after an abortive armed rising by his supporters in Macedonia and the islands. Essad Pasha was assassinated in Paris during the Peace Conference; Alexander of Yugoslavia met a similar fate at Marseilles in 1934. Franchet d'Espérey was thrown from his car while driving across the Tunisian desert in 1933. Remarkably he survived; perhaps fortunately, a long convalescence prevented him from welcoming King Alexander at the start of his fatal visit.

When the Second World War broke out, Franchet d'Espérey and Pétain, his coeval, were the only two living Marshals of

Grand Couronné, showing the 'Devil's Eye' (arrowed)

Salonika, 1917: the aftermath of the Great Fire

General Todorov and officers of the Bulgarian High Command

Serbian signaller in the Moglena mountains

The Serbian front line: deep trenches are impossible on the rocky
hills of Macedonia

General Franchet d'Espérey inspects a British Guard of Honour at Constantinople,
February 1919: General Sir Henry Maitland Wilson behind

Spahis of the Jouinot-Gambetta Brigade

France. D'Espérey's health was too poor for him to undertake any responsible duties. As the all-conquering Germans moved southwards in 1940 he retired to the unoccupied zone, convinced that France would triumph in the end. Although his political sympathies had (like Pétain's) been with the extreme Right, he would take no part in the melancholy charade of Vichy. On his desk he kept a loaded revolver which, he announced, he would fire at any German who crossed the threshold of his study: none did. His strength began to ebb away in the spring of 1942. Once he was heard to murmur faintly, 'Budapest, Vienna, Berlin – Clemenceau and Foch would not have it'. He died on July 8th 1942. Five years later his coffin was interred in the Invalides, where it lies beside the tomb of Napoleon and the greatest soldiers of France. In death there was none to question his true merit as a military commander.

General Milne lived on until March, 1948. Chief of the Imperial General Staff for seven years, he was raised to the peerage in 1933 – 'Field-Marshal Baron Milne of Salonika and of Rubislaw, County Aberdeen'. Like d'Espérey, he remained loyal to the men who had served under him. As Patron of the Salonika Reunion Association he strove to foster and preserve 'the comradeship of the Balkans', and to a remarkable extent he succeeded. The S.R.A. has continued to flourish since his death: even today its quarterly magazine, *The Mosquito*, has a circulation of nearly two thousand. In its modest way, the Association has served as a link between Britain and Greece despite all the political vicissitudes of the last quarter of a century. It has 'adopted' a village of some sixty families, Mavroplagia, near Kilkis, halfway between Salonika and Doiran; and it lends support to a Gymnasium School in the city itself. On several occasions members of the S.R.A. have made 'pilgrimages' to the old battlefields in Macedonia. Few associations of ex-servicemen have achieved such a corporate identity.

To most returning veterans, Salonika is unrecognizable today. The map of Macedonia itself looks unfamiliar, for the place-names have been hellenized. The inhabitants, too, are different: the Turks have gone; the Jewish population suffered grievously in the Nazi occupation; and Greek settlers have moved in from Asia Minor and the south. Yet the most striking change is, of course, in the general appearance of the city. The White Tower still stands at the end of the waterfront and the old Turkish citadel straddles the north-eastern corner of the ramparts as it has done for centuries. But much else is new. In the nineteen-twenties Salonika was re-planned by a French architect and it is now a city of boulevards and open squares with a long line of ferro-concrete hotels looking out across the bay towards Olympus. There is a modern university, a large athletics stadium and a smart bathing-station on the sands leading to Karaburun. At Mikra an airport accommodates three daily flights from Athens, an hour's flying time away. Each September an international fair on a permanent site behind the White Tower – at the head of the Avenue Franchet d'Espérey – serves as a shop-window for East and West. Before the Great Fire two dozen minarets dominated the city skyline: only one is still standing today.

The Kajmakcalan and the Moglena Mountains remain virtually inaccessible, but it is possible to take a bus along the Seres Road to the Struma (now free from the malarial mosquito) or a train to Lake Doiran, which is still a restricted military zone. Pip Ridge and the Grand Couronné lie beyond the frontier in Yugoslavia; there are holiday chalets at Doiran Town and the Yugoslav travel brochures assure the tourist that the fishing is excellent. In 1927 an impressive memorial was unveiled on what had been known as Colonial Hill: it overlooks the scene of the tragic assaults of 1917 and 1918. It is here, on the bare slopes of the hills around the lake, that one is most aware of the echoes of a distant war. Furrows in the uncultivated earth trace the line of disused trenches.

There is no public memorial to the men of Salonika in Britain itself. But each day a few visitors come to the quiet village of Burghclere, on the borders of Berkshire and Hampshire. There Sir Stanley Spencer sought to capture the tragic beauty of warfare in Macedonia in a series of murals on the walls of a private chapel, dedicated to the memory of an Army Service Corps officer, Lieutenant Sandham: it is the tribute of a sensitive artist to his fallen comrades and, as such, it is something more than a personal shrine. In London, too, the Salonika Army is not quite forgotten. Each year, on the Sunday nearest to the Bulgarian Armistice, a narrowing circle of veterans gather at the Cenotaph in Whitehall to remember the sacrifice of the men who fell on the hills around Doiran or along the Struma or who died in the hospitals of Macedonia.

Later battles have long since thrust the 'Ifs' and 'Whys' of the Salonika campaign away from public discussion. Old arguments have become warp spun into the fabric of history, like the follies of the Boer War or the extravagances of the Crimea. But with the lapse of almost half a century it becomes easier to see the achievement of the Armies of the Orient in perspective. Much of the old controversy seems oddly artificial, perhaps because it was fought over the wrong issues. No one today would seriously maintain that the defeat of Bulgaria by itself precipitated the collapse of the Hohenzollern and Habsburg Empires. The main German Army had to be vanquished in the field before peace could be assured, and that defeat took place in France and Flanders. But supposing it had not been possible to breach the Hindenburg Line at the end of September, 1918? The only alternative way of entering Germany and of forcing Hindenburg and Ludendorff to move their divisions back to defend their own soil lay in the threat posed by the allied army on the Danube. And Franchet d'Espérey's men were in central Europe because each of the allied contingents had performed the task assigned to it in the September battles, the French, Serbs and Italians in the Moglena, the British and Greeks less spectacularly to the east. D'Espérey's offensive was a reinsurance against failure by Foch. His men were not, as it happened, required to move into Germany; but that is no reason for doubting the reality of their triumph – the rout of the Bulgarian Army and an advance across four hundred miles of mountain in six weeks.

Yet there remains one unresolved question about the whole campaign: if it was possible to break through so decisively in 1918, would not a determined offensive earlier in the war under a resolute joint commander, backed by London and Paris, have had the same result? Milne argued two years before the final victory that once the Bulgars were dislodged from the positions they were then holding, they would lose their will to wage war and he was right. Had the Allies occupied strategic points in Bulgaria at any time up to the summer of 1917, Roumania would have stayed a belligerent and a route would have been opened up to southern Russia. With Turkey isolated and Austria-Hungary under Emperor Karl already favouring peace, there is no reason why the 'props' should not then have been knocked away from under the German war machine, before Hindenburg could transport enough divisions to south-eastern Europe to stabilize the Front. But it was not to be. Macedonia was outside the compass of established military thought. Men of little imagination see only what touches their eyes; the beckoning indentations of the Vardar and the Morava lay beyond their range of vision.

Notes on Sources

CHAPTER ONE: THE ARRIVAL

The main sources for this introductory chapter are: Cyril Falls, *History of the Great War, Military Operations: Macedonia* (London, 1933), Vol. 1, chapters 2 and 3; Sir Julian Corbett, *History of the Great War: Naval Operations* (London, 1923), Vol. III, chapter 9; M. Larcher, *La Grande Guerre dans les Balkans* (Paris, 1929), chapter 3; Luigi Villari, *The Macedonian Campaign* (London, 1922), chapters 1, 4 and 9; G. Ward Price, *The Story of the Salonica Army* (London, 1917), chapter 2. Topographical references to Salonika in the early twentieth century may be found in *Murray's Handbook to Turkey-in-Europe* (London, 1912). A brief extract from the diary of one of the first soldiers to land at Salonika was printed in *The Mosquito* (the official journal of the Salonika Reunion Association) for June, 1960. For Sir Bryan Mahon's earlier career, see *Dictionary of National Biography*; and for criticism of his rôle at Suvla, Alan Moorehead, *Gallipoli* (London, 1956), chapter 13, and Lord Hankey, *The Supreme Command* (London, 1961), Vol. 1, chapter 36.

CHAPTER TWO: PLANS AND POLICIES

The fullest account of the coming of war in the major European capitals is in Barbara Tuchman's brilliant book, *August, 1914* (London, 1962), chapters 6, 7, 8 and 9. For the background of the Balkan Wars, for British distrust of Serbia and for Russian suspicion of Greece, see C. A. Macartney and A. W. Palmer, *Independent Eastern Europe* (London, 1962), chapters 1 and 2 and the sources cited therein. The military conferences discussed in the later sections of this chapter are covered by Professor Falls in *Macedonia* and by Lord Hankey.

There are several good histories of modern Greece: J. Mavrogordato, *Modern Greece, 1800–1931* (London, 1931); E. S. Forster, *A Short History of Modern Greece* (rev. ed., London, 1958); N. G. Svolonos, *Histoire de la Grèce Moderne* (Paris, 1953). Professor Forster's book gives the fullest account of events in Salonika, where he served as a British liaison officer at French Headquarters, but he is reticent on relations between the major Allies. The early career of Venizelos is covered by Doros Alastos, *Venizelos* (London, 1942); the map which he had on his wall as a student is mentioned on p. 13. I have used Alastos and Forster for the meeting between Venizelos and King Constantine on September 23rd, 1915 and for the speech of Venizelos on October 4th. Venizelos is criticized in G. F. Abbott, *Greece and the Allies* (London, 1922). Constantine's point of view is given by Prince Nicholas of Greece in his *Political Memoirs* (London, 1928) and, rather haphazardly, in his *My Fifty Years* (London, 1926); see also G. M. Melas, *Ex-King Constantine and the War* (London, 1920).

Marshal Franchet d'Espérey described his pre-war journeys in Austria-Hungary and the Balkans in an introduction to Larcher, *La Grande Guerre dans les Balkans*, and part of the November Memorandum is printed as an Appendix to that book. Further details about d'Espérey and his plan are included in General Azan's biography, *Franchet d'Espérey* (Paris, 1949). Azan also prints extracts from d'Espérey's letters to his friend, Le Chatelier. Poincaré's recollections of his visit to d'Espérey and of the discussions of January, 1915, are, on his own admission, confused, *Memoirs* (London, 1926), Vol. II, chapter 1. In particular, he maintains that d'Espérey's plan did not reach him until January 6th 1915. This seems to me to be highly improbable; Poincaré was evidently thinking of a second visit made by d'Espérey's emissary to him on that date. I have taken December 1st as the day on which the memorandum was brought to Paris on the evidence in Azan. Suarez, *Briand: Sa vie, son oeuvre avec son journal* (Paris, 1939) suggests that the conversation about the Balkans on January 1st was begun on Briand's initiative. Marius-Ary and Leblond, *Galliéni Parle* (Paris, 1920), vol. II, stake a claim for their hero, General Galliéni.

Hankey prints his Christmas memorandum in *The Supreme Command*, Vol. I, chapter 23. The same chapter considers the general discussion on rival theatres of war in January, 1915. Lloyd George's paper is in his *War Memoirs* (London, 1934), chapter 10. His foreign travels are narrated by Frank Owen in his biography, *Tempestuous Journey* (London, 1954), which also discusses his friendship with the Crosfield family. Lloyd George's letters to his brother are quoted in William George, *My Brother and I* (London, 1958). For the opposition of the Westerners at this stage, see Sir William Robertson, *Soldiers and Statesmen* (London, 1926), Vol. II, and Sir Charles Callwell, *Experiences of a Dug-Out* (London, 1920). The evolution of Kitchener's views on Salonika are given a chapter on their own in Ballard, *Kitchener* (London, 1930).

There are accounts of the War Council of January 13th 1915, in Lloyd George, Hankey and Robertson; in Churchill, *The World Crisis* (London, rev. ed. 1939), Part 2, chapter 5; in Magnus, *Kitchener* (London, 1959); and in J. A. Spender and Cyril Asquith, *Asquith* (London, 1932), Vol. II.

The telegram to Venizelos quoted on page 27 is printed in Hankey, p. 278. Hankey also mentions the postponement of the bombardment of the Dardanelles Forts – an incident curiously ignored by Alan Moorehead, from whose excellent narrative I have taken other references to the Gallipoli campaign.

General Sarrail's war memoirs, *Mon Commandement en Orient, 1916–18* (Paris, 1920) show his character at its sourest, but remain an important source. Other phases of his early career are covered, in a rather odd fashion, by P. Coblentz, *The Silence of Sarrail* (London, 1930). The most detailed diplomatic history of French policy is Albert Pingaud, *Histoire Diplomatique de la France pendant la Grande Guerre* (Paris, 1938), Vol. I, part 2, chapter 3 and part 3, chapter 1, and Vol. II, part 4, chapters 4 and 5.

The German side of events in 1915 is given in Falkenhayn's memoirs, *General Headquarters and its Critical Decisions* (London, 1919).

CHAPTER THREE: WINTER WAR

Joffre's directive of October 3rd is printed in the official French war history, *Les Armées françaises dans la Grande Guerre* (Paris, 1925), Vol. VIII, annexe 101; see also, Larcher, P. 76. The official French history (Vol. VIII, part I) and Falls, *Macedonia*, are the main sources for Allied movements up the Vardar and for their withdrawal. Ward Price, *Story of the Salonica Army*, chapters 2 and 3, is a useful supplement to Falls. The best account in English of the Serbian retreat is J. C. Adams, *Flight in Winter* (Princeton, New Jersey, 1942); documents are printed in Milan Nedić *Srpska Vojska na Albanskoj Golgoti* (Belgrade, 1937). Extracts from the diaries of members of the 10th Division are printed in *The Mosquito* for September and December 1959; see also the March 1960 issue. Sarrail's account of the de Lardmelle incident in *Mon Commandement* needs to be supplemented by the official histories and by the references to de Lardemelle in Azan's *Franchet d'Espérey*. Falkenhayn discusses the dispute over halting on the Greek frontier in *General Headquarters and its Critical Decisions*, pp. 96–97; his decision is criticized in Hoffman, *The War of Lost Opportunities* (New York, 1925), but appears to be justified by the entries in Gallwitz, *Meine Führertatigkeit im Weltkriege* (Berlin, 1929). There is also a clear analysis of this particular problem in Larcher, and a succinct account of the breach between Falkenhayn and Conrad in Cruttwell, *History of the Great War* (Oxford, 1934), chapter 14. For Austrian aspirations in the Balkans (and particularly at Salonika) before the War, see A. J. May, *The Habsburg Monarchy, 1867–1914* (Cambridge, Mass., 1951).

For Joffre's visit to London on October 29th, see Hankey, Robertson and Falls, *Macedonia*. The political problems of the Viviani Government and the succession of Briand are described by the former French deputy, Georges Bonnefous, in *Histoire Politique de la Troisième République* (Paris, 1957), Vol. II, pp. 91–101. Kitchener's journey to Gallipoli and Greece is narrated in Magnus, *Kitchener*, and Moorehead, *Gallipoli*. The conferences at Calais and Chantilly may be reconstructed from Falls, Hankey and Robertson; Asquith's formal statement at Calais is printed in Falls, p. 63. The clearest narrative of the 'Salonika or Gallipoli?' dilemma is in Hankey, Vol. II.

CHAPTER FOUR: 'THE GREATEST INTERNMENT CAMP'

Sarrail's description of his defensive preparations around Salonika forms Chapter 4 of *Mon Commandement*; Falls, *Macedonia*, Vol. L, pp. 85–95 gives the British account. It may be supplemented by Chapters 4 and 5 of Ward Price's *Story of the Salonica Army* and by a short section in Chapter 2 of H. Collinson Owen, *Salonica and After* (London, 1919). See Newbolt *Naval Operations* (London, 1928), Vol. IV, p. 127 (and Falls, p. 93) for the naval dispositions around the Salonika base. The use of vehicles fitted with caterpillar treads ('*tracteurs blindés*') is described by their inventor, J. Archer, *L'Enigme de la Guerre* (Paris, 1938). For the activity of the consular staff in the enemy legations see Falls and Ward Price and Sarrail's own account in *Mon Commandement*, pp. 73–76. German comment may be found in *Der Weltkrieg, 1914 bis 1918 Die militarischen Operationem zu Lande* (Berlin, 1933), Vol. IX, p. 315. On the destruction of the bridge at Demir Hissar, see Sarrail, *Mon Commandement*, pp. 94–96. For events in Greece early in 1916, see Forster, *Short History of Modern Greece*, pp. 100–101. The Karaburun operations are described in Newbolt, *Naval Operations*, Vol. IV, pp. 131–2 and (extensively) in Ward Price, *Salonica Army*, pp. 95–99. The calculation about the amount of wire used in the entrenched camp (P. 53) is based on statistics given by Professor Falls in *Macedonia*, Vol. 1, p. 91; for the refusal of fire-extinguishers and other supply problems (P. 59), again see Falls, pp. 101–102.

The Russian proposal for a joint advance on Budapest is noted in *Armées Francaises dans la Grande Guerre*, Vol. VIII, part 1, pp. 399–400. The same volume considers Sarrail's request for reinforcements on p. 413; his own account of his problem is in *Mon Commandement*, pp. 76–79. On British subordination to Sarrail for a simulated offensive, see *Armées Francaises*, Vol. VIII, part 1, p. 420. The Bulgarian who believed the War was 'really over' (p. 57) is quoted in *Der Weltkrieg*, Vol. IX, p. 305; and Falkenhayn's abortive plan to launch a spring offensive in Macedonia is discussed in detail in the same volume, pp. 316–22.

The Chantilly military conference of March 12th 1916, and the inter-allied conference in Paris a fortnight later are reported by Falls, p. 110; *Armées Francaises*, Vol. VIII, part 1, pp. 427–8; Hankey, *Supreme Command*, Vol. II, p. 482; and Larcher *Grande Guerre*, pp. 127–8. For the movement of the Serbs to Salonika see the same volume of *Armées Francaises*, pp. 471–8; Falls, p. 119–21; Compton Mackenzie, *Greek Memories* (London, 1939), pp. 108–10; and the last section of De Ripert d'Alauzier, *Un Drame Historique: La Résurrection de l'Armée Serbe* (Paris, 1923).

The destruction of the Zeppelin on May 5th is described by Ward Price, pp. 70–72; see also Falls, p. 114. Professor Falls has an account of the actions between the Sherwood Rangers and the German Uhlans, pp. 112–13; and in *The Mosquito* for December 1959 there is an article by a veteran of these skirmishes, illustrated by a contemporary sketch.

Joffre's letter to Robertson of April 25th 1916, is printed in Annexe 1 to *Armées Francaises*, Vol. VIII, part 1, no. 280, and extensively quoted in Larcher, p. 129. For British reactions see Falls, pp. 116–18; Robertson, *Soldiers and Statesmen*, Vol. II, p. 104; and Hankey, Vol. II, p. 501. The Downing Street Conference of June 9th 1916, is summarized by Falls on p. 136 and covered extensively by Lloyd George in *War Memoirs* (Volume 1 of 1938 edition), pp. 319–20. There is no biography of Field-

Marshal Lord Milne and he appears to have destroyed most of his papers; but see the entry in *Dictionary of National Biography*.

Sarrail prints the telegram in which he described his visit to Athens in *Mon Commandement*, pp. 100–2; see also, *Armées Françaises*, Vol. VIII, part 1, Annexes part 3, p. 446. The Fort Rupel incident and its immediate consequences are considered by Falls (pp. 124, 130 and 132) and by Forster, pp. 102–3. For the naval demonstration in the Cyclades see Newbolt, *Naval Operations*, Vol. IV, pp. 133–4; and for its effect on Athens, see Compton Mackenzie, *Greek Memories*, pp. 155–65. Life in Salonika in the summer of 1916 is described by Collinson Owen, *Salonica and After*, pp. 20–51.

The secret session of the Chamber of Deputies in Paris is fully reported by Georges Bonnefous, *Histoire Politique de la Troisième République*, Vol. II, pp. 145–50, from which the extract from Delcassé's speech is taken. The French attitude over Salonika is seen against the general background of parliamentary conflict with the military command in Chapter 6 of J. C. King, *Generals and Politicians* (Berkeley, 1951).

For examples of Clemenceau's hostility to the Salonika expedition, and Sarrail's reaction to the 'gardeners of Salonika' jibe, see Paul Coblentz, *The Silence of Sarrail*, pp. 108–16.

CHAPTER FIVE: THE BATTLE FOR MONASTIR

Roumanian policy towards the Allies is treated with considerable detail by Albert Pingaud, *Histoire Diplomatique de la France pendant la Grande Guerre*, Vol. I, part 2, chapter 3 and Vol. II, part 4, chapter 1 and part 5, chapter 2; see also Larcher, *La Grande Guerre dans les Balkans*, chapter 4; and Macartney and Palmer, *Independent Eastern Europe*, chapter 2 and other sources cited therein. Falls deals with the effect of the Roumanian proposals, p. 133, pp. 138–43 and pp. 153–4. See, also, Sarrail's comments, *Mon Commandment*, chapter 9.

The Bulgarian offensive of August 1916 is described from the Bulgarian side in Nedeff, *Les Opérations en Macédoine: L'Epopée de Doiran* (Sofia, 1927), pp. 45–83; see also Ward Price, *Salonica Army*, chapter 10. For reactions in Athens, see Compton Mackenzie, *Greek Memories*, pp. 220–3. On Sarrail's conference of August 20th and his plans for the September offensive, see *Mon Commandement*, pp. 367–9. The account of the storming of the Kajmakcalan and of the battles for Florina, Kenali and Monastir is based, primarily, on *Armées Francaises*, Vol. VIII, part 2, pp. 1–327 and annexes 1 and 2. These annexes include directives for, and reports from, the Serbian Army as well as the French. Some of the French orders are reproduced in *Mon Commandement*, pp. 370–85. Sarrail gives a hostile portrait of Cordonnier in *Mon Commandement*, chapters 11, 13, 14, 15 and 16. Cordonnier gives his version in *Ai-je Trahi Sarrail?* (Paris, 1930), chapters 11, 12, 13, 14, 15. It is a relief to turn from these embittered accounts to the judicious assessment of Professor Falls, *Macedonia*, Vol. I, pp. 184–8. Ward Price was present on the Monastir Front at the height of the battle and his narrative (*Story of the Salonica Army*, chapters 11 and 12) is a gem of war reporting. The part played by the Italians is described by Villari in *The Macedonian Campaign*, pp. 45–48. A semi-official German account is to be found in Strutz, *Herbstschlacht in Mazedonien: Cernabogen*, 1916 (Berlin, 1925); it is hardly sympathetic to the Bulgars. The reaction of German G.H.Q. to the demands from the Macedonian Front may be traced in *Der Weltkrieg*, Vol. XI (Berlin, 1937), chapter 5, especially pp. 345–6; see, also, the same volume pp. 195–6. The British M.P. who informed the monks at Mt Athos of the Monastir victory was L. S. Amery; see his *My Political Life*, Vol. II: *War and Peace, 1914–1929* (London, 1953), p. 87. For the impressions of a British visitor to the Kajmakcalan twenty years later, see Rebecca West, *Black Lamb and Grey Falcon* (London, 1941), Vol. II, chapter 1.

The British actions along the Struma and south of Doiran are described at length in Falls, *Macedonia*, Vol. I, chapters 8 and 9. An officer in one of the cyclist companies (Lieutenant G. W. Holderness) has written an article of reminiscences of this forgotten aspect of warfare in *The Mosquito* for March, 1960. There is an interesting contemporary assessment of British difficulties 'along the Seres Road' in Harold Lake's *In Salonica with our Army* (London, 1917), chapter 3.

CHAPTER SIX: POLITICS AND KNAVISH TRICKS

Salonika's turbulent political history is summarized interestingly and concisely in Apostolos P. Vacalopoulos, *A History of Thessaloniki* (Institute for Balkan Studies, Salonika, 1963); the book also contains chapters on the economic development of the

city. There is a convenient account of French investment policy
in the Ottoman Empire at the beginning of the twentieth century
in W. W. Gottlieb, *Studies in Secret Diplomacy* (London, 1957),
pp. 20–21. Villari voices Italian suspicion of Sarrail's alleged
commercial interests in *The Macedonian Campaign*, pp. 59–60.

For the revolution in Salonika see Falls, *Macedonia*, Vol. I,
pp. 208–9; Forster, *Short History of Modern Greece*, p. 111; Ward
Price, *Story of the Salonica Army*, pp. 106–12; Collinson Owen,
Salonica and After, pp. 163–4; Sarrail, *Mon Commandement*, chapter
12. The officer's diary to which reference is made on p. 94 was
kept by Captain W. Dudden, R.A.M.C.; a typewritten version,
illustrated with attractive drawings and water-colours, is pre-
served in the Imperial War Museum Library. The quotation
comes from p. 12; the typescript is dated 1920.

Diplomatic exchanges in Athens are reported by Compton
Mackenzie in *Greek Memories*, pp. 221–3 and pp. 230–70. Sir
Compton also gives an account of the impression made by the
arrival of the Allied squadron in the same section. Newbolt,
Naval Operations, Vol. IV, chapter 5, part 1, has a detailed survey
of the naval problem. Dartige du Fournet, *Souvenirs de Guerre
d'Un Amiral* (Paris, 1930), chapters 8 and 9 are the memoirs of
the Allied naval commander at this stage.

King George V's letter to Asquith of September 4th is printed
in Harold Nicolson, *King George V* (London, 1952), pp. 281–2.

The account of Venizelos's movements is based on Alastos,
Venizelos, pp. 171–2; Compton Mackenzie, *Greek Memories*,
pp. 278–9; and J. C. Lawson, *Tales of Aegean Intrigue* (London,
1920), chapter 5.

The misfortune of the wealthy citizens in Salonika who sought
to avoid enlistment in the National Army is described by L. S.
Amery, who was at G. H. Q. at the time of the Revolution, in
My Political Life, Volume II, p. 84. Other eye-witnesses have
testified to the extreme reluctance of the Greeks from the mainland to volunteer for the National Army.

The worsening situation in Athens may be studied in Compton
Mackenzie's *Greek Memories* and in Dartige du Fournet's *Souvenirs*. Suarez, *Briand*, Vol. IV (Paris, 1940), chapter 1 sees these
events as they appeared from Paris. The Admiral's contempt for
intelligence reports was noted by Compton Mackenzie, who was
present when the Admiral said, '*Excellence je m'en fiche des ren-
seignements*' (*Greek Memories*, p. 369).

For the events of December 1st–2nd, 1916, see Dartige du

Fournet, *Souvenirs*, chapters 19 and 20; Mackenzie, *Greek Memories*, pp. 376–408; the report of Major C. D'O. Harmar, R.M.L.I. quoted in Newbolt, *Naval Operations*, Vol. IV, p. 168; the French military attaché's report, *Armées Francaises*, Vol. VIII, part 2, annexe no. 1085; and the Queen of Greece's letter to the Kaiser quoted in Forster, *Short History*, pp. 120–1. The subsequent correspondence of Constantine and George V is summarized by Sir Harold Nicolson in *King George V*, p. 283. For the effect of these events in Athens on the attitude of the authorities in Salonika, see Falls, *Macedonia*, Volume I, pp. 225–30.

CHAPTER SEVEN: SPRING OFFENSIVE

For changes in the French Government and administration in December 1916, see Suarez, *Briand*, Vol. IV, chapter 3, and Bonnefous, pp. 213–21; and for Sarrail's attitude at this time see his *Mon Commandement*, pp. 220–7, and *Armées Francaises*, Vol. VIII, annexe 1097. On the formation of the Lloyd George Government see Frank Owen *Tempestuous Journey*, chapters 17 and 18; his physical collapse is mentioned on p. 353. The London Conference is covered by Larcher, pp. 184–6.

On the Rome Conference of January 1917 see: Lloyd George, *War Memoirs*, chapter 47; Sarrail, pp. 214–17; Suarez, Vol. IV, pp. 104–15; Larcher, pp. 187–9; Falls, *Macedonia*, Vol. I, pp. 253–255; Hankey, pp. 606–12; Robertson, *Soldiers and Statesmen*, Vol. II, pp. 135–7; Victor Bonham Carter, *Soldier True* (London, 1963), pp. 200–3; Spears, *Prelude to Victory* (London, 1939), pp. 36–37; *Armées Francaises*, vol. VIII, part 2, pp. 377–80 and annexes nos. 1441 and 1442. The meeting between Sarrail and Lloyd George is described by Lloyd George himself in *War Memoirs*, p. 846 and by Sarrail in *Mon Commandement*, p. 216 and p. 217; Hankey, who was also present, prints an extract from his diary in Supreme Command, p. 612. Robertson's comment on Sarrail is from a private letter intended to be shown to King George V and printed in *Soldier True*, p. 202. Milne's assessment of the situation on October 30th 1916 is discussed in some detail in Falls, pp. 193–6.

The disintegration of the Seres Road after heavy rain is described by Ward Price, *Story of the Salonica Army*, pp. 243–4. The Italian operations are covered extensively in Villari, *The Macedonian Campaign*, pp. 105–12 and 122–4. On the Santi Quaranta route see also, Falls, p. 259; Sarrail, p. 224; Larcher, p. 196;

Armées Francaises, Vol. VIII, part 2, p. 382 and annexes nos. 1451 and 1477.

Sarrail's plan of February 1917 is summarised in *Armées Francaises*, Vol. VIII, part 2, pp. 391–2 and in Falls, pp. 294–5. See also the annexes to *Armées Francaises*, nos. 1518, 1520, 1550. For intelligence reports of the relative strength of the opposing forces, see annexe no, 1558. Milne's change of emphasis from Seres to Doiran is discussed by Falls on p. 295; and see *Armées Francaises*, annexe no. 1550.

For the Calais Conference of February 1917 and its repercussions in Salonika, see Spears, p. 157 (from which the quotation on p. 116 is taken); Robertson, Vol. II, pp. 136–7; Bonham Carter, *Soldier True*, pp. 212–18; Sarrail, pp. 402–3; Larcher, p. 194; and *Armées Francaises*, Vol. VIII, part 2, p. 397 and annexe no. 1585.

The early fighting around Lake Prespa may be followed in Ward Price, pp. 193–4; *Armées Francaises*, Vol. VIII, part 2, pp. 428–39; and Falls, p. 296 (who also mentions the Serb rising south of Niš which is exhaustively covered by Milivoje Perović, *Toplicki Ustanak*, Belgrade, 1954). For the German air squadron see Heydemarck, *War Flying in Macedonia* (London, n.d. ? 1938); and for the response from the R.F.C. and R.N.A.S. see Ward Price, pp. 190–1 and H. V. Jones, *The War in the Air* (Oxford, 1935), Vol. V, chapter 6. On the use of gas shells by both sides see Falls, pp. 300–1 and Nedeff, *Les Opérations en Macédoine*, p. 88.

For the conference of St Jean-de-Maurienne see Falls, pp. 301–302 (from whom the remarks of Robertson are quoted) and Hankey, pp. 633–4; cf. Robertson, *Soldiers and Statesmen*, Vol. II, pp. 142–3.

On Yanesh, see Collinson Owen, *Salonica and After*, pp. 74–75 and the reference to 'those gorgeous sunsets' on p. 173 of A. J. Mann, *The Salonika Front* (London, 1920), a book which includes delightful illustrations in colour by W. T. Wood. A less attractive picture of Yanesh appears in H. A. Jones, *Over the Balkans and South Russia* (London, 1923), p. 66. On the Grand Couronné position, see Nedeff, p. 85–86 (whence the quotation on p. 120 is taken); Ward Price, pp. 197–9; Collinson Owen, pp. 220–9; Villari, p. 128; and Wood's illustration on p. 76 of Mann's book. See, also, *The Mosquito* for December 1961 and March 1962.

The Operations Order for the attack of April 24th forms Appendix 7 of Falls, *Macedonia*, Vol. I. On the action of April 24th and the following days, see the same volume, pp. 302–16;

Nedeff, pp. 108–18; and Ward Price, pp. 199–200. For Sarrail's postponement of the general offensive, see *Armées Francaises*, Vol. VIII, annexe no. 1786.

The Allied decision to withdraw some British units from Macedonia in June is mentioned by Falls, p. 318; but see, more fully, *Armées Francaises*, Vol VIII, part 2, p. 482 and annexes nos. 1825, 1826, 1900 and 1902. Milne's letter of May 2nd is printed in full in Falls, p. 346. For his decision not to mount his next attack at dawn, see the same volume, p. 319.

The Operations Order for the British action on May 8th–9th is printed as Appendix 8 of Falls, Vol. I. The action itself is described on pp. 321–31 of the same volume; see also Ward Price, pp. 202–4; Villari, p. 129, Nedeff, pp. 118–24; and *Armées Francaises*, Vol. VIII, annexes nos. 1858 and 1868. On British casualties, see Falls, Vol. I, p. 331, and compare the final figures given in Appendix 21 of *Macedonia*, Vol. II.

The joint allied offensive of May 9th is fully described in *Armées Francaises*, Vol. VIII, part 2, pp. 457–72 and annexes 1856, 1860, 1861, 1862, 1866. It is covered more succinctly in Falls, pp. 340–1. On the Italian contribution see Villari, pp. 130–132 and *Armées Francaises*, Vol. VIII, part 2, p. 467 and annexe no. 1854. For the Russians see annexes 1871, 1878, 1931, 1945. On the breakdown in command on May 10th, see Falls, p. 341, Villari, p. 132 and *Armées Francaises* annexe no. 1870. The British naval guns attached to the Serbian Second Army are mentioned in *Armées Francaises*, annexe no. 1966; and in the reminiscences of Dr A. A. Greenwood in *The Mosquito* for December 1963. For the operations on the Struma Front, see Falls pp. 334–8; Sarrail, pp. 250–3; Ward Price, p. 205; and *Armées Francaises* annexes nos. 1878, 1925, 1975.

The peculiar behaviour of the Serbian First Army is discussed by Falls on p. 343 and Villari, p. 133. See, also, the exchange of messages between Sarrail and Douchy in *Armées Francaises*, annexes nos. 1912, 1914, 1933 and 1937. For the end of the offensive, see annexes nos. 1961 and 1962.

CHAPTER EIGHT: CONSPIRACY, MUTINY AND FIRE

Sarrail's contemporary reaction to the failure of the offensive may be gathered from *Armées Francaises*, Vol. VIII, annexe 1966. His later explanations may be found in *Mon Commandement*, pp. 251–2. For Milne's view see Falls, *Macedonia*, Vol. I, pp. 343–345 and Vol. II, p. 3. The attitude of the Italians and Serbs is covered by Villari, *Macedonian Campaign*, pp. 134–6.

Sarrail's criticism of the Serbs (quoted on p. 132) is taken from *Armées Francaises*, annexe 1982. The letter from Bojović is printed as annexe 1607; for Sarrail's reply, see annexes 1688, 1717 and 1718.

On the Black Hand and the Salonika Trial of Apis: Milan Z. Zivanović, *Pukovnik Apis: Solunski Proces 1917* (Belgrade, 1955); B. Nesković, *Istina o Solunksom Procesu* (Belgrade, 1953); Wayne S. Vucinich, *Serbia between East and West* (Stanford, 1954; pp. 104–105); H. Uebersberger, *Oesterreich zwischen Russland und Serbien* (Cologne–Graz, 1958), pp. 267–302. The quotation on p. 134 is from the study by Zivanović (p. 58), who was the nephew of Apis. See also, *Armées Francaises*, vol VIII, part 2, pp. 394–5; and Sarrail, *Mon Commandement*, p. 257. For the re-alignment of the Serb Army, see *Armées Francaises*, annexes 1704, 1719 and 1739; and Sarrail, *Mon Commandement*, p. 399.

The position of the Russian Brigade after the Spring Offensive is covered by: *Armées Francaises*, Vol. VIII, part 2, pp. 502–3; Vallari, *Macedonian Campaign*, pp. 185–8; Sarrail, *Mon Commandement*, pp. 261–3. My prime source for the Russian troops on the Macedonian Front is the article by Dragomir Mitrović, 'Revolucija u Rusiji i Ruske Trupe na Solunskom Frontu' in the Yugoslav periodical, *Istoriski Glasnik* for 1957 (parts 3 4), pages 17–24. The quotation on the falling morale of the Russian troops (p. 137) is from Dietrichs's report to Sarrail of May 18th 1917, printed as annexe 1945 of *Armées Francaises*. On the Russian riot at Vertikop in 1918, see *The Mosquito* for December, 1963. The Russian mutinies on the Western Front are narrated by Richard Watt in *Dare Call It Treason* (London, 1964), chapters 12 and 16.

On the activity of Jonnart and the abdication of King Constantine, see: Hankey, *Supreme Command*, pp. 634–7; Sarrail, *Mon Commandement*, Chapter 24; Villari, *Macedonian Campaign*, pp. 146–148; Falls, *Macedonia*, Vol. I, chapter 15; *Armées Francaises*, Vol. VIII, part 2, chapter 16; Forster, *Short History of Modern Greece*, pp. 126–30.

For the grievance of the French Army over shortage of leave and for the mutiny of 57th Division, see Sarrail, *Mon Commandement*, pp. 264–5 and Falls, *Macedonia*, Vol. II, p. 11. On the French Western Front mutinies, see Richard Watt *Dare Call It*

Treason, chapters 11, 12 and 16. For General Grossetti's generous interest in the welfare of his troops, see Bernard Sarrigny, *Trente Ans avec Pétain* (Paris, 1959), p. 31. For Sarrail as a centre of gossip, see Villari, pp. 58–59.

The shipping problem and the U-boat menace to communications with Salonika are most clearly shown in Newbolt, *Naval Operations*, Vol. IV, pp. 306–14. On the Bralo–Itea–Taranto route; *Armées Francaises*, Vol. VIII, part 2, pp. 490–3; Collinson Owen, *Salonica and After*, chapter 15; Villari, p. 170.

For the incidence of malaria in Macedonia, see Falls, *Macedonia*, Vol. II, pp. 7, 58, 293–4 and 351. See also, Ward Price, *Story of the Salonica Army*, pp. 251–4; and *The Mosquito* for September, 1960. The withdrawal to summer positions in the Struma Valley is narrated by Falls in *Macedonia*, Vol. II, pp. 72–74.

For the section on the recreational activities and interests of the British units in Macedonia, I have primarily used Collinson Owen's, *Salonica and After*, Ward Price's *Story* and Woods, *Salonika Front*; supplemented by issues of *The Mosquito* for September 1959 (on Dr Vaughan Williams) and for December, 1962 (for 'The Roosters'). The British Lieutenant's request for coffee to be dropped on a German aerodrome (quoted on p. 144) is taken from Heydemarck, *War Flying in Macedonia*, p. 57. The incident of the hounds who crossed the Bulgarian lines is told in Falls, *Macedonia*, Vol. II, p. 9; and Professor Falls mentions the Horse Show attended by Sarrail (*ibid*, p. 8). For an Italian view of the British aptitude for amateur dramatics, see Villari, pp. 78–79; and see, also, his comments on *The Balkan News*, p. 162. A considerable collection of back-numbers of *The Balkan News* is available in the Library of The Imperial War Museum.

On the British attitude to the Salonika expedition in the summer of 1917 and on the Paris and London conferences of July and August, 1917, see: Hankey, *Supreme Command*, pp. 684–5, 687–90; Robertson, *Soldiers and Statesmen*, pp. 142–3; Falls, *Macedonia*, Vol. II, pp. 3, 11–12. On the view of Smuts, see Lloyd George, *War Memoirs*, Vol. I, pp. 911–12. Robertson's paper of July 29th is printed in Falls, pp. 3–4; his private letter to Haig (from which extracts are quoted on p149.) is included in Bonham Carter, *Soldier True*, p. 269. Lloyd George's estimate of the respective military value of a Division in Salonika and in Palestine is given by Hankey, *Supreme Command*, p. 687. The letter in which Lloyd George asked the French to dismiss Sarrail is printed by Lloyd George in *War Memoirs*, Vol. II, pp. 1913–14. On Sarrail's brusque treatment of Milne, see *Mon Commandement*, p. 267.

The movement of the Tenth Division is described by Falls in *Macedonia*, Vol. II, pp. 13, 14, 15, 17.

I have used accounts of the Great Fire in: Collinson Owen, *Salonica and After*, chapter 8; Falls *Macedonia*, Vol. II, pp. 21–23; C. V. Usborne, *Blast and Counter-Blast* (London, 1935), chapter 17; Wood, *Salonika Front*, chapter 1; Villari, *The Macedonian Campaign*, pp. 179–82; and the reminiscences of Mr A. Beeby-Thompson in *The Mosquito* for March, 1958. I have also used information supplied by my father who was at Base headquarters during the Fire. On the high incidence of fires in Salonika, see Vacalopoulos, *History of Thessaloniki*, p. 107.

CHAPTER NINE: THE FALL OF SARRAIL

For Italian irritation with Sarrail, see Villari, *The Macedonian Campaign*, pp. 172–5. Bertie's distrust of Sarrail is evident in many entries in Lennox (ed.) *The Diary of Lord Bertie, 1914–1918* (London, 1924), notably Vol. II, pp. 21–22 and pp. 134–5. See, also, Lloyd George *War Memoirs*, Vol. II, p. 1913–14. The letter from Painlevé (which is quoted on p.154) appears in Sarrail, *Mon Commandement*, p. 268.

For the British raids on Pip Ridge, see Falls, *Macedonia*, Vol. II, pp. 15–16. The Italian attacks in the Crna are described by Villari, *Macedonian Campaign*, p. 183.

On Albania in general, see the Foreign Office Historical Section Handbook no. 16, *Albania* (London, 1918) and J. Swire, *Albania: The Rise of a Kingdom* (London, 1929). Some of the fighting is described by Ward Price, *Salonica Army*, pp. 285–93. On the capture of Pogradec, see Sarrail, *Mon Commandement*, pp. 279–80; Villari, *Macedonian Campaign*, pp. 183–4; Falls *Macedonia*, Vol. II, pp. 16–17; and *Armées Francaises*, vol. VIII, part 2, pp. 513–25. For the Victory Procession in Paris in 1919, see Falls, *Macedonia*, Vol. II, p. 283. On Essad Bey's earlier life, see Swire, *Albania, passim*. For Essad Bey in Salonika and at Pogradec, see: Ward Price, *Salonica Army*, p. 294; Villari, *Macedonian Campaign*, pp. 163–4; Collinson Owen, *Salonica and After*, p. 155; Sarrail, *Mon Commandement*, p. 281 and p. 414; Falls, *Macedonia*, vol. II, pp. 32–33. On the abortive resumption of the offensive after the fall of Pogradec and the discomfiture of the

Italians, see *Armées Francaises*, Vol. VIII, part 2, pp. 528–9. Additional information on the objections of Pašić is in Sarrail, *Mon Commandement*, p. 280. For the raids by units of XVI Corps, the reoccupation of the 'Winter Line' in the Struma, and the raid by the Argyll and Sutherland Highlanders, see Falls, *Macedonia*, Vol. II, pp. 24–30 and pp. 44–45.

On Clemenceau, Malvy and Almereyda see: Lloyd George, *War Memoirs*, Vol. II, chapter 73; Bonnefous, *Histoire Politique de la Troisième République*, Vol. II, pp. 303–4, 313–18 and 354–5; Watt, *Dare Call It Treason*, pp. 260–3; King, *Generals and Politicians*, pp. 182–3, 186, 202–3; Bertie, *Diary*, Vol. II, pp. 159, 163, 168, 170–2, 175–7, 184–7; Adam, *Treason and Tragedy* (London, 1929), pp. 101–36. On the links between Sarrail and the confidential documents found at Almereyda's home, see Villari, *Macedonian Campaign*, pp. 188–9; and Bonnefous, *Histoire Politique*, p. 306.

For the Supreme War Council at Versailles, see: Lloyd George, *War Memoirs*, pp. 1620–1 and 1914; Hankey, *Supreme Command*, Vol. II, chapters 68, 69 and 70; Alastos, *Venizelos*, pp. 183–4; and Falls, *Macedonia*, Vol. II, pp. 46–47.

The French War Council's decision to recall Sarrail is described by Poincaré, *Au Service de la France*, Vol. IX, pp. 402–3. For other matters relating to Sarrail's recall, see Sarrail, *Mon Commandement*, p. 290 and pp. 293–4; Falls, *Macedonia*, Vol. II, pp. 46–7; Bertie, *Diary*, p. 236.

On the projected coup d'etat by Caillaux, see: Bonnefous, *Histoire Politique*, pp. 370–1; J. Caillaux, *Mes Prisons* (Paris, 1920), p. 73; J. Caillaux, *Mes Mémoires* (Paris, 1947), Vol. III, p. 193; Poincaré, *Au Service de la France*, Vol. X, pp. 7, 8, 16.

CHAPTER TEN: GUILLAUMAT

On the offer of the post of Commander-in-Chief to Franchet d'Espérey and his refusal in December, 1917, see Azan, *Franchet d'Espérey*, pp. 163–4. For the decision to appoint Guillaumat: Poincaré, *Au Service de la France*, Vol. IX, p. 403.

The directive handed to Guillaumat and the additional comments by Foch are printed, in translation, in Falls, *Macedonia*, Vol. II, pp. 318–21; see also Larcher, *Grande Guerre dans les Balkans*, p. 280; *Armées Francaises*, Vol. VIII, part 2, pp. 563–4 and annexe 2314.

The defensive preparations in Macedonia may be studied in *Armées Francaises*, Vol. VIII, part 2, pp. 588–93 and 602–4. The changes in the French administrative command are covered by the same volume, p. 572 and p. 580; as also are Franco-Italians relations in Albania, *ibid*, pp. 567–8. The British account of these developments is in Falls, *Macedonia*, Vol. II: defence, pp. 53–58 and 70–76; Franco-Italian relations, p. 51.

Haig's proposal at Compiègne on January 24th 1918 is discussed by Lloyd George, *War Memoirs*, pp. 1633–4. For the artillery reinforcement of the British Salonika Army, see Falls, *Macedonia*, Vol. II, pp. 58–59 and pp. 61–62. There are several accounts of the replacement of Robertson by Wilson: Hankey, *Supreme Command*, Vol. II, pp. 768, 776, 779; Bonham Carter, *Soldier True*, pp. 324–30; Lloyd George, *War Memoirs*, pp. 1673–1693. For Lloyd George's subsequent irritation with Wilson see Hankey, *Supreme Command*, Vol. II, p. 830. The unkind comment on Wilson's attitude to politicians; Cruttwell, *History of the Great War*, pp. 500–1.

On General Bordeaux's mission to the Greek Army, see: *Armées Francaises*, Vol. VIII, part 2, pp. 490–2, 548–52 and 577–8; Falls, *Macedonia*, Vol. II, pp. 67–68. On King Alexander's treatment of Greek troublemakers, see *Armées Francaises*, Vol. VIII, part 2, pp. 578–9 (and footnotes).

On the rivalry between Pašić's 'Greater Serbia' idea and the Yugoslav Committee, see Macartney and Palmer, *Independent Eastern Europe*, pp. 52–53 and p. 71 (and the sources cited therein). For the Yugoslav Volunteers from Russia, see Ante Mandić, *Fragmenti za Historiju Ujedinjenja* (Zagreb, 1956), pp. 39–49. (Dr Mandić was the chief spokesman for the Yugoslav Committee in Petrograd). There are brief accounts of their tribulations in Villari, *Macedonian Campaign*, pp. 192–3 and Falls, *Macedonia*, Vol. II, pp. 68–69.

For Guillaumat's report to Foch on March 1st, see Larcher, *Grande Guerre dans les Balkans*, p. 281; *Armées Francaises*, Vol. VIII, part 3, pp. 7–9 and annexe 2414; and Azan, *Franchet d'Espérey*, p. 181.

On the British and Greek actions on the Struma in April 1918 see Falls, *Macedonia*, Vol. II, pp. 80–85. The joint Franco-Italian advance in Albania is discussed in the same volume, pp. 91–92 and more fully in *Armées Francaises*, Vol. VIII, part 3, pp. 46–58.

For accounts of the Skra di Legen actions, see: *Armées Fran-*

caises, Vol. VIII, part 3, pp. 36–42; Falls, *Macedonia*, Vol. II, pp. 89–91 and Larcher, *Grande Guerre dans les Balkans*, pp. 224–5. Bulgarian reactions to the battle (which they called 'Yarebitchna') are noted in Nedeff, *Les Opérations en Macèdoine*, pp. 178–179 and p. 182; and are adversely criticized by Landfried, *Der Endkampf in Mazedonien* (Berlin, 1923), pp. 132 ff. Villari, *Macedonian Campaign*, pp. 197–8 emphasizes the effect of the Skra combat on Greek public opinion, and the quotation on p. 178 is taken from his account.

CHAPTER ELEVEN: 'DESPERATE FRANKIE'

The gesture of respect to Guillaumat at the boxing championships is described by Collinson Owen, *Salonica and After*, pp. 126–7. The account of the interview between Franchet d'Espérey and Clemenceau is in Azan, *Franchet d'Espérey*, pp. 176–177. Clemenceau refers briefly to the appointment of d'Espérey in *Grandeurs et Miseres d'une Victoire* (Paris, 1930), p. 104; d'Espérey's note to Le Chatelier on leaving Paris is printed by Azan, p. 178.

On Franchet d'Espérey's character, see: Azan, pp. 283–6; A Grasset, *Franchet d'Espérey* (Paris, 1920), pp. 8–10; Robert d'Harcourt, *Le Fauteuil du Maréchal Franchet d'Espérey* (Paris, 1947), pp. 40–41 and p. 44. For a shrewd Italian estimate, see Villari, *Macedonian Campaign*, pp. 201–2. Criticism of his impulsiveness occurs several times in Serrigny, *Trente Ans avec Pétain* (Paris, 1959), pp. 137 and 146–7. Haig's assessment is in John Terraine, *Douglas Haig: The Educated Soldier* (London, 1963) p. 97. The account of Franchet d'Espérey's attitude when he took over the Fifth Army is in E. L. Spears, *Liaison, 1914* (London 1930), p. 397–8.

The 'savage vigour' remark appears in d'Harcourt, *Fauteuil*, p. 43. For d'Espérey's reaction to existing plans see Azan, pp. 181–182, and d'Harcourt, p. 29. Clemenceau's telegram of interim instructions is printed in *Armées Francaises*, Vol. VIII, part 3, annexe 293. For the visit to Yelak, see Azan, pp. 182–3 and *Armées Francaises*, Vol. VIII, part 3, pp. 75–76 and annexes 357 and 381. The entry in d'Espérey's diary after the meeting is quoted by d'Harcourt in *Fauteuil*, pp. 29–30.

The 'summary study of a joint offensive' forms annexe 376 to *Armées Francaises*, Vol. VIII. For Clemenceau's directive and d'Espérey's reactions see Azan, p. 185; Larcher, *Grande Guerre*

dans les Balkans, annexe 18 and 19; and *Armées Francaises*, Vol.
VIII, part 3, pp. 77–82.

For the meeting at Versailles on July 2nd between Clemenceau
and Lloyd George, see Falls, *Macedonia*, Vol. II, p. 105; Lloyd
George, *War Memoirs*, p. 1917 (which contains the quotation
printed on p. 189); *Armées Francaises*, Vol. VIII, part 3, pp. 155–
156. For the Trianon meeting of July 11th see, *ibid*, p. 157 and
Falls, p. 106. The correspondence between Milne and General
Bliss is summarized by Falls on p. 108; and Professor Falls also
deals with the objections of the C.I.G.S. to an offensive, p. 110.
The Versailles meeting of military representatives is covered by
Larcher, p. 227–8 and by Falls, pp. 110–11.

On the hoisting of guns on the Floka, see F. Feyler, *La Campagne de Macédoine* (Geneva, 1920), Vol. III, pp. 37–40; and
Azan, p. 191. Italian activity in Albania at this time is described
by Villari, *Macedonian Campaign*, pp. 203–5; he also mentions
d'Espérey's neglect of Essad, p. 212. For General Henrys's plan
see annexes 502 and 712 of *Armées Francaises*, Vol. VIII, part 3.
The same volume prints the plan of General d'Anselme as
annexe 749, and the proposals of Mišić, with the amendments of
d'Espérey as annexes 515 and 688: it discusses the preparation
of the plans, pp. 175–84; see also Azan, p. 190 and Falls, p. 128.
On Milne's failure to get all the men and material he required,
see Falls, pp. 112–17; on the high incidence of Spanish influenza,
see the same volume, p. 166: and on Milne's plans, pp. 135–9.
Franchet d'Espérey's instructions of July 24th, ordering the
British to participate in a general offensive when attacks elsewhere 'have made a certain progress' is printed as Appendix 7
of Falls, *Macedonia*, Vol II. For criticism of Milne's subsequent
timing of the attack, see Charles Packer, *Return to Salonika* (London, 1964), p. 118. Franchet d'Espérey's general instructions for
the exploitation are printed as Appendix 11 of Falls, *Macedonia*.
D'Espérey's awareness of the danger in concentrating on detail
is taken from Azan, p. 192.

For Guillaumat's visit to No. 10 Downing Street, and the
conference there see: Hankey, *Supreme Command*, Vol. II, p. 837;
Lloyd George, *War Memoirs*, pp. 1917–18. For Guillaumat's
activities in general at this stage see the article by Lieutenant-
Colonel Lepetit, 'La Genèse de l'Offensive de Macédoine' in
Revue Militaire Francaise (Paris), July 1922, pp. 41–42. The telegram authorizing d'Espérey to open the offensive forms annexe
910 of *Armées Francaises*, Vol. VIII, part 3. D'Harcourt (p. 33)

prints the comment made by d'Espérey in his diary when the telegram reached him.

CHAPTER TWELVE: 'THE ENEMY IS IN RETREAT'

For Mišić on the Floka and the signal to open fire, see Falls, *Macedonia*, Vol. II, p. 147. The German who wrote of the 'iron storm' of shells is General D. Dieterich who compiled the semi-official monograph, *Weltkriegsende an der Mazedonischen Front* (Berlin, 1926): the reference is to p. 26. I have used this work (pp. 26–28) for the German reactions to the attack. The British exploratory feint on the Roche Noire Salient is vividly described by a participant, F. G. Ingamells, in a brief memoir, *On the Salonika Front*, 1916–1918 (Salonika Reunion Association, Norwich, 1944). An account of the capture of the Vetrenik, the Kravicki Kamen, the Dobropolje and the Sokol is given in *Armées Francaises*, Vol. VIII, part 3, pp. 315–17, supplemented by annexes 964, 973, 975–81, 985, 1003–14. For the assault on the Kozyak, the same volume of the French history, pp. 317–18 (with annexes 999, 1000, 1015–17, 1031) and Dieterich, *Weltkriegsende*, pp. 35–37.

On von Scholtz's request to Hindenburg for assistance, see Dieterich, p. 48, Falls, p. 194 and appendix 16. For the reaction to the request at Spa, see Hindenburg, *Aus meinem Leben* (Berlin, 1920), p. 370 and p. 372, and Ludendorff, *Meine Kriegserrinungen* (Berlin, 1919), pp. 578–9. For Rušev and the Bulgarian Second Division, see Dieterich, *Weltkriegsende*, p. 37.

The code message to open the attack on Doiran appears in H. A. Jones, *Over the Balkans and South Russia*, p. 111. The fullest account of the situation at Doiran on the eve of the battle and of the fighting on the XII Corps front is in Falls, Vol. II, pp. 159–172. An account from the Bulgarian side is in Nedeff, *Les Opérations en Macédoine*, pp. 223–42. See, also, Collinson Owen, *Salonica and After*, pp. 284–53. The account by a survivor of the 11th Welch Regiment, J. E. Vipond, appeared as an article, 'In Bulgar Hands' in *The Mosquito* for June, 1958. For the XVI Corps attack, see Falls, Vol. II, pp. 172–7 and the recollections of a veteran of the 28th Division, Charles Packer, *Return to Salonika*, pp. 125–35. On the fighting of September 19th, see: Falls, pp. 178–86; Nedeff, pp. 245–55; Collinson Owen, 254–8.

For Nerezov, Todorov and the conference at Prilep, see Nedeff, p. 225; Dieterich, *Weltkriegsende*, pp. 47–49; Falls, pp.

193–5. On the reactions of the Bulgarians to the order to retreat, see Nedeff, pp. 283–6.

The quotation from an airman, printed on p. 213 appears in Jones, *Over the Balkans*, p. 122. For the effect of bombing, see Jones, pp. 123–4; Collinson Owen, pp. 261–2. Stanley Spencer's impressions of the Allied advance are printed in the authorized biography of the artist, Maurice Collis, *Stanley Spencer* (London, 1962), p. 57.

For the attack on the Dzena Mountains and its consequences, see *Armées Francaises*, vol. VIII, part 3, pp. 322–9. The Italian assault on Hill 1050 is fully covered by Villari, *Macedonian Campaign*, pp. 234–9. D'Espérey's jubilant message of September 22nd recording that the enemy was in retreat on the whole front is printed as Appendix 17 of Falls, *Macedonia*, Vol. II.

The fullest record of the advance of the French colonial cavalry is to be found in the memoirs of its commander, F. L. Jouinot-Gambetta *Uskub* (Paris, 1920). He quotes from his letters showing his hopes of reaching Germany on p. 24; describes the meeting with Franchet d'Espérey on p. 28; comments on the fall of Prilep on p. 32. On Gradsko, see the record of Dieterich, *Weltkriegsende*, pp. 94–98 which has especial importance as Dieterich was commander of the composite force defending the town. For the importance attached by the German High Command to Gradsko, see Hindenburg, *Aus meinem Leben*, pp. 370, 374–5; the quotation of the improbability of the French reaching Skopje is taken from p. 375 and Franchet d'Espérey's annotation of this passage is mentioned by Azan on p. 289 of his biography.

General Pruneau's letter on the sorry state of the 17th Colonial Division is quoted by C. Photiades, *La Victoire des Alliès en Orient* (Paris, 1920), pp. 184–5. Jouinot-Gambetta continues his narrative over the Babuna Pass and into the mountains in *Uskub*, pp. 48–82. The approach to Skopje and the fall of the city are described in the same book, pp. 79–90. Extracts from this passage have appeared in English translation in Richard Thoumin, *The First World War: History in the Making* (London, 1963) pp. 498–499. For a German account of the defence of Skopje, see Dieterich, *Weltkriegsende*, pp. 122–6.

CHAPTER THIRTEEN: ORIENT EXPRESS

For the British and Greek advance into Bulgaria, see Falls

Macedonia, Vol. II, pp. 223–36. There is a detailed account of the entry into Bulgaria by a veteran of the Derbyshire Yeomanry, C. R. Allcock, entitled 'Saw the Bulgars Surrender' in *The Mosquito* for September, 1962.

For the strain of the war on Bulgaria, see P. Gentizon, *Le Drame Bulgare* (Paris, 1923). On Lukov and Ferdinand, see Villari, *Macedonian Campaign*, p. 246: Villari also has a clear account of American policy towards Bulgaria, p. 209. A highly critical assessment of Lukov is contained in Dieterich, *Weltkriegsende*, p. 249.

For the armistice negotiations with Bulgaria and the movements of the Bulgarian plenipotentiaries, see: Falls, *Macedonia*, Vol. II, pp. 228, 230, 233 and 250 (with the terms of the Armistice printed in full, pp. 251–3); Azan, pp. 196–200; Photiades, *La Victoire*, p. 130. The armistice terms are also printed by Lloyd George in his *War Memoirs*, pp. 1946–7. For the effect of the Bulgarian surrender in London, see Hankey, *Supreme Command*, Vol. II, p. 840. Churchill's description of the reaction in Paris is in *The World Crisis*, p. 1397. For German reactions, see Ludendorff, *Meine Kriegerrinungen*, pp. 581–3; and Hindenburg, *Aus meinem Leben*, pp. 372–80; also Lloyd George (quoting German sources), *War Memoirs*, pp. 1944–5. Hindenburg's decisive appeal of October 3rd is printed by Prince Max of Baden, *Memoirs* (London, 1928), Vol. II, p. 19: the suggestion that Hindenburg was seeking to excuse failures on the Western Front by placing the blame on the troops in Macedonia was first made by that incorrigible Westerner, Sir William Robertson, in *Soldiers and Statesmen*, Vol. II, p. 147.

There is a detailed description of the intrigues against d'Espérey in Paris and Clemenceau's proposal to send Guillaumat to replace him in Azan's biography, pp. 201–4. For d'Espérey's intention to press forward into Germany, see Azan, p. 211 (from which the quotation on p. 227 is taken), Larcher, *La Grande Guerre*, p. 250 Falls, *Macedonia*, Vol. II, p. 277; d'Harcourt, *Fauteuil*, pp. 35–36. For Italian ambitions Photiades, *La Victoire*, p. 203.

Falls analyses the discussions between d'Espérey and Milne in *Macedonia*, Vol. II, pp. 257–60. On Lloyd George's attitude to Constantinople and on the discussions between Clemenceau and Lloyd George, see: Hankey, *Supreme Command*, Vol. II, pp. 840–3; Lloyd George, *War Memoirs*, pp. 1947–50, Larcher, pp. 287–9; Azan, pp. 213–14. For the Devonshire Regiment in Roumania, see Falls, p. 282.

o*

The fullest account of the British advance to the frontier of Turkey and the subsequent occupation of strategic points on the Straits is contained in Falls, pp. 262–71. The quotation from the reminiscences of a former member of the R.F.A. is taken from the article 'The March to Turkey' by E. A. Armstrong in *The Mosquito* for December, 1963. There is another interesting article on this subject entitled 'Rendezvous in Dedeagach' by G. J. Davidge in *The Mosquito* for March, 1959.

On the advance of the French and the Serbs from Skopje to the Danube, see *Armées Francaises*, Vol. VIII, part 3, pp. 376–93 and 440–68. There is an interesting account of the activities of Serb irregulars (which claims that they captured several thousand prisoners and entered Belgrade before the regular Serb Army) in an article by B. Hrabak, 'Ucesce Stanovistva Srbija u Proterivariju Okupatora Oktobra 1918 Godine' in *Istoriski Glasnik* (Belgrade) 1958, parts 3/4, pp. 25–59. The account of the German retreat in Dieterich, *Weltkriegsende*, pp. 164–75 is much more comprehensive than the cursory treatment given to the ending of the war in the Balkans in volume XIII of the official German history, *Der Weltkrieg*.

D'Espérey's abortive proposal to carry his front to Germany in collaboration with the Italians is printed in Larcher, *La Grande Guerre*, p. 252. His comparison with 1809 is also cited by Larcher, p. 253. His journey from Salonika to Belgrade is outlined by Azan, p. 228.

The fullest accounts of the negotiations with the Hungarians are in Azan, pp. 228–32; and by Karolyi himself in *Faith without Illusion* (London, 1956), pp. 130–7. The terms of the Hungarian Military Convention are printed as annexe 23 of Larcher (pp. 289–92).

I am grateful to Dr J. B. Hoptner for having verified from the National Archives in Washington the presence of United States troops (the 2nd Battalion, 332nd Infantry) at Kotor (Cattaro) from November, 1918 to the spring of 1919.

D'Espérey's dairy entry of November 11th 1918 is printed in Azan's biography, p. 235.

CHAPTER FOURTEEN: 'WITHOUT THE LAUREL'

For the movements of the British divisions after the end of the war, see Falls, *Macedonia*, Vol. II, pp. 306–9. D'Espérey's reactions are considered by Azan in his biography, pp. 238–60. For Bishop Winnington-Ingram's letter see *The Times* for 8th November, 1918; and for Milne's article, see the special War Graves Supplement to *The Times*, 10th November, 1928.

The projects for intervention in Salonika in the Second World War are well-documented: see M. Weygand, *Rappelé au Service* (Paris, 1950), vol. 3, pp. 21–23; A. Cretzianu, *The Lost Opportunity* (London 1957), pp. 35–36; Macartney and Palmer, *Independent Eastern Europe*, p. 416. For the German invasion of Greece in 1941, see A. Papagos, *The Battle of Greece 1941–41* (Athens, 1949) and Field-Marshal Lord Wilson of Libya, *Eight Years Overseas* (London, 1950). For Hitler's fears of Salonika as a British base, see Macartney and Palmer pp. 434–5. On Franchet d'Espérey's last days, see Azan, pp. 278–80 and Robert d'Harcourt, *Le Fauteuil . . .*, p. 39 and p. 47.

Sections of the murals in the Sandham Memorial Chapel at Burghclere are reproduced in the biography of Sir Stanley Spencer by Maurice Collis.

Bibliography

1. Official Publications

CORBETT, Sir Julian, *History of the Great War: Naval Operations*, Volume III (London, 1923).

FALLS, Cyril, *History of the Great War: Military Operations, Macedonia*, Volume I (London, 1933), Volume II (London, 1935).

FOREIGN OFFICE, Historical Section Handbook no. 14, The Yugoslav Movement (London 1918), no. 16, Albania (London, 1918).

JONES, H. A., *History of the Great War: The War in the Air*, Volume V (London, 1935).

MINISTERE DE LA GUERRE, Etat-Major de l'Armée, Service Historique, *Les Armées Francaises dans la Grande Guerre*, Volume VIII and Annexes (Paris, 1925–1934).

NEWBOLT, Sir Henry, *History of the Great War: Naval Operations*, Volume IV (London, 1928).

REICHKRIEGSMINISTERIUM, *Der Weltkrieg, 1914–1918*, Volumes IX, XI, XIII (Berlin, 1936 *et seq.*).

2. Memoirs and Biographies of Leading Personalities

ALASTOS, D., *Venizelos* (London, 1942).

AMERY, L. S., *My Political Life*, Volume II (London, 1953).

AZAN, General Paul, *Franchet d'Espérey* (Paris, 1949).

BALLARD, C. R., *Kitchener* (London, 1930).

BONHAM CARTER, V., *Soldier True* (London, 1964).

CAILLAUX, J., *Mes Prisons* (Paris, 1920).

CAILLAUX, J., *Mes Mémoires* (Paris, 1947).

CALLWELL, Sir Charles, *Experiences of a Dug-Out* (London, 1920).

CHURCHILL, Sir Winston, *The World Crisis* (London, 1923–31) (All references are to the 1939 edition).

CLEMENCEAU, G., *Grandeurs et miseres d'une victoire* (Paris, 1930).

COBLENTZ, P., *The Silence of Sarrail* (London, 1930).

CORDONNIER, General E. L. V., *Ai-Je Trahi Sarrail?* (Paris, 1930).

DICTIONARY OF NATIONAL BIOGRAPHY, Articles on General

Sir Bryan Mahon and Field Marshal Lord Milne, etc.

FALKENHAYN, General E. V., *General Headquarters and its Crucial Decisions* (London, 1919).

FOURNET, Admiral Dartige du, *Souvenirs de Guerre d'un Amiral* (Paris, 1930).

GALLWITZ, General Max von, *Meine Führertatigkeit im Weltkriege* (Berlin, 1929).

GEORGE, D. LLOYD *War Memoirs* (London, 1934 *et seq.*) (All references are to the 1938 edition).

GEORGE, William, *My Brother and I* (London, 1958).

GRAHAM, S., *Alexander of Yugoslavia* (London, 1938).

GRASSET, A., *Franchet d'Espérey* (Paris, 1920).

GREY OF FALLODON, Viscount, *Twenty-Five Years*, Volume II (London, 1925).

HANKEY, Lord, *The Supreme Command, 1941–1918* (London, 1961).

HARCOURT, Robert D', *Le Fauteuil du Marechal Franchet d'Espérey*, Discours de Reception de M. le Comte Robert d'Harcourt a l'Académie Française (Paris, 1947).

HINDENBURG, Field-Marshal Paul von Beneckendorff, und, *Aus meinem Leben* (Berlin, 1920).

HOFFMANN, General Max, *The War of Lost Opportunities* (New York, 1925).

JOUINOT-GAMBETTA, General F. L., *Uskub* (Paris, 1920).

KAROLYI, Mihaly, *Fighting the World* (London, 1925).

KAROLYI, Mihaly, *Faith without Illusion* (London, 1956).

LENNOX, Lady A. Gordon, *The Diary of Lord Bertie, 1914–1918* (London, 1924).

LUDENDORFF, General Erich, *Meine Kriegserrinerungen* (Berlin, 1919).

MACKENZIE, Sir Compton, *Greek Memories* (London, 1939).

MAGNUS, Sir Philip, *Kitchener* (London, 1959).

MARIUS-ARY and LEBLOND, *Gallieni Parle*, Volume II (Paris, 1920).

MAX, Prince, of Baden, *Memoirs*, Volume II (London, 1928).

OWEN, Frank, *Tempestuous Journey* (London, 1954).

POINCARÉ, President Raymond, *Au Service de la France*, Volumes II–X (Paris, 1926–1933).

ROBERTSON, Field Marshal Sir William, *Soldiers and Statesmen* (London, 1926).

SARRAIL, General Maurice, *Mon Commandement en Orient* (Paris, 1920).

SERRIGNY, General Bernard, *Trente Ans avec Pétain* (Paris, 1959).

SPENDER, J. A. and ASQUITH, C., *Asquith* (London, 1932).

SUAREZ, G., *Briand: Sa Vie, son Oeuvre avec son Journal*, Volume IV (Paris, 1939).

TERRAINE, John, *Douglas Haig: The Educated Soldier* (London, 1963).

TREVELYAN, G. M., *Grey of Fallodon* (London, 1937).

WEYGAND, General M., *Rappelé au Service* (Paris, 1950).

WILSON, Field Marshal Lord, of Libya, *Eight Years Overseas* (London, 1950).

3. Reminiscences of the Salonika Campaign

(The most useful single source for personal reminiscences of British veterans is *The Mosquito*, the quarterly organ of the Salonika Reunion Association, published in London since 1928. Articles from *The Mosquito* are cited in the Notes on Sources, above.)

BUDDEN, W., *Leaves from a Salonika Diary* (Typescript deposited in the Imperial War Museum, London, 1920).

BURR, Malcolm, *Slouch Hat* (London, 1935).

BURGESS, Alan, *The Lovely Sergeant* (London, 1963) (A biography of Flora Sandes).

CASSON, S., *Steady Drummer* (London, 1935).

COLLIS, Maurice, *Stanley Spencer* (London, 1962) (A biography including extracts from the artist's letters).

DAVID, Robert, *Le Drame Ignore de l'Armée d'Orient* (Paris, 1927.

DAVIS, R. H., *With the French in France and Salonika* (London, 1916).

DAY, H. C., *Macedonian Memories* (London, 1930).

FRAPPA, J-J., *Makedonia: souvenirs d'un officier de liaison en Orient.* (Paris 1921).

HEYDEMARCK, Hauptmann, *War Flying in Macedonia* (London, 1938).

HUTTON, I. Emslie, Lady, *With a Woman's Unit in Serbia, Salonika and Sebastopol* (London, 1928).

INGAMELLS, F. G., *On the Salonika Front, 1916–1918* (Norwich, 1944).

LAKE, H., *In Salonica with our Army* (London, 1917).

LAWSON, J. C., *Tales of Aegean Intrigue* (London, 1920).

MANN, A. J., *The Salonika Front* (London, 1920).

OWEN, H. Collinson, *Salonica and After* (London, 1919).

PACKER, Charles, *Return to Salonika* (London, 1964).

SANDES, Flora, *An English Woman Sergeant in the Serbian Army* (London, 1916).

SELIGMAN, V. J., *Macedonian Musings* (London, 1918).

SELIGMAN, V. J., *The Salonica Side-Show* (London, 1919).

SMITH, R. S., *A Subaltern in Macedonia and Judea* (London, 1930).

USBORNE, C. V., *Blast and Counter-Blast* (London, 1935).

WALSHE, Douglas, *With the Serbs in Macedonia* (London, 1920).

4. Other Books

ABBOTT, G. F., *Greece and the Allies* (London, 1922).

ADAM, G., *Treason and Tragedy* (London, 1929).

ADAMS, J. C., *Flight in Winter* (Princeton, 1942).

ARCHER, J., *L'Enigme de la Guerre* (Paris, 1938).

BARKER, Elizabeth, *Macedonia: its place in Balkan Power Politics* (London, 1950).

BOGICEVIĆ, Milos, *Le Procès de Salonique, Juin, 1917* (Paris, 1927).

BONNEFOUS, Georges, *Histoire Politique de la Troisième République*, Volume II (Paris, 1957).

CRUTTWELL, C. R. M. F., *A History of the Great War* (London, 1934).

DALBIAC, P. N. *History of the 60th Division* (London, 1927).

DIETERICH, General D., *Weltkriegsende an der Mazedonischen Front* (Berlin, 1926).

EDMONDS, Brigadier-General Sir James, *A Short History of World War I* (London, 1951).

FALLS, Cyril, *The First World War* (London, 1960).

FEYLER, F., *La Campagne de Macédoine* (Geneva, 1920).

FORSTER, E. S., *A Short History of Modern Greece, 1821–1956* (rev. ed., London, 1958).

GENTIZON, P., *Le Drame Bulgare* (Paris, 1923).

GORCE, Paul-Marie de la, *La République et son Armée* (Paris, 1963).

GOTTLIEB, W. W., *Studies in Secret Diplomacy* (London, 1957).

HIGGINS, Turnbull, *Winston Churchill and the Dardanelles* (London, 1964).

HAUMANT, L., *La Formation de la Yougoslavie* (Paris, 1930).

HELMREICH, E. C., *The Diplomacy of the Balkan Wars* (London, 1937).

JONES, H. A., *Over the Balkans and South Russia: 47 Squadron R.A.F.* (London, 1923).

KERNER, R. J. (ed.), *Yugoslavia* (Berkeley, U.S.A., 1949).

KING, J. C., *Generals and Politicians* (Berkley, U.S.A., 1951).

LANDFRIED, O., *Der Endkampf in Mazedonien* (Berlin, 1923).

LOGIO, G. C., *Bulgaria, Past and Present* (Manchester, 1936).

MACARTNEY, C. A. and PALMER, A. W., *Independent Eastern Europe* (London, 1962).

MANDIĆ, Ante, *Fragmenti za Historiju Ujedinjenja* (Zagreb, 1956).

MAVROGORDATO, J., *Modern Greece, 1800–1931* (London, 1931).

MAY, A. J., *The Hapsburg Monarchy, 1867–1914* (Cambridge, Mass., 1951).

MELAS, G. M., *Ex-King Constantine and the War* (London, 1920).

'MERMEIX' (Gabriel Terrail), *Fragments d'histore, 1914–19* Volume IV, Part 2, *Sarrail et les armées d'Orient* (Paris, 1920).

MICHEL, P. H., *La Question de l'Adriatique, 1914–18* (Paris, 1938).

MILLER, W., *A History of the Greek People, 1821–1931* (London, 1931).

MURRAY's *Handbook to Turkey-in-Europe* (London, 1912).

NEDEFF, Lieutenant-Colonel, *Les Opérations en Macédoine: l'Epopée de Doiran* (Sofia, 1927).

NESKOVIĆ, B., *Istina o Solunskom Procesu* (Belgrade, 1953).

PAPAGOS, General A., *The Battle for Greece, 1940–1941* (Athens, 1949).

PEROVIĆ, M., *Ustanak na juga Srbije 1917: Toplicki ustanak* (Belgrade, 1954).

PHOTIADÈS, C., *La Victoire des Alliés en Orient* (Paris, 1920).

PINGAUD, A., *Histoire Diplomatique de la France pendant la Grande Guerre* (Paris, 1938 *et seq.*).

PRICE, W. H. C., *The Balkan Cockpit* (London, 1915).

PRICE, G. Ward, *The Story of the Salonica Army* (London, 1917).

PRIBICEVIĆ, Svetozar, *La Dictature du Roi Alexandre* (Paris, 1933)

RIPERT d'Alauzier, *Un Drame Historique: La Résurrection d l'Armée Serbe* (Paris, 1923).

SARRAUT, M. and REVOL, J., *Un Episode du Drame Serbe* (Paris, 1919).

SCHRAMM VON THADDEN, E., *Griechenland und die grossen Mächte, 1912–23* (Gottingen, 1933).

SCIAKY, L., *Farewell to Salonika* (London, 1946).

SFORZA, Carlo, *Fifty Years of War and Diplomacy in the Balkans* (New York, 1940).

SLIPICEVIĆ, F., *Prvi svjetsi Rat* (Belgrade, 1956).

SPEARS, Brigadier-General E. L., *Liaison, 1914* (London, 1930).

SPEARS, Brigadier-General E. L., *Prelude to Victory* (London, 1939).

STAVEIANOS, L. S., *The Balkans since 1453* (New York, 1958).

STRUTZ, G., *Herbstschlacht in Mazedonien: Cernabogen* (Berlin, 1921).

SVOLONOS, N. G., *Histoire de la Grèce Moderne* (Paris, 1953).

SWIRE, J., *Albania: The Rise of a Kingdom* (London, 1929).

TAYLOR, A. J. P., *The First World War* (London, 1963).

THOUMIN, Richard, *The First World War: History in the Making* (London, 1963).

TUCHMAN, Barbara W., *August, 1914* (London, 1962).

UEBERSBERGER, H., *Oesterreich zwischen Russland und Serbien* (Cologne Craz, 1958).

VACALOPOULOS, Apostolos P., *A History of Thessaloniki* (Salonika, 1963).

VILLARI, L., *The Macedonian Campaign* (London, 1922).

WATT, Richard M., *Dare Call It Treason* (New York, 1963).

WEST, Dame Rebecca, *Black Lamb and Grey Falcon* (London, 1941).

WORMSER, Georges, *La République de Clemenceau* (Paris, 1961).

ZIVANOVIĆ, Milan Z., *Pukovnik Apis: Solunski Proces, 1917* (Belgrade, 1955).

5. *Articles in Periodicals*

HRABAK, Bogumil: 'The participation of the inhabitants of Serbia in the expulsion of the occupying forces in October, 1918' (In Serbo-Croat), *Istoriski Glasnik* (Belgrade, 1958) parts 3/4, pp. 25–50.

HRABAK, B. and DZAMBAZOVSKI, K.: 'Serbian Social Democrats on the Salonika Front and in Corfu in the years 1916–18' (In Serbo-Croat), *Istoriski Glasnik* (Belgrade, 1961) parts 1/4, pp. 151–97.

LEPETIT, Colonel: 'La genèse de l'offensive de Macédoine', *Revue Militaire Française* (Paris, 1922), July, pp. 28–43.

MITRVIĆ, Dragomir: 'The Russian Revolution and Russian Troops on the Salonika Front' (In Serbo-Croat), *Istoriski Glasnik* (Belgrade, 1957) parts 3/4, pp. 17–24.

Index

(Alternative place names in italics)

Achi Baba, 120

Adalia, Italian troops moved from Macedonia to, 237

Alamein, El, battle of, 129

Albania: Serbs retreat into, 41; fighting in (September, 1917), 155, 156, 157, 158, 159; Italian designs on, 155, 158, 169, 236; Republican 'Government' of, 156, 157; French and Italian operations in (May, 1918), 174–175; Italian operations in (Sept.–Oct., 1918), 193, 232; rival Powers claim, 236

Albanians: irregulars reach Salonika, 74; in action south of Lake Prespa, 88; fight under Essad, 156, 157, 158

Albion, H.M.S., British battleship, 11, 55

Alexander I, King of Greece: accession, 139; reconciliation with Venizelos, 139, 153; visits Salonika, 171

Alexander, Prince-Regent of Serbia and subsequently King of Yugoslavia: in Albanian retreat, 42; visits liberated Monastir, 90; alleged conspiracy against, 133–135; and offensive in the Moglena, 184, 185, 186; receives d'Espérey in Serbia, 234; assassinated (1934), 240; mentioned, 171, 172

Alexandria, 59, 64

Allenby, General Sir Edmund (1861–1936), 147, 170, 229

Almereyda, Miguel, German agent in France, 159, 160, 161

Andrew, Prince of Greece, 54, 97

Angheliki, Greek ship attacked by U-boat, 100

Apis, see Dimitriević

Armensko, 83

Armistices: Austro-Hungarian, 233, 234, 235; Bulgarian, 224, 242; German, 226, 231, 236, 238; Turkish, 229, 231

Arras, battle of, 130

Arz von Straussenburg, General, chief of the Austro-Hungarian General Staff, 203

Askold, Russian cruiser, 55

Asquith, Herbert Henry, British prime minister: and war against Turkey, 26; and reluctance to keep troops at Salonika, 1915, 46, 47, 49, 50; resignation, 108

Athens: political situation in 1915 in, 13; visit of Kitchener to, 48; visit of Sarrail to, 65; naval threat to (spring, 1916), 68; panic among Entente sympathizers in, 76; Entente fleets threaten (autumn, 1916), 96, 101; Allied troops land in, 102, 104; fighting in (Dec., 1916), 104–107; changing attitude to war in, 177–178; in the Second World War, 240

Athos, Mount, Serbian monks celebrate Monastir victory, 90.

Aulard, Alphonse, French historian, 33

Australia, South Slav volunteers come to Salonika from, 173

Austria-Hungary: and outbreak of war, 17–18; covets Salonika, 45–46; possibility of separate peace, 147, 243; effect of four years of war on, 203; possible despatch of troops to Macedonia, 203; disintegration of, 233–234

Austro-Hungarian Army: invades Serbia, 1914, 18; invades Serbia in 1915, 32, 36; in action against Italians and French in Albania, 113, 155–156, 175; reinforcements for Serbian Front in 1918, 225; resistance in Serbia, 232

Babuna Pass, Serbian Macedonia, 40, 78, 216, 217

Bailloud, General, French soldier, 38, 39

Balfour, Arthur James, British statesman: 26, 229

Balkan News, newspaper published by British Salonika Army, 145

Balkan Wars (1912–1913), 14, 19, 20, 206, 221

Banica, 84

Batachin, 80

Belasica Planina, mountains on Serbo-Bulgarian frontier, 77, 114, 193, 221

Belasnica, river in Serbian Macedonia, 204

Belgrade: in campaigns of 1914–15, 22, 23, 32, 34; liberation of in 1918, 232, 233; meeting of Karolyi and d'Espérey in, 234–236; visits of d'Espérey to, 234, 237

Below, General von, commander of Army Group at Skopje, 87, 88

Benazet, Paul, French deputy and friend of d'Espérey, 22, 102, 103, 165

Bertie, Francis, Lord, British ambassador in Paris, 153, 162
Berovo, 222
Beshik (*Besikium*), lake in Greek Macedonia, 51, 52
Biklishta, Greek village near Albanian frontier, 157
Bizerta, dissident Serbs interned in, 135
Blace, Serbian town, 41
'Black Hand', Serbian terrorist organization, 133–135
Blaga Planina, line of hills south of Belasica Planina, 193, 206, 209
Bliss, General Tasker H., American soldier, 190, 191
Bojadief, General, commander of Bulgarian First Army, 75, 86
Bojović, General, chief of staff of Serbian Army, 77, 129, 132, 133, 135, 185
Bonaparte, Napoleon, 15, 21, 22, 163, 164, 234, 241
Bordeaux, General, head of French mission to Greek Army, 171
Boresnica, 81
Boris, Prince (later King) of Bulgaria, 215
Bosphorus, 228, 231
Boxer Rising, service of d'Espérey and Guillaumat in suppression of, 22, 166
Bralo, supply port for Entente armies, 141, 168
Bratianu, Ion, Roumanian prime minister, 71, 72, 74
Breslau, German warship, 229
Briand, Aristide, French prime minister: enthusiast for Salonika campaign, 23, 50, 63; heads French Government, 47, 49, 50, 108, 109; defends his Balkan policy, 69, 70; at Rome Conference, 110; fall of, 117; mentioned, 85, 96, 97, 153
Briggs, Lieutenant-General C. J., commander of British XVI Corps, 128, 221
British Army:
Army Corps
XII Corps, 117, 118, 122, 193, 205, 206, 209, 210, 214
XVI Corps, 64, 122, 125, 127–128, 159, 174–175, 193, 214, 221
Brigades
29th Brigade, 13
65th Brigade, 210
66th Brigade, 209
77th Brigade, 210
78th Brigade, 121, 123
79th Brigade, 120
85th Brigade, 128
Divisions
10th Division, 13, 15, 37, 38, 40, 41, 44, 114, 128, 142, 150
22nd Division, 74, 119, 121, 122, 124, 145, 208

26th Division, 119, 120, 125
27th Division, 64, 114, 144, 200, 221, 237
28th Division, 114, 128, 142, 144, 206, 221
29th Division, 27
60th Division, 109, 121, 122, 124, 144, 146, 147
Units (Regiments, etc.)
Argyll and Sutherland Highlanders, 159, 210
Cheshire Regiment, 175, 209
Cycle Battalion, 77
Derbyshire Yeomanry, 221, 223
Devonshire Regiment, 120, 121, 231
East Kent Regiment (The Buffs), 128
Gloucestershire Regiment, 124
Hampshire Regiment, 14, 120
King's Shropshire Light Infantry, 209
Rifle Brigade, 175
Royal Army Medical Corps, 144
Royal Berkshire Regiment, 121, 214
Royal Field Artillery, 231
Royal Fusiliers, 128
Royal Scots Fusiliers, 210
Scottish Rifles, 123, 210
Sherwood Foresters, 61
South Lancashire Regiment, 209
South Wales Borderers, 208
Welch Regiment, 208
Wiltshire Regiment, 120, 121
Worcestershire Regiment, 121
British Salonika Army: original administrative arrangements of, 59; participation in attacks of August 1916, 79; actions of in October 1916, 85–86; change in Headquarters status of, 111; participation in Spring Offensive of 1917, 115–125; reduction in strength of, 122; casualties in 1917 attacks, 125; living conditions within during 1917, 142–145; ridiculed on English music-hall stage, 145, 238; strength relative to Palestine army, 148; deprived of facilities by Salonika Fire, 152; Boxing Championship of (1918), 179; C.I.G.S. proposes replacement of British units within by Indian troops, 191; participation in final offensive of 1918, 194–195, 205–211, 213–214; advance into Bulgaria of, 220, 223–224; end of fighting for, 230; advance into Turkey of, 231; post-war treatment of veterans in, 238–239; annual memorial service for, 242.
Brod, 82, 84
Brussilov, General, commander of the Russian Eighth Army, 68, 69, 136
Bucharest, 71, 90, 231; Treaty of (1913), 19
Budapest, 22, 236, 241
Bulgaria: Balkan Wars and, 19–20; traditional friendship with Britain, 19,

33; inclination to support Central Powers, 19, 30; entry into the war, 36; friction with Austria-Hungary over Salonika's future, 46; effect of long period of war upon, 222; republic proclaimed within, 223; negotiation and conclusion of an Armistice, 223, 224

Bulgarian Army (*in general*): casualties in Balkan Wars, 19; first skirmishes with the French and the British, 39–40; unwilling to march into Greece (Jan. 1916) 57–58; anticipated Sarrail's offensive by attacking in August 1916, 75–76; and Sarrail's eventual attack, 80, 86, 87–89; strength in Macedonia in February 1917, 114; significance of Doiran for, 120; strengthened by Germans in May, 1917, 126; casualties in Albanian fighting, 156; on the Struma, 175; surprised at the Skra di Legen, 176; low morale after the Skra di Legen attacks, 177; surprised by assault on the Dobropolje, 197; stubborn resistance of, 201; failure to check the Serbs, 204; in second battle of Doiran, 205–211; possible counteroffensive of rejected by Germans, 211–212; severely bombed in retreat, 213–214; ineffectual defence of Skopje, 219; casualties in three years of war, 221–222; revolt of units in Sofia, 223; demobilized by Armistice terms, 224

Bulgarian Army (*Units*): First Army, 77, 86, 199, 211, 212, 213; Second Army, 128, 222; Second Division, 203, 204, 211; Third Division, 204, 211, 212, 213, 214; Fourth Division, 218; 30th Regiment, 200

Burges, Lieutenant-Colonel, South Wales Borderers; awarded Victoria Cross, 208

Burghclere, Hampshire; memorial chapel, 242

Butkovo (*Kerkinitis*), Greek valley south of Bulgarian frontier, 143

Caillaux, Joseph, French politician, 31, 160, 161, 163, 164

Calais Conferences: September 11th, 1915, 32; October 5th, 1915, 36; December 4th, 1915, 49–50; February 26th, 1917, 116.

Canea, (*Khania*), 98.

Caporetto, Battle of, 161

Carinthia, 237

Carson, Sir Edward: sees need to aid Serbia, 36; resigns from Cabinet over failure to help Serbs, 46

Cattaro (*Kotor*), 42, 236

Chamber of Deputies, lower house of French parliament, 69–70, 108–109, 117, 160, 163

Chantilly, headquarters of French commander-in-chief, 38, 47, 49, 59, 60, 61, 108

Charpy, Colonel (later General), chief of staff to d'Espérey, 167, 186

Chemin des Dames, battles of, 138, 165, 180

Chios, Greek island, 98

Churchill, Winston: and Dardanelles, 26, 27; and Bulgarian Armistice, 225

Clemenceau, Georges, French statesman: coins 'Gardeners of Salonika' jibe, 70; press campaign against Almereyda and Malvy, 159–160; appointed prime minister, 160; hostility to Sarrail, 160–161, 162; dismisses Sarrail, 163; investigates treasonable activities of Caillaux, 163; wishes to appoint d'Espérey as Sarrail's successor, 165; appoints Guillaumat, 166; summons Guillaumat back to Paris, 180; dismisses d'Espérey from Western Front command, 180; interview with d'Espérey before sending him to Salonika, 181; sends directive to Salonika, 187; justifies appointment of d'Espérey to Lloyd George, 189; answers British complaints about d'Espérey's planning of offensive, 191; authorizes d'Espérey to open offensive, 196; and Bulgarian Armistice, 223, 227; wishes to replace d'Espérey by Guillaumat, 227; attitude to Germany, 227–228; desire to end the war swiftly, 228; angry with d'Espérey for his independent spirit at end of the war, 229, 230, 239

Colonial Hill, war memorial, 242

Compiègne, French headquarters at, 108, 130, 169, 226

Constantine I, King of the Hellenes; military career, 20, 67, 171; succession, 20; friendship with German Kaiser, 20, 138; ambitious to occupy Constantinople, 20–21; attitude to Serbia, 21; illness in 1915, 30; disputes with Venizelos, in 1915, 34–36; visited by Kitchener (1915), 48; and Fort Karaburun, 55; receives Sarrail, 65; his political activity in 1916, 94, 95, 96, 97, 102–107; deposed, 138–139.

Constantinople, 20, 21, 26, 29, 32, 147, 228, 229, 230, 231

Conrad von Hötzendorf, Field Marshal, chief of Austro-Hungarian General Staff, 22, 32, 45–46.

Consuls, Enemy, at Salonika, 12–13, 53, 54

Cordonnier, General, French commander subordinate to Sarrail, 74, 78, 81–85, 88, 111, 114, 161

Corfu (*Kerkira*), 42–43, 60, 168

Corfu Pact (1917), 173
Crete, 98, 100
Crna, river in southern Serbian Mace-
donia, 40, 78, 79, 86, 87, 88, 89, 113,
114, 115, 125, 128, 129, 130, 155, 169,
204, 205, 206, 214, 215
Croatia, 172, 233
Crosfield, Sir Arthur, friend of Lloyd
George and Venizelos, 24
Czecho-Slovakia, 230, 233
Czechs, 225, 227, 232, 235

Danglis, General, Greek soldier and
commander-in-chief, 98, 99, 193
D'Anselme, General, French comman-
der of Army Group in Macedonia, 193,
214, 228
Danube, river, 32, 36, 78, 147, 228, 229,
230, 231, 234; flotilla on, 233
Dardanelles, 23, 26, 27, 28, 29, 31, 37,
43, 55, 96: Dardanelles Committee, 28
Dartige du Fournet, Vice-Admiral,
French commander of Allied naval
squadron off Salamis in 1916, 101–107
Dedeli, headquarters of Bulgarian First
Army, 199, 213
Dedeagatch (Alexandroupolis), 19, 231
Delcassé, Theophile, French statesman:
hostility to Salonika Expedition, 47,
69, 70
Demir Hissar (Sidhirokastron), 54, 66
Dietrichs, General, commander of Rus-
sian Brigades in Macedonia, 136–137
Dimitrievic, Dragutin, Colonel, Serbian
soldier and political conspirator, alias
"Apis", 133–135
Dinjić, Colonel, Serbian soldier, 133
Djevdjeli (Gevgelija), 221
Dobropolje, mountain on Greco-Serbian
frontier, 125, 127, 129, 155, 185, 186,
187, 192; battle of the Dobropolje,
200–204
Dobrusevo, 216
Doiran (Dhoijani), lake and town: fighting around in 1915, 40–41, 44; fighting
around in 1916, 74, 76, 78, 79, 115;
significance of, for the Bulgars, 115,
116; British committed to fight at,
115; preparations for first battle of
Doiran, 119–120; course of first battle
(April–May, 1917), 121–125; raids in
the autumn of 1917, 159; links with
the Skra di Legen action, 176; in
operational plans of the summer of
1918, 193; second battle of Doiran
(September, 1918), 205–211; Bulgars
retreat from, 212–213; after the
battle, 238, 242; mentioned, 114
Douchy, General, French liaison officer
with Serbs, 129
Drama, 77, 144
Dresden: d'Espérey's desire to march
upon, 21, 227, 228

Dreyfus Case: and Sarrail, 30
Drina, river, 18, 233.
Duncan, H.M.S., British battleship, 102
Dušan, Stephen, medieaval Serbian war-
rior-king, 79, 80, 90
Dzena, mountain, stormed by French
and Greek troops, 214

E 11, H.M. Submarine, 229
Elliott, Sir Francis, British Minister in
Athens, 35, 95
Eleusis, 96
Embeirikos, Greek shipowner, 99
d'Espérey, Franchet: see Franchet d'Es-
pérey
Essad Bey Pasha, Albanian General, 156,
157, 158, 162, 193, 240
Exmouth, H.M.S., British battleship, 102

Falkenhayn, General Erich von, Chief of
the German General Staff: and in-
vasion of Serbia in 1915, 32, 33, 34,
36; dispute with Conrad over in-
vasion of Greece, 45–46; reverses his
Balkan policy, 57–58; sends German
divisions to Macedonia, 75
Fashoda, Kitchener and, 43
Ferdinand, King of Bulgaria, 19, 222, 223
Ferrero, General, Italian soldier, 193
Fisher, Lord, Admiral of the Fleet, 26
Flocca's Restaurant, Salonika, 152
Floka, mountain, summit eyrie of Serbs,
185, 186, 192, 197, 200
Florina; fall of, 75–76; re-captured, 81,
82, 83; mentioned, 216
Foch, Ferdinand, General (later, Marshal of France): made chief of the
French General Staff, 165; instructions to Guillaumat, 167; and appointment of d'Espérey to Salonika command, 180, 181, 182; favours British
advance on Constantinople, 229; not
prepared to permit d'Espérey to
march into Germany, 234, 236, 241;
death, 240, mentioned, 163
France: treaty rights in Greece, 11;
traditional friendship with Serbia, 18;
at war with Turkey, 18; extent of
German occupation in 1914–1915, 24;
decision to send aid to Serbia, 37;
governmental changes of 1915 in, 47;
conflict with Britain over retention of
force at Salonika in December, 1915,
47–50; attitude to Sarrail in 1916, 85;
commercial interests in Greece and
Turkey, 93; policy towards Venizelos, 95, 99, 103; recognition of Venizelist Government, 104, 107; objections to withdrawal of British from
Salonika, 148–149; the political crisis
leading to appointment of Clemenceau
as prime minister, 160; danger of
coup d'état in 1917, 163; in favour of

Macedonian offensive in 1918, 189, 191, 192; and veterans of Salonika Army, 238

Franchet d'Espérey, General (later, Marshal of France), Louis Felix: desire for French Army on the Balkan Front in 1914–1915, 21, 22, 25, 45, 165, 227; early career, 21–22; prefers Western Front to Salonika command in December 1917, 165–166; dismissed as commander of Army Group of the North and ordered to Salonika, 180–181; interview with Clemenceau, 181; journey to Salonika, 182; appearance and character, 182–184; arrival in Salonika, 184; visits Serbian headquarters at Yelak, 184–187; determines on Dobropolje offensive, 186–187; displeased with Clemenceau's directive, 187; appointment of, attacked by Lloyd George, 189; authorized to prepare for an offensive, 192; seeks Clemenceau's intervention to secure shells for Milne's army, 194; his general battle instructions, 195; sends staff-officer to Rome by air to secure Italian co-operation, 196; receives authority to begin offensive, 196; confers Croix de Guerre on 7th Battalion, South Wales Borderers, 208; his supply problem, 212; aware of danger of his troops being trapped, 214; orders cavalry to advance, 215; intercepts Jouinot-Gambetta at Dobrusevo, 216; learns of fall of Skopje, 220; and Bulgarian Armistice terms, 223–224; mistrusted in Paris, 226–227; wishes to march on Dresden, 227; anxious to carry the war into Germany, 227, 234, 241; informs Milne of his Danubian plans, 228, 229; ordered to liberate Serbia but to send British troops into Turkey, 230, 233; travels from Salonika to Belgrade, 234; receives Karolyi in Belgrade, 235–236; orders advance into Hungary, 236; returns to Salonika and learns of German Armistice, 236; at Constantinople, 237; created Marshal of France (1922), 238; in North Africa, 238, 239, 240; last days, death (1942) and burial, 241; mentioned, 29, 102, 197, 199, 209, 242, 243

French Army (in general): in Macedonian campaign of 1915, 38, 39–40, 43–44; in battle for Monastir, 81–85, 88–89; in Spring Offensive of 1917, 125–127; mutinies in France, 138, 139, 140, 141; mutiny in Salonika, 140; problem of leave, 140, 141, 154; participation in the battle of the Dobropolje, 197, 200–201, 203–204; advances into Serbia, 232; liberates

South Slav lands, 236; refusal to learn lessons from Macedonian campaign, 239

French Army (Units) Divisions: 57th, 39, 140, 156, 76th, 116; 122nd, 43, 44; 156th, 13, 15, 38, 156; 16th Colonial, 125, 126; 17th Colonial, 126, 201, 216. Spahis, 215, 217, 218, 219, 237. Zouaves, 88, 140, 206, 210

French, General Sir John, commander of B.E.F. in France: on possible Salonika campaign, 25; 26

Galerius, Roman Emperor, 13

Gallieni, Joseph, General; favours French active participation in a Balkan campaign, 25, 47, 49; mentioned, 182

Gallipoli, 11, 13, 26, 28–29, 40, 46, 48, 49, 50, 229

Gallwitz, General von, commander of the German Eleventh Army, 58, 75

Gambetta, Leon, French statesman, 215

Gas: use of, by the Bulgars, 117; by the British, 117, 206; difficulty of securing gas shell from Britain, 194

George, D. Lloyd; see Lloyd George

George I, King of the Hellenes, 20

George V, King of England, etc.: concerned at French republican movement in Greece, 96–97; attitude to Greek monarchy after Zappeion incident, 106

George, Princess, of Greece, 97

Georgia (Russia), 237

German Army (in general): and invasion of Serbia in 1915, 32–36; and possible invasion of Greece, 45, 58; and battle for Monastir, 86, 87, 88; changing Greek opinion of, 177; Kaiserschlacht offensive on the Western Front, 179–180; and Bulgarian defeatism, 197, 199, 200; attitude of Supreme Command to the Dobropolje offensive, 202–203; in the defence of Skopje, 219; reinforcements from the Crimea, 223; German troops under Bulgarian Armistice terms, 224; effect of Bulgarian Armistice upon Supreme Command, 225

German Army (Units): Eleventh Army, 126, 199, 212, 224; 217th Division, 223, 225; Saxon Jäger Regiment, 200, 204; Alpine Corps, 225.

Germany: outbreak of war in 1914, 17–18; contempt for the Salonika defences, 62; intelligence agents learn of projected offensive (1918), 199; possible invasion of, 227, 234, 241; capitulation, 236

Gilman, Major-General Webb, Chief of Staff, British Salonika Army, 148

Goeben, German warship, 229

Golesnica Planina, mountains in Serbian
Macedonia, 218
Gradsko, 205; capture of, 216, 217
Grand Couronné, 120, 121, 123, 125,
205, 208, 209, 213, 238, 242
Great Britain: treaty rights in Greece,
11; coming of war in 1914, 17; distrust of Serbia, 17-18, 33; partiality
for Bulgaria, 19, 33, 63; Government
considers alternatives to campaign in
France, 26-27; enthusiasm for Gallipoli, 26, 27, 28; Government reluctant
to authorize advance into Macedonia,
36; evacuation of Salonika or Gallipoli, 48-49, 50; equivocal attitude
towards Greece (1916), 94, 102,
106-107; attitude of public to Salonika
expedition, 145, 146; relative merits
of Salonika Front and Palestine Front,
148-149; reluctance of Government to
accept Macedonian offensive in 1918,
189, 190, 191, 192; consent given to
offensive, 196; reception of news of
Bulgarian collapse, 224; military dispositions tend to make Britain more
interested in Near East than Central
Europe, 230; veterans of Salonika
ignored, 238, 239 (See also 'British
Army', etc.)
Greece: neutrality in 1914, 11, 20, 21;
Balkan Wars and, 19-20; ambitions at
expense of Turkey, 21; obligations to
Serbia, 21, 27, 28; and Gallipoli campaign, 28, 29; internal politics in 1915,
29, 30, 34-36; indignation at expulsion of consuls from Salonika, 54; re-
fuses passage to reconstituted Serbian
Army, 60; internal politics in 1916,
65; blockaded by Allied warships in
spring of 1916, 68; Venizelist revolt
in, 95, 98-100; Allied demands on
(1916), 96, 101-104, 106-107; deposition of King Constantine, 137-138;
popularity of the war after the Skra
di Legen victory, 177-178; failure of
Greater Greece Idea, 237; in Second
World War, 240.
Greek Army (in general): attitude to
arrival of Allies at Salonika, 12; distrust of Venizelos among officers, 20,
36; relations with Sarrail, 51, 54, 65,
66; and surrender of Fort Rupel, 66;
and surrender of Kavalla, 77-78; and
Salonika Revolution, 95; and creation
of National Army, 99-100; reorganization by General Bordeaux, 171;
mutiny in, 171; on Struma Front in
May, 1918, 175; participation in
seizure of Skra di Legen, 175-177;
operational plans for September offensive of 1918, 192-193; in second
battle of Doiran, 206, 209, 210; and
Smyrna 237

Greek Army (units): Fourth Army
Corps, 77; Seres Division, 206, 210,
213; Crete Division, 209, 210, 221
Grey, Sir Edward, British Foreign Secretary, 26, 27, 28, 33, 50, 96, 101
Groener, General Wilhelm; and proposed German invasion of Greece
(1916), 58
Grossetti, General, French Army commander on Macedonian Front; 114,
125, 129, 140, 167
Guillaumat, General Marie Louis
Adolphe, commander of the Army of
the Orient: as successor to Sarrail,
166; early career and character,
167-168; defensive scheme, 168; relations with Allied commanders, 169;
plans offensive operations, 174; and
Skra di Legen, 176-177, 178; recalled to Paris, 178, 180; attend
British Boxing Championships, 179;
passes d'Espérey's train, 182; delegate
to Allied military conference of July,
1918, 189-190; visits London and
Rome, 196; considered as successor
to d'Espérey, 227; death, 240; mentioned, 181, 184, 185
Gumendye, 175

Haig, Sir Douglas, British Field Marshal,
commander of B.E.F.; 146, 149, 169,
170; impressions of d'Espérey, 183
Hamilton, Brigadier-General, commander of British advance-party to Salonika, 14, 15, 35
Hamilton, General Sir Ian, British commander at Gallipoli, 35
Hankey, Colonel Sir Maurice, secretary
of Committee of Imperial Defence,
etc.: at Gallipoli, 15; plan for Balkan
Front, Christmas 1914, 23, 25; and
despatch of force to Salonika, 32; and
Joffre in October, 1915, 47; attends
Rome Conference, 109, 110; 'charmed'
by Sarrail, 111; on Bulgarian Armistice, 224; attends Anglo-French conference of October, 1918, 229-230
Henrys, General, commander of the
French Army in Macedonia, 167, 169,
184, 193, 204, 215, 216
Hill 340, Doiran, 208
Hill 1050, Crna Front, Italian Division
and, 113, 155, 193, 215
Hindenburg, Field-Marshal Paul von
Beneckendorff und,: becomes Chief of
the Great (German) General Staff, 75;
attitude towards Macedonia in 1916,
86-87; received requests for German
divisions to check d'Espérey's offensive, 202; treats it as a minor matter,
203; his subsequent comments on
d'Espérey's offensive, 217; orders
troops to Balkan Front, 223; and Bul-

garian collapse, 224, 225; seeks a new army for the Serbian Front, 225; insists on asking for peace terms, 226; mentioned, 46, 211, 239
Hitler, Adolf; interest in Salonika as a base in 1941, 240
Hong Kong: Serbian troops shipped through, 174
Hungary: revolution in, 234–236; occupied by d'Espérey's Army, 236, 237

Influenza: in British Salonika Army (1918), 194
Iron Gates, on the Danube, 228, 229
Ismailia, 59
Italian Army: arrival of 35th Division at Salonika, 73; participation in battle for Monastir, 78, 79, 87, 89; in heavy fighting at Hill 1050, 113; participation in spring offensive of 1917, 125, 126, 127; main Italian army defeated at Caporetto, 101; operations in Albania, 174–175; participation in Macedonian offensive of 1918, 193, 215; returning prisoners-of-war seek to reach, 218; main Italian army victorious in 1918, 233
Italy: and Serbian retreat to the Adriatic, 42; decision to send troops to Salonika, 63; willing to accept British advice on Macedonian operations, 64; and Rome Conference, 109; unresponsive to plea for more active Balkan policy, 110–111; hostility of Italians to Sarrail, 131, 153, 158, 162, ambitious policy in Albania, 155, 158, 159, 169; relations of Italians with Guillaumat, 169, 196; approval of participation of troops in Macedonian offensive, 196; as residual legatees of Habsburgs on the Adriatic, 228; and Padua Armistice, 233
Itea; as supply port for Salonika Armies, 141, 168

Jerusalem, capture of, 147, 170
Jacquemot, General, French soldier: and capture of Pogradec, 156, 157, 158
Joffre, General Joseph (later, Marshal of France), commander in chief of the Armies of France: and early plans for a Balkan Front, 23, 25; and Western Front problems in 1914 and 1915, 24–25, 29; dismisses Sarrail from command of Third Army, 30; directive to Sarrail in Salonika, 38; in London (Oct. 1915), 47; and Calais Conference of Dec, 1915, 49; insists on retention of force at Salonika, 50; wishes for active operations from Salonika in 1916, 56–57; reluctance to release British divisions from Salonika, 59–60; proposes offensive (April, 1916),

62–64; orders suspension of offensive (Dec., 1916), 91; retired and becomes Marshal of France, 108; mentioned, 182
Jonnart, Charles, Allied High Commissioner in Athens (1917), 138–139
Jouinot-Gambetta, General F. L., commander of French cavalry brigade: marches from Florina to Skopje, 215, 216, 217, 218–220; in Hungary, 237
Jumeaux Ravine, Doiran, 122, 123, 206, 208

Kajmakcalan, mountain: stormed by Serbs, 79–81; mentioned, 120, 136, 185, 200
Kalamaria, headquarters of British Salonika Army, 65, 143
Karaburun (Karaburnu): seizure by Allies of Greek fort at, 54, 55, 56, 57, 66; mentioned, 12, 242.
Karl, Emperor of Austria and King of Hungary, 147, 203, 243
Karolyi, Mihaly, Hungarian revolutionary, 234–236
Kavalla, 22, 68, 76, 77
Kenali, 75, 82, 84, 85, 87, 88
Kerensky, Alexander, 137
Khalkidike Peninsula, 100
Kilindir (Kalindria), 120
Kitchener, Lord, British War Minister: and Mahon, 15; attitude towards Balkan Front, 26, 27; and War Council of January, 1915, 26; meets Joffre and Sarrail, 32; opposed to Serbian preventive attack on Bulgaria, 33; at Calais Conference of October, 1915, 36–37; and Mahon in 1915, 40; visits Dardanelles, Salonika and Athens, 43, 48; attitude to Salonika force at end of 1915, 48, 49, 50; unwilling to see British troops under French command, 57; seeks return of British divisions from Salonika in 1916, 59; and Milne, 65
Klagenfurt, 237
Kolubara, battle of, 23
Koritsa, 74, 155, 169
Kosovo: in Serbian retreat, 40, 41, 42
Kosturino: Bulgarian village entered by British troops, 221, 223
Koundouriotis, Greek prime minister, 98, 99, 102
Kovess, Field Marshal von, Austrian soldier, 232
Kozyak, mountain, 186, 192, 201, 202, 204
Kragujevac, 41
Krusha Range, 209
Kun, Bela, Hungarian communist, 237
Kyustendil, Bulgarian headquarters, 211, 212, 222, 223

Lamia, 141, 171
Langaza (*Langadhas*), 51, 52
Lardemelle, General de, French soldier, 43–45, 81, 111, 114
Larissa, 76, 108, 141, 171
Latona, H.M.S., British warship, 151
Law, Andrew Bonar, member of British War Cabinet: supports Salonika Expedition, 36, 47
Leblois, General, French soldier, 81, 85, 87
Lebouc, General, French soldier, 131
Le Chatelier, friend of Franchet d'Espérey, 181, 227
Lesbos, Greek island, 98
'Little Entente', 230
Ljubljana, 233
Ljumnica, 176
Lloyd George, D., British prime minister: champions Balkan Front idea, 23–25; the reasons for his interest in the Balkans, 24; hostility of British generals towards, 25; attitude towards Salonika campaign in 1916, 46; on Joffre in April 1916, 64; becomes prime minister, 108; and Rome Conference, 109–112; meets Sarrail, 111–112; hostility to Salonika Expedition (1917), 118; more interested in Palestine, 118, 147; and deposition of Constantine, 138; fails to secure dismissal of Sarrail, 146–147; wishes to move a division to Palestine, 148; forced to compromise over Salonika with Allies, 149; and Robertson's fall, 149; and dismissal of Sarrail, 153, 162; complains of d'Espérey's appointment, 189; and Bulgarian peace, 224; more interested in Constantinople than in Central Europe, 228; wishes to place British Salonika Army under Allenby, 229; angry with d'Espérey, 229, 230
Loos, battle of, 32, 36, 47
Ludendorff, General Erich: in partnership with Hindenburg, 75, 202, 225; and Macedonia, 86, 202; and the *Kaiserschlacht*, 179, 180, 182; mentioned, 18, 46, 211
Lukov, General, commander of the Bulgarian Second Army, 222, 223, 224
Lyautey, General (later, Marshal of France), 22, 110, 115, 117

Machukovo, 85, 86, 121
Mackensen, Field-Marshal August von, 41
Mackenzie, Compton, 96, 104
Mafeking: Mahon relieves, 15
Mahon, General Sir Bryan, commander of British troops in Macedonia: arrival at Salonika, 15; earlier career, 15; initial instructions, 38; and fighting of 1915, 40; visited by Kitchener, 48;

and the enemy consuls, 54; and Karaburun, 55; superseded by Milne, 64
Malaria, 46, 64, 142–143, 194, 242
Malinov, Alexander, Bulgarian prime minister, 222, 223, 224
Malvy, Louis, French Minister of the Interior, 159, 160, 161
Marne, battles of, 31, 166, 180
Mavroplagia, 241
Messimy, Adolphe, French Minister of War, 167
Michaud, General chief of staff to Sarrail, 167
Mikra, 60, 242
Millerand, Alexandre, French Minister of War, 31, 32
Milne, General Sir George (later Field-Marshal Lord Milne), commander-in-chief of the British Salonika Army: appointed to command at Salonika, 64; earlier career, 64–65; and Sarrail's determination to control Salonika, 66–67; and participation in autumn offensive of 1916, 72, 73; attends Rome Conference, 111; optimism on probability of Bulgarian collapse, 111; wishes British to fight at Doiran rather than Seres, 115; and Calais Conference of 1917, 116; and first battle of Doiran, 119, 122, 124; visits Prince Regent Alexander, 135–136; on importance of mosquito nets, 143; appreciates need for relaxation, 144–145; on bad terms with Sarrail, 150; improved relations with Guillaumat, 169; receives artillery reinforcements, 170; confident of success in 1918, 190–191; requests reinforcements, 191; Greek divisions under command of, 192; and War Office inability to send shells, 194; his operational plans for 1918 offensive, 194–195; and second battle of Doiran, 209, 210; learns of Bulgarian retreat, 213; orders pursuit of enemy, 214; and Bulgarian request for Armistice, 223; and d'Espérey's desire to send British troops to Danube, 228–229; champions Salonika veterans in the press, 239; and Salonika Reunion Association, 241; later years and death, 241
Milner, Lord, British statesman, 149, 195, 229
Mišić, General (later *Voivode*), Serbian soldier: and storming of the Kajmakcalan, 79–81; reluctance to attack in 1917, 129; appointed Serbian chief of staff, 185; favours attack on Dobropolje, 185; and d'Espérey, 186–187; transmits signal to open offensive, 197, 203; orders Serbian troops to keep up pressure, 202; mentioned, 213; death, 240

Moglena Mountains, 113, 117, 122, 125, 126, 127, 128, 129, 185, 237, 242, 243
Moglenitsa, river, 186, 192
Mombelli, General, Italian soldier, 137, 169
Monastir (Bitolja), 20, 75, 79, 81, 82, 86, 87; capture of, 88–90, 92, 108, 109, 110, 111, 122, 125, 126, 127, 140, 155, 156, 158
Monte Cassino, 120
Montenegro, 19, 41, 60
Moorehead, Alan, 28
Morava, river, 22, 27, 32, 228
Morocco, 22
Mudros, British base at, 11, 13, 14, 28, 35, 231
Mules, 14, 15, 113
Murray, General Sir Archibald, 47

Negotin, 39
Nerezov, General, commander of Bulgarian First Army, 199, 211, 216
Nicholas, Prince of Greece, 97
Nicholas II, Tsar of Russia, 50, 97, 136
Niš, 32, 38, 39, 228, 232, 234
Nivelle, General Robert, French soldier, 30, 31, 108, 112, 116, 130
Norseman, British transport, 55
Novak, 216

Ochrid, Lake, 20, 114, 125, 137, 155, 157, 158, 159, 174
Ochrid, town, 158
Olympus, Mount, 13, 109, 117, 242
Orfano, Gulf of, 51
Orle, 126, 136
Ostrovo, Lake, 79, 133

Packer, Charles, 195
Painlevé, Paul French prime minister, 117, 153, 154, 156, 159, 160, 161
Palestine, 112, 147, 148, 150
Paracin, capture of, 233
Pašić, Nikola, Serbian prime minister, 42, 134, 135, 153, 157, 158
Passchendaele Ridge, battle of, 161
Patty Ravine (Doiran), 123, 124
Pec, 41
Pechaev, 222
Pétain, Philippe, General (later, Marshal of France): shirks responsibility of recalling Sarrail, 162–163; and d'Espérey, 165, 166, 186; in Second World War, 240, 241; mentioned, 30, 31, 130, 180, 181
Peter, King of Serbia, 18, 42
Petit Couronné (Doiran), 120, 121, 123, 124, 205, 208, 210
Pettiti, General, Italian soldier, 79, 90
Phaleron Bay, 98, 104, 105
Pip Ridge (Doiran), 120, 123, 205, 206, 209, 213, 238, 242
Piraeus, 96, 98, 102, 103, 137

Piton Rocheux (Doiran), 209
Pogradec, capture of, 155, 156, 157, 158
Poincaré, Raymond, President of France: visits d'Espérey, 22; and memorandum on Balkan offensive, 22–23; and appointment of Briand, 47; and appointment of Clemenceau, 160
Politis, Venizelist foreign minister, 99
Port Arthur, Serbian volunteers pass through, 174
Ploesti oilfields, 91
Prespa, Lake, 88, 114, 116, 125, 137, 157
Prilep, 84, 89, 90, 114, 199, 200, 211, 212, 214, 216
Prizren, 41, 232
Prosenik, 175
Provins, d'Espérey's headquarters in France, 181, 187
Pruneau, General, French soldier, 216, 217
Putnik, Marshal, Serbian chief of staff in Albanian retreat, 41, 42

Rabrovo, 213
Radical Socialist Party (French), 31, 161
Radomir, 223
Rendina Gorge, 51
Reuter, General von, German soldier, 202, 203, 204
Ribot, Alexandre, French prime minister, 117, 138, 152, 160, 161
Rijeka (Fiume), 233
Robertson, General Sir William (later Field-Marshal): appointed C.I.G.S., 56; hostile to Salonika Expedition in 1916, 56, 59, 60, 62–64; and autumn offensive of 1916, 72; at Rome Conference, 109, 111; meets, and distrusts, Sarrail, 111–112; and Calais Conference of 1917, 116; wishes to withdraw troops from Salonika in 1917, 146, 148, 149; irritation with British political leaders, 149; replaced as C.I.G.S. by Wilson, 170
Roche Noire Salient, attack on, 194, 200
Rome: inter-allied conference of January 1917, 109–112, 113, 116, 153; Guillaumat visits, 196
'Roosters', British Salonika Army concert-party, 144
Roques, General, French Minister of War, 161
Roumania: Balkan Wars and, 19; possible entry into war in 1915, 27, 28, 29, 71; entry into war in 1916, 72, 74; invaded, 83, 86, 90–91, 131; renewal of contact with in 1918, 228, 230, 231, 236; in inter-war period, 230.
Royal Air Force, 213–214, 221
Royal Flying Corps, 73, 117, 144
Royal Marines, 51, 55, 105
Royal Naval Air Service, 117
Rupel, Fort, 66, 68, 75

Rupel Gorge, 54, 77, 86, 212
Rusev, Major-General, Bulgarian soldier, 203, 204
Russia: treaty rights in Greece, 11; at
  war with Turkey, 18; plea for aid, 26;
  possible participation in Salonika
  Expedition, 27; insists on keeping open
  Balkan Front, 50; proposes joint
  advance to Budapest, 56; offensive in
  Galicia in 1916, 68–69, 71–72; and
  Roumanian Front, 74, 75; Revolution in, 118, 137; Russian troops in
  France mutiny, 136
Russian Brigades in Macedonia: arrival,
  73; and advance on Monastir, 82–84,
  89; and seizure of Orle, 125–126;
  weariness of brigades in 1917, 136–137;
  effect of Russian Revolution upon,
  136–138; withdrawn from Front, 137;
  mutiny at Vertikop, 137.

Sabac, 18
Sackville-West, Major-General, 189, 190,
  191
St Jean-de-Maurienne Conference
  (1917), 118, 122, 146
Salamis, 96, 102
Salonika (*Thessaloniki*): arrival of British
  and French at, 11–16, 34; description
  of, 13–14, capture of, in Balkan Wars,
  19, 20; assassination of King George
  at, 20; Sarrail reaches, 38; Kitchener
  visits, 43, 48; Austria covets, 45–46;
  Entrenched Camp at, 51–53; expulsion of consuls from, 53–54; bombing
  of, 53, 54, 117; arrival of Serbs at, 60;
  Zeppelin shot down at, 61; proclamation of state of siege in, 66, 68; effect
  of eight months of occupation upon,
  68; arrival of Russians at, 73; arrival
  of Italians and Albanians at, 73; commercial potentialities of, 92–93; republican revolution in, 94–95, 99;
  Venizelos lands at, 98; execution of
  alleged Serbian conspirators at, 135;
  mutiny of French troops in, 140; Great
  Fire of (1917), 150–152, 238; Guillaumat at, 167; visit of King Alexander to,
  171; d'Espérey at, 184; Allied troops
  leave, 237; in second World War,
  240; appearance today, 241–242
Salonika Reunion Association, 241
Salonika Trial, 134–135
Samos, 98
Sandham, Lieutenant, R.A.S.C., 242
Santi Quaranta, 111 113, 155, 169
Sarajevo, 17, 134, 233
Sarrail, General Maurice: dismissed
  from Third Army command, 30; early
  career, 30–31, 160–161; appointed to
  Army of the Orient, 31–32; informed
  that Salonika was his destination, 33;
  arrival there, 38; directive from Joffre,

38; and aid to the Serbs in retreat,
  38–41, 43; dispute with de Lardemelle, 43–45; establishes defensive
  line at Salonika, 51; and enemy consuls, 53–54; and destruction of
  Struma bridge, 54; and Karaburun
  Fort, 54, 55, 56; relations with Mahon,
  64, 65; visit to Athens, 65; angry at
  Fort Rupel surrender, 66; and state of
  siege in Salonika, 67; and Bulgarian
  attack of 1916, 75–76, 78–79; in conflict with Cordonnier, 81–85; and capture of Monastir, 87–90; political intrigue and, 92; his commercial interests, 93; and Venizelist revolution, 94–
  95, 99–100, 107; criticized by George
  V, 97; wishes to attack Greek royalists,
  108–109; attends Rome conference,
  109–112; meets Lloyd George, 111–
  112; plans Spring Offensive of 1917,
  113–115; seeks clarification of Calais
  Conference decisions, 116; postpones
  Spring Offensive, 122; on bad terms
  with Italians, 126, 127; conduct of
  Spring Offensive, 127, 129, 130; personal responsibility for its failure,
  131–132; and Black Hand conspiracy
  132, 133, 135; his marriage, 139; and
  French mutiny, 140; survives British
  request for his recall, 146–147; bad
  relations with Milne, 150; further
  Allied complaints about, 153, 159,
  162; his Albanian policy, 155–159;
  his links with Caillaux, 160–161,
  163–164; dismissed by Clemenceau,
  162, 163; retires to Montauban,
  163–164; removal of his staff from
  Salonika, 166, 167; mentioned, 184,
  185, 195; later years and death, 240
Sava, river, 32, 36, 232
Scholtz, General von, commander of
  German Army Group in Macedonia,
  199, 200, 202, 204, 205
Scottish Women's Suffrage Federation, 42
Scourge, H.M.S., British destroyer, 42
Seeckt, General Hans von, 58, 182
Serbia: inaccessibility of, 11, 12; war
  aims of, 17–18; invaded by Austria
  (1914), 18, 22–23; Balkan Wars and,
  19; military convention with Greece,
  21, 33; invaded in 1915, 32, 33, 34;
  appeals for Allied aid, 33; overrun
  by Central Powers, 34, 41; flight to
  Corfu, 42–43; political rivalry in, 134–
  135; objections to British withdrawal,
  148–149; conditions of occupation of,
  172; and South Slav volunteers,
  173–174; liberation of, 231–233
Serbian Army (*Divisions*): Drina, 80;
  Sumadija, 127, 201; Timok, 135, 202;
  Vardar, 174; Yugoslav, 201, 202, 216,
  233

Serbian Army (*in general*): in 1914 campaign, 23; in 1915 campaign, 32, 41; in retreat through Albania, 41–43; re-constituted at Salonika, 60–61; moved to the Macedonian Front, 73; and Bulgarian attack (1916), 75, 76, 77; and the Kajmakcalan, 79; and fall of Monastir, 87–90; and Spring Offensive of 1917, 125, 127, 129; malaise of (1917), 132–136; oversea reinforcements for, 172–174; assaults Sokol, Vetrenik and Kozyak, 200, 201, 202; develops the offensive, 203–205, 214–215; advances into Serbia, 231–233; occupies Yugoslav districts, 236

Seres (*Serrai*), 73, 76, 77, 85, 114, 115

Seres Road, 15, 113, 150, 168, 179

Skopje (*Uskub*): 38, 39, 40, 87, 216, 217, 218; capture of, 219–220; 221

Skouloudis, Greek premier, 65, 68

Skra di Legen; capture of, 175–178; 180, 185, 187, 206

Smuts, General (later Field-Marshal): critical of Salonika Expedition, 146, 147, 149

Sofia, 36, 78, 114, 221, 223, 234, 236

Sokol, Mountain, 185, 186, 193, 199, 200, 201

Somme, battles of, 64, 82, 96, 109

Spears, Brigadier-General E. L., 183

Spencer, (Sir) Stanley, British artist, 214, 242

Starigrad, 218

Stavros (*Skala Stavros*), 51, 143–144

Stepanović, General, commander of Serbian Second Army, 125, 127

Steuben, General von, commander of the German Eleventh Army, 199, 212

Struga, 158

Struma (*Strimon*), river, 46, 54, 73, 76, 85, 90, 114, 115, 127–128, 142, 143, 144, 150, 159, 175, 193, 237, 242

Strumica, 39, 213, 223

Sumadija, 233

Supreme War Council: meeting in Nov. 1917, 161–162; meeting in July, 1918, 189; subordinates occupation of Germany to Foch, 234

Suvla, landing at (1915), 13, 15

Sveti Vrach, headquarters of Bulgarian Second Army, 212, 222

Tannenberg, battle of, 18

Taranowski, General, commander of Russian Brigades, 137

Taranto, 141

Todorov, General, acting Bulgarian commander-in-chief, 211, 212, 216, 223

Topcider, 233

Thessaly, 103, 107, 138, 139, 154

Tiflis, British troops sent from Struma to, 237

Toulon, 15

Trianon Palace, Versailles, Allied military conference (1918), 189–190, 191

Trumbić, Ante, Yugoslav political leader, 173

Tsarevo Selo, 222

Turkey: entry into the war, 18; and Balkan Wars, 19; British decision to attack, 26; section of Macedonian Front taken over by troops of, 100; size of contingent in Macedonia, 114; British interest in occupying, 118, 229; concludes Armistice, 231

Typhus, 23, 32, 42, 58

U-boats, German submarines, 55, 60, 69, 118, 140, 141, 146

United States of America: as a neutral power, 112; as an Associated belligerent, 139, 228; South Slav volunteers from, 172; and final offensive, 190, 191; and Bulgarian Armistice, 223; sends battalion to Kotor, 236

Vardar (*Axios*), river, 11, 12, 22, 27, 32, 38, 39, 40, 51, 52, 54, 73, 78, 85, 175, 176, 215, 216

Vaughan-Williams, (Sir) Ralph, 144

Vazov, General, Bulgarian soldier, 206

Veles (*Titov Veles*), 39, 40, 43, 78, 218, 219

Venizelos, Eleutherios, Greek statesman: attitude to use of Salonika by the Allies, 12, 35–36; early career, 20; ambitions, 20–21; wish to enter war in 1914, 20–21; and Lloyd George, 24; urged to assist Serbia, 27–28; and Gallipoli, 28–29; resigns as premier (March, 1915), 29; wins election, 30; seeks Allied assistance, 33; dispute with Constantine, 34–35; resigns (Oct. 1915), 36; visited by Sarrail, 67; reluctant to become French puppet, 95; flight to Crete, 97–98; heads Provisional Government, 98–100; recognized as constitutional premier, 139; seeks dismissal of Sarrail, 153, 162; post-war career and death, 237, 240; mentioned, 94, 134

Verdun, battle of, 31, 57, 58, 59, 69

Vertikop, 137

Vetrenik, mountain, 185, 186, 192, 193, 197, 199, 200, 201

Via Egnatia, 14, 151

Victory Procession in Paris (1919), 156, 238

Vienna, 21, 234, 241

Vittorio-Veneto, battle of, 233

Viviani, René, French premier, 23, 31, 47

Vodena (*Edhessa*), 75

Vostarene, 133, 134

War Committee, British, 50, 62
War Council, British, 23, 26, 28
Weygand, General Maxime: wishes to
 use Salonika as a base in 1939, 240
White Tower (Salonika), 13, 152, 241,
 242
Wilson, Field Marshal Sir Henry,
 C.I.G.S., 170, 191, 196
Wilson, General Maitland (Field Mar-
 shal Lord Wilson of Libya), 240
Wilson, Lieutenant-General Sir Henry
 Maitland, commander of the British
 XII Corps, 118, 119, 122, 160, 205,
 209, 210, 231, 240
Wilson, President Woodrow, 226, 228,
 235
Winckler, General von, German soldier,
 75, 86, 87, 88

Winnington-Ingram, Dr A. F. (Bishop of
 London), 238

Yanesh (*Metallikon*), 118–119, 120, 205,
 209, 223
Yelak, Serbian advanced headquarters,
 185, 186
Ypres, battles of, 25, 65, 82
Yugoslavia, 172–173, 230, 237, 239, 240,
 242

Zagreb (*Agram*), 233
Zaimis, Greek premier, 36, 68
Zappeion (Athens), shooting at, 104–105,
 106, 107, 108
Zymbrakakis, Colonel (later General),
 Greek soldier, 95, 99, 100, 106, 171,
 176, 206